THE
SHACKLED
CONTINENT

ROBERT GUEST

THE SHACKLED CONTINENT

Power, Corruption, and African Lives

Smithsonian Books
Washington

Published in 2004 in the United States of America
By Smithsonian Books
in association with Macmillan,
an imprint of Pan Macmillan Ltd
Pan Macmillan, 20 New Wharf Road, London N1 9RR
Basingstoke and Oxford

ISBN: 1-58834-214-X

Library of Congress Cataloging-in-Publication Data
Guest, Robert.
The shackled continent : power, corruption, and African lives /
Robert Guest.
p.   cm.
Includes bibliographical references and index.
ISBN 1-58834-214-X (alk. paper)
1. Political corruption—Africa.   2. Africa—Politics and
government—1960–   3. Africa—Social conditions—1960–
4. Poverty—Africa.   I. Title.
JQ1875.A55C6378   2004
960.3'2—dc22   2004052131

Manufactured in the United States of America

10 09 08 07 06 05 04   1 2 3 4 5

To Emma, for holding the babies while I slipped off to write

Contents

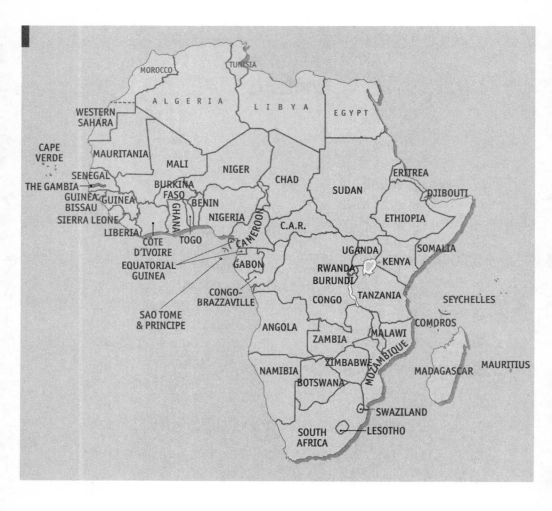

PREFACE

It was not much of a road block: a heap of branches and a broken fridge with a cow's skull on top, painted the orange, white, and green of the flag of Côte d'Ivoire. But the rebels manning it had guns and rocket-propelled grenades, so we stopped.

There were about fifty of them, and they were determined to look tough. Some strutted around shirtless, with sashes of bullets wrapped around their chests. Others wore T-shirts with death's heads on them. Most sported reflective sunglasses, and all except the most senior officer waved their weapons around carelessly. Several were drunk. It was 10:30 on a hot Ivorian morning, but the top was off the plastic jerry can of *koutoukou*, a throat-scalding local palm spirit, and young rebels were gulping it from battered tin cups.

They told us to get out of the car. I was traveling with Kate Davenport, another British journalist, and Hamadou Yoda, our Ivorian driver and guide. None of us wanted trouble, so we got out, stood in the road, and tried politely to explain our business while they searched our bags.

In my bag, one of them found the corrected first draft of this book, which I was hoping to read on spare evenings during this trip to report on Côte d'Ivoire's civil war. It was a thick block of paper, held together with a rubber band. The rebel picked it up, waved it in my face, and demanded to know what it was. "It's a book," I said. "What's it about?" he asked.

"It's about the abuse of power in Africa. It describes how men with guns, like you, have impoverished an entire continent," I wanted to reply, but of course I said nothing of the sort, though it would have been true.

In five years of reporting on Africa, I've grown accustomed to seeing power abused. Some of the less media-savvy politicians are quite open about it.

1

I once had a conversation with the governor of a remote part of Namibia, where a minor uprising had just been put down with energetic brutality. Several hundred people had been tortured and then released without charge, presumably because they were innocent. Asked whether he was sorry that innocent people had been tortured, the governor told me his only regret was that he had not been able to take part in the beatings himself. I couldn't think of any more questions after that.

Africa* is in a bad way and this book is my attempt to explain why. I think it's an important question and one that needs to be answered if the continent is ever to recover. But I don't think the gravity of the topic is an excuse for dull writing, so I've tried to keep the narrative vivid and punchy. Whenever it makes the argument more digestible, I've thrown in real-life examples. Some may be startling, but none, I hope, is gratuitous. The anecdote in Chapter 4 about the prostitute in the lift illustrates a serious point.

On re-reading the text, it occurs to me that I've left out a lot of the good things about Africa. The kindness of its people, their passion for life, the extraordinary hospitality of the poorest of the poor, the joy of Congolese rumba music, the sunset over the Okavango delta; the list goes on. But this is a book about why Africa is poor, so it has to grapple with war, pestilence, and presidents who think their office is a license, literally, to print money.

Africa has endured its share of evil leaders. The more colorful tyrants, such as Idi Amin and Mobutu Sese Seko, are well known. What is less well known is that, with so few effective checks on arbitrary power in Africa, its well-meaning leaders have often done great harm, too. Julius Nyerere, the revered former Tanzanian president, sincerely hoped to make his people better off by forcing millions of them into giant collectives, but instead he almost destroyed his nation's capacity to feed itself.

The rebels at that Ivorian road block probably also thought they were fighting for a noble cause. To be fair, the government

* By "Africa," I mean sub-Saharan Africa. This book does not deal with the Arab countries of North Africa.

they hoped to overthrow was indeed an unpleasant one. But their revolution did not topple it. Rather, it split the country in two and exposed wide swathes of it to rape and pillage.

Not that we were badly treated. They only held us for an hour. We were given seats in the shade, near an old tape deck belting out dance tunes, and our guard kept offering us swigs of *koutoukou*. At one point, we watched him respectfully help a couple of old ladies up an earthy bank they had to climb in order to be questioned. All in all, this was a relatively disciplined group of rebels, which was a relief. But it would have been better if there had been no war, no road blocks, and no need to ask men with guns for permission to go about one's daily business.

Acknowledgments

Barbara Smith, my editor at the *Economist*, has been a delight and an inspiration to work for. Stuart Evers, my editor at Macmillan, has shown a lighter touch in handling the manuscript than that Ivorian rebel I mentioned. Thanks to my agent, Andrew Lownie, for selling the book, and to James Astill, Tony Hawkins, Steve King, Philip Marsden, Anthea Jeffrey, and Broo Doherty for their helpful comments.

Among the many who have shared with me their insights and experiences, I am particularly grateful to Shantha Bloemen, Paul Collier, Ahmed Diraige, Nima El-Bagir, Comfort Ero, François Grignon, Heidi Holland, Dick Howe, Victor Mallet, Mesfin Wolde Mariam, Deligent Marowa, Strive Masiyiwa, Andy Meldrum, Fred M'membe, John Robertson, Themba Sono, Thomas Sowell, Brian Williams, Nashon Zimba, and Faides Zulu. Of course, none of these excellent people should be blamed for any of my mistakes.

Finally, a word of thanks to the Cameroonian policeman I met at the thirty-first road block between Douala and Bertoua for unwittingly providing me with the best quote in the book.

London, August 2003

INTRODUCTION: WHY IS AFRICA SO POOR ?

The helicopter swooped low over the floodwaters of southern Mozambique. The South African airmen sitting in the rear, legs dangling out of an open doorway, strained their eyes for a glimpse of survivors. I sat behind them, taking notes.

Poking out from the leaves of a tree that, despite the deluge, had somehow stayed upright, the pilot saw a scarlet shawl on a stick, waving to attract our attention. He took the helicopter down, and as we drew closer, the blast from its rotorblades flattened the canopy to reveal twenty-two Mozambicans clinging to the branches to avoid the churning waters below.

To rescue these people required hovering dangerously close to the tree, but the pilot did not hesitate. An airman rappeled down and strapped a little girl into his spare harness. The two were then winched back up. The airman quickly but gently handed the girl to his mate and rappeled down again. And again, and again, and again, until all twenty-two of the people in that tree were safely on board the helicopter.

The refugees had all tried to save their most treasured possessions from the flood. Most carried sacks of half-rotten corn or bundles of damp clothes. One man wore a miner's helmet – a status symbol in a country where the best-paid workers are often those who toil in the gold and platinum mines of neighboring South Africa. Another fellow had salvaged his hut's wooden front door and was distraught when the airman told him that there was no room for it on board. A thin old man was told that he could not keep his pet dog, but the airman relented when he signaled, by pointing to the dog and then to his mouth, that the animal was for food. The dog defecated with fear when pulled into the helicopter, adding a new stench to an atmosphere already rank with the smell of large numbers of unwashed bodies crammed into a small cabin.

By the time the airmen had finished plucking people out of trees and from thatched rooftops, there were at least sixty in a machine that would have felt crowded with ten. I found myself pressed against a bag of pots and pans, with a mother of two and her children sitting on my leg. But it was only a thirty-minute flight to the refugee camp, where everyone was obviously grateful to be put down. The refugees had no language in common with the airmen. They spoke no English or Afrikaans, and the airmen knew no Shangaan or Portuguese. So they thanked their rescuers with gentle nods as they were ushered out of the helicopter and across a field to the nearest feeding station. The airmen smiled and nodded back and then flew off to pull more people out of trees. A baby girl was born in a Mozambican tree that day; both child and mother were rescued.

Perhaps a million southern Africans lost their homes in the floods of March 2000. Mozambique, the poorest country in the region, was also the worst affected. At the time, it was still recovering from two decades of civil war that had reduced many people to wearing tree bark and eating wild berries. The country had done well in the late 1990s, its economy expanding at a scorching pace, albeit from a wretchedly low starting point. Then, suddenly, the Zambezi, Save, and Limpopo rivers swelled to rushing torrents up to eighty miles wide, drowning villages and hurling livestock into the Indian Ocean. Countless Mozambicans, who were struggling so determinedly to pull themselves out of poverty, had just been knocked back down by several billion tons of muddy water.

Back in the capital, Maputo, I was in a taxi heading for dinner when my mobile telephone buzzed. It was Phil, an old friend from back home in Britain. His Internet company had floated that morning, making him a millionaire. I congratulated him and asked him to tell me all about it. He started to gush but then paused. "What's that noise?" he asked, referring to a hubbub in the background. I told him. It was a throng of half-naked street kids, tapping on the taxi windows and begging for change. Phil took this in and said: "Well, that certainly puts things into perspective."

I calculated that, at current income levels, it would take an average Mozambican 10,000 years to earn what my friend earned that day. As it happens, Phil lost it all again when the dot.com market crashed. But somehow that does not make the contrast any less striking. He's young, he's clever, and he lives in a country where talent is amply rewarded. He'll probably make another fortune some other way. For the Mozambican street kids, the prospects are not quite so good. They are young, too, but they live in Africa, the poorest continent on earth, and the only one that, despite all the technological advances that are filling stomachs and pockets everywhere else, has actually grown poorer over the last thirty years.

The numbers are staggering: half of sub-Saharan Africa's 600 million people live on just sixty-five cents a day, and even this figure is misleadingly rosy. Many Africans rarely have any money at all. They build their own homes, often out of mud and sticks. They grow their own food. When the rains fail, they go hungry. And when the rains are too heavy, as in Mozambique, they lose their homes. The median African country has a gross domestic product (GDP) of only $2 billion – roughly the output of a small town in Europe. Not even Africans want to invest in Africa – about 40 percent of Africa's privately held wealth is held offshore.[1]

As a journalist covering Africa, I've come face to face with some of the human consequences of economic failure. I've seen ragged children foraging for lunch in an Angolan trash pile and listened to Ethiopian nomads describing what it feels like to starve.

I don't imagine that I can change any of this, but I do believe that it can change. Any country inhabited by human beings has the potential to grow rich. We know this because many countries have already done so. If Africa is to succeed too, it is crucial to understand what has gone wrong in the past. Just why is Africa so poor?

This book is an attempt to grapple with that question.

In historical terms, Africa's plight is not unusual. Since humans first stopped being apes, most have lived short and hungry lives. The way the poorest Africans live today is not much different from the way most Europeans lived until the industrial revolution. In fact, modern Africans live longer than Europeans or Americans did before the twentieth century, largely because so many useful medicines that were invented elsewhere – antibiotics, for example – have become cheap enough for Africans to buy.

It is not much comfort for Africans, however, to hear that other people were equally poor a hundred years ago. Even cattle-herders in the foothills of Lesotho know that, today, the rest of the world is much richer than they are. Any African who occasionally watches television can see that people in America live lives of unimaginable luxury, with bulging fridges, soft clothes, and big cars that even teenagers can afford. Why, they ask, is life in Africa not like that?

Some blame geography. It is certainly a factor. Most African countries are tropical. Rich nations tend to have temperate climates: roughly 93 percent of the people in the world's thirty richest nations live in temperate zones. The tropics tend to be poor: of the forty-two countries that the World Bank classified in 1999 as "Heavily Indebted Poor Countries" (HIPCs), thirty-nine either were in the tropics or consisted largely of desert. The only three temperate HIPCs – Malawi, Zambia, and Laos – were land-locked.[2]

The Victorians believed that hot weather drains a man's strength. A more likely link between climate and poverty is that hot countries are home to all manner of diseases that affect both people and their livestock. Africa has the worst of them: malaria, yellow fever, rare but deadly viruses such as Ebola, and a host of energy-sapping parasites. Down a cup of dirty water in Nigeria, for instance, and you may find yourself infested with threadlike, meter-long guinea worms, which cause a painful fever and can, for months, make you too tired to work. You can cure guinea-worm infestation by waiting till the worm's end bursts through the skin and then wrapping it around a stick and tugging it out slowly and gently over the course of several days. But Africans can't do much about the climate that allows such horrors to thrive, and it is hard to build a prosperous, efficient society when you are riddled with parasites or shaking with fever.

Another popular culprit for Africa's ills is history. Many Africans argue that the continent's current problems spring largely from the traumas that Europeans visited on Africa, such as slavery.

It's an emotive argument. In the eighteenth and nineteenth centuries, millions of Africans were kidnapped, chained, squashed into the fetid holds of slaving ships, and taken across the Atlantic. Many died before they reached the other side. Those who reached the Americas were set to work, unfree and unpaid, on plantations. Those who stayed behind in Africa lived in fear that they would not escape the clutches of the slave raiders the next time they came. This fear and the constant loss of healthy adults were massively disruptive to African societies.

Slavery was not introduced to Africa by Europeans. Arab slavers arrived earlier than the Portuguese, British, and French, and Africans were enslaving each other centuries before even the Arabs arrived. In fact, slavery was common in most parts of the world before the British started trying to crush it, and Africa was no exception. By one estimate, between 30 and 60 percent of Africans were slaves before the Europeans arrived.[3] The shipping of slaves to America could be seen as an extension of Africa's internal market: many African chiefs saw no wrong in selling slaves to European traders, and some even protested when the trade was banned. None of this excuses the European slavers, of course. Judged by today's standards, their behavior was abominable, and even by the standards of the day it was cruel and rapacious.

Of course, slavery is evil. But it is implausible to blame it for all of Africa's modern problems. Practically all nations have endured slavery at some point. Probably everyone alive today is descended from slaves (and from slave-owners, too). Thirty or forty generations ago in Europe, the vast majority of people were serfs: bonded laborers, tied to the land, forced at their lord's whim to fight for him, sleep with him, or harvest his corn.

Granted, if you are African, your closest slave ancestors probably lived more recently than the medieval serfs from whom most Europeans are descended. But the transatlantic slave trade ended in the nineteenth century. Slavery continued in much of East Asia and the Middle East for decades longer. In a few African countries, notably Sudan and Mauritania, it still exists, though both governments deny it.

Long after slavery was abolished, most of Africa remained subject to European colonial rule. Since most African countries were still colonies until the 1960s or 70s, it is easy to find colonial roots for modern problems. If the rulers of Congo today treat their subjects as a leopard treats a herd of impala, one can argue that they learned the habit from the Belgians. If the rulers of Sudan and Burundi manipulate ethnic grievances to stay in power, they probably learned that from their former colonial masters, too.

The colonists left deep scars. But they also left behind some helpful things, such as roads, clinics, and laws. If colonialism was what held Africa back, you would expect the continent to have boomed when the settlers left. It didn't.

Perhaps, then, the problem is that the legacy of colonialism remained, even after the colonists had gone. Up to a point, this is true. Africa's borders are still a source of trouble. Arbitrarily penciled onto inaccurate maps when European powers carved up the continent in the nineteenth century, today's national boundaries split tribes in half and lump mutually hostile ethnic groups together. This often causes tension and sometimes bloodshed. But African countries have themselves determined not to tamper with the colonial borders, for fear that this might spark new conflicts rather than end old ones.

Some Africans argue that their continent has been crippled by what Steve Biko, a South African revolutionary, called a "colonization of the mind." White rulers thought their black subjects inferior. The fact that the more technologically advanced European powers conquered most of Africa with relative ease doubtless led some Africans to wonder whether this might be true. Even today, some argue, Africans' lack of confidence prevents them from fulfilling their potential. There may be something in this, but over 70 percent of Africans alive today were born after independence.[4] And examples from other countries suggest that unpleasant colonial experiences need not doom a country to eternal penury.

Korea, for example, was annexed by Japan in 1910 and freed only when America dropped atomic bombs on Hiroshima and Nagasaki. While they ruled Korea, the Japanese colonists tried to destroy the local culture and to cow the population into servitude. They banned the Korean language, barred Koreans from universities, and systematically desecrated the country's most sacred hilltop shrines. They shipped young Korean men to Japan to provide forced labor in mines and munitions factories or conscripted them to serve in the Imperial army. They drafted more than 100,000 Korean women, some as young as twelve, to serve as sex slaves in military brothels. And the ordeal did not end with liberation. Soon after the colonists left, Korea was plunged into a civil war that cost a million lives and split the country in two.[5]

With such a traumatic history, Korea would have every excuse for failure. But the southern, capitalist part, which was as poor as Ghana in 1953, is now twenty times richer. Taiwan, Hong Kong, Malaysia, and Singapore – all ex-colonies – are all now affluent and peaceful. So are Ireland, Australia, and Massachusetts. Africa's colonial legacy, though influential, cannot explain all that is awry today.

Another problem with blaming the legacy of colonialism for Africa's current woes is that it gives little clue as to how these woes could be ended. History, like geography, cannot be changed. Grieving for past wrongs is natural and human, but it can also provide an excuse for despair. If today's problems are the fault of the West, the obvious thing to do is to demand that the West should solve them. The trouble with this approach is twofold. First, today's Westerners do not feel particularly guilty about the sins of dead people who happened to come from the same country. Second, efforts by rich countries to solve Africa's problems have, over the last few decades, been spectacularly unsuccessful.

Put differently, countries that prosper tend to do so by their own efforts. Outsiders can help, but only on the margins. Thabo Mbeki, South Africa's president, has predicted an "African renaissance" but says that this renaissance will only succeed "if its aims and objectives are defined by the Africans themselves, if its programmes are designed by ourselves and if we take responsibility for the success or failure of our policies."[6]

Countries grow wealthy in much the same way that individuals do: by making things that other people want to buy or by providing services that others will pay for. There are exceptions. Just as some individuals inherit wealth, so some countries are rich simply because they have a lot of oil and not many citizens. But by and large the route to prosperity is through thrift, hard work, and finding out what other people want in order to sell it to them.

Britain first grew rich, in the nineteenth century, by using newly invented industrial techniques to produce cheaper and better textiles, steel, railways, and other goods, which both locals and foreigners were keen to buy. Japan grew rich in the twentieth century by adopting and improving manufacturing techniques invented elsewhere, in order to make better and cheaper cars, semiconductors, and fax machines. America is the world's richest country today because so many people crave American movies, medicines, airplanes, and banking services. Africa, by contrast, hardly produces anything that the rest of the world wants to buy. With a tenth of the world's population, Africa's share of world trade is a miserable 2 percent. The continent exports minerals, such as oil and copper, and crops, such as cocoa, coffee, and tobacco. But few African countries turn their minerals into manufactured goods, and hardly anyone buys African software or insurance. To understand why Africa is so poor, we must first ask why Africa is so unproductive.

The great African novelist, Chinua Achebe, said of his homeland: "The trouble with Nigeria is simply and squarely a failure of leadership. There is nothing basically wrong with the Nigerian character. There is nothing wrong with the Nigerian land or climate or water or air or anything else. The Nigerian problem is the unwillingness or inability of its leaders to rise to the responsibility, to the challenge of personal example which are the hallmarks of true leadership."[7]

Substitute "Africa" for "Nigeria" and this is a pretty good summary of what holds the continent back. Since independence, Africa's governments have failed their people. Few allow ordinary citizens the freedom to seek their own fortunes without official harassment. Few uphold the rule of law, enforce contracts, or safeguard property rights. Many are blatantly predatory, serving as the means by which a small elite extracts rents from everyone else. Predatory governments usually make their countries poorer, as in Nigeria and the Central African Republic. Worse, when power confers riches, people sometimes fight for it, as in Congo and Liberia.

INTRODUCTION: WHY IS AFRICA SO POOR?

The shackled continent

Nowhere exemplifies how an authoritarian government can stifle a nation's ability to create wealth better than Robert Mugabe's Zimbabwe. Mugabe is interesting because he is one of the last reigning members of the first generation of post-independence African leaders, and he rules in a way that suggests he has not learned much from his contemporaries' mistakes. He seizes private property, thus sending a deafening warning to foreign and local investors alike: "Do not put your money into Zimbabwe." He also tries to alter the laws of economics by decree. He fixes the price of gas at below what it costs to import it, so the pumps run dry. He tries to create money by printing it and so causes hyper-inflation. These policies have failed as utterly in Zimbabwe as they have everywhere else they have been tried and have made Zimbabweans much poorer than they were at independence. But although most of his people would love to get rid of Mugabe, they have not been able to because he rigs elections to keep himself in power.

Mugabe governs like the guerrilla commander he once was. He gives orders and expects them to be obeyed. He regards his opponents as enemies to be crushed. The details of how his people earn their daily bowl of cornmeal mush do not interest him in the slightest. He thinks the economy is like the land he once fought for. There is only a fixed amount to go around, and if you want a bigger share, you have to take it by force.

For most of the time since independence, the majority of African countries have been ruled by men with similarly authoritarian ideas. Kwame Nkrumah led the way, imposing a one-party state on Ghana, the first colony to win independence after the Second World War. Other African leaders followed suit, declaring that their own irremovable governments would henceforth control everything of importance. They nationalized everything from mines and factories to bicycle-repair shops,

13

staffed them with ruling-party cronies, and then ran them into the ground.

For a while, they were able to disguise the fact that they were not producing much by borrowing huge sums of money from foolish Western banks and governments. This created a temporary illusion of prosperity. Some of the borrowed cash was spent on free healthcare, education, and loans to farmers, but much of the money was wasted on prestige projects: dams, conference halls, steel mills erected far from the nearest port and over budget, and so on. Little of the money was invested in such a way that it actually produced a return, so African governments eventually found themselves unable to service their loans, let alone repay them.

Since the collapse of the Soviet Union, some things have improved. Marxism is out of fashion, democracy is in. Almost all African countries have held multi-party elections, and many have attempted free-market economic reforms. But old attitudes persist. In many African countries, reforms have been pursued fitfully and without enthusiasm, which may explain why they have so rarely succeeded.

Laissez-faire is not popular in Africa. Nkrumah is still a hero to most Ghanaians, who remember his generous spending but not the fact that he used the accumulated surplus of the colonial period to finance his social programs, which collapsed when the money ran out.[8] Robert Mugabe enjoys a curious popularity too, at least among Africans who do not live in Zimbabwe. Many see him as a strong black leader standing up to intimidation by Western governments, which refused to recognize his stolen election victory in 2002. They cannot fail to notice that Zimbabwe has grown poorer under his rule but swallow his line that this is the fault of a Western conspiracy.

Unchecked power is a swift route to riches, especially in countries with abundant natural resources. Africa is fabulously well endowed with precious minerals, which is one reason why so many people are prepared to fight for a share of power.

In Congo, for example, half a dozen armies and several rebel factions have been battling for control of some of the world's richest deposits of diamonds, cobalt, and tantalum. In Angola, a four-decade-long scramble for loot ended only in 2002, when the rebel leader, Jonas Savimbi, was shot and killed.

In both these cases, and several others besides, minerals have provided not only the motive but also the means for war. Governments use oil revenues to buy helicopter-gunships. Rebels capture diamond mines, sell the stones, buy weapons, and carry on fighting.

That such struggles make Africa poorer than it would otherwise be is obvious: armies marching through your cornfields are bad for your harvest. What is not so obvious is how such wars can be stopped and Africa's mineral wealth turned from a curse into a blessing.

Even in African countries where men with guns do not routinely plunder villages, property rights are rarely secure. Most African peasants do not own the land they cultivate. In some countries, the state owns all the land. In others, individual ownership is allowed, but because of an over-prescriptive and under-competent bureaucracy, it can take ten years and untold hassle to obtain formal title. The same is often true of the houses where the urban poor live.

This matters enormously. Lack of clear ownership means that poor Africans cannot use their property as collateral in order to obtain loans. Without access to credit, farmers find it hard to afford the tools and seeds that might make them more productive, and would-be entrepreneurs find it hard to get started.

A Peruvian economist, Hernando de Soto, estimated that the value of "dead capital" in poor countries – that is, property which cannot be capitalized because of the lack of a title deed – is roughly forty times the foreign aid received throughout the world since 1945. In Africa, the unexploited value of informal urban shacks and informally owned fields is almost a trillion dollars, which is about three times the annual GDP of all the countries south of the Sahara.[9]

Another obstacle to African prosperity is AIDS. Despite all the advances of modern medicine, life expectancy has fallen in much of Africa in the last two decades; in some countries it is less than forty. The main reason is the human immuno-deficiency virus (HIV), which destroys the body's immune system. Thirty million Africans are infected with HIV. Three quarters of the world's AIDS deaths occur in Africa: nearly five Africans die of the disease every minute.[10]

Poverty speeds the epidemic's spread. Those who cannot afford television find other ways of passing the evening. Many Africans cannot afford antibiotics and so cannot cure other sexually transmitted diseases, which leaves them with open sores through which the virus can pass.

Migration and war help the virus to cross borders. Laborers and traders flock from the poorest African countries, such as Mozambique, to the richer ones, such as South Africa. Migrant miners often live in single-sex hostels for eleven months of the year, surrounded by prostitutes. At Christmas, they go home and infect their wives. Truck drivers carry the virus for thousands of miles, from one rest-stop brothel to another. Africa's wars create surges of refugees, some of whom have no other means of support but sex work. Soldiers, with their regular pay and disdain for risk, are more likely to contract HIV than civilians and horribly prone to spread it, forcefully, when they march through enemy villages.

Most important, the virus is spread through sex, something which most Africans do not wish to discuss. This is part of the problem. In Kenya, Christian and Islamic groups have burned sex-education pamphlets and condoms in protest at what they see as the encouragement of promiscuity. South Africa's president, Thabo Mbeki, has suggested that foreigners who say Africa has a big AIDS problem are in fact hinting that Africans are immoral savages: "We are blamed as criminals and seen as human beings of a lower order that cannot subject its passions to reason . . . as natural-born, promiscuous carriers of germs, unique in the world, doomed to a mortal end because of our unconquerable devotion to the sin of lust."[11]

There is a simpler explanation. People who worry about AIDS in Africa do so because the disease threatens to kill more people than all the continent's wars put together and multiplied by ten. And in countries where a quarter of the adult population is infected, it is clear that someone has been having unsafe sex. Without frank discussion of what exactly people are doing in bed and behind bushes, it will be impossible to curb the epidemic.

There are myths that must be rebutted: some young African women believe that without regular infusions of sperm, they will not grow up to be beautiful. In parts of southern Africa, men believe that they can cleanse themselves of the virus by passing it on to a virgin. In Kenya, some think they can achieve the same effect by having sex with a madwoman.

AIDS has devastated African families. The disease strikes people in their productive prime. Breadwinners sicken, so households lose their income just as their medical bills soar. Daughters drop out of school to help nurse their parents. When the virus kills, millions of orphans are left behind. And yet there is hope. A few countries, notably Uganda and Senegal, have fought the epidemic with great success. In Uganda, after a loud and inventive anti-AIDS campaign, adult HIV prevalence crashed from 30 percent in 1992 to 5 percent in 2002.[12]

Even the most stable societies would find it hard to cope with African rates of HIV infection. African societies, however, are often chronically unstable. Most Africans still feel more loyalty to their tribe than to the young nation-states of which they are citizens. Because tribal loyalties are so strong, wily politicians can often stir up conflicts between tribes as a means of cementing their hold on power. This phenomenon is not unique to Africa, of course. From the pogroms of medieval Europe, through the rape of Nanjing, to the Balkans and the Middle East today, unscrupulous politicians have often inflamed tribal passions, usually with vile consequences. But in recent years the worst ethnic clashes have been disproportionately African. The 1994 Rwandan genocide was probably the worst tribal massacre since the Holocaust. On a smaller scale, ethnic violence is common in Burundi, Nigeria, Côte d'Ivoire, and several other African countries.

Ethnic conflict is not inevitable in Africa. Tanzania has dozens of tribes, but Tanzanian politicians have not sought to inflame their differences, and the country has been peaceful since independence. The Rwandan genocide is usually portrayed as the result of ancient and implacable tribal hatreds, but I would argue that without predatory politics, it would not have happened. Members of the Hutu tribe did not spontaneously slaughter their neighbors, the Tutsis. The genocide was meticulously planned by Hutu politicians, who sought thereby to keep themselves in power and Tutsis out of it. Their radio station urged Hutus to fear, hate, and finally kill their neighbors. A secretly organized militia coordinated the bloodletting, arming Hutus who took part and slaughtering those who refused. Roughly 800,000 Tutsis and moderate Hutus were murdered in six weeks, making it the swiftest genocide on record. Rwanda is an extreme example, but the same problem – the tribalization of politics – afflicts most African countries.

In Nigeria, home to at least 250 ethnic groups and split between Muslims in the north and Christians and animists in the south, politicians look to their kith and kin for support, often by reminding them of how much they detest the tribe next door. Once in power, Nigerian politicians tend to put as many people as possible from their own tribe onto the public payroll. This is nice for them but not quite so good for Nigerian public services, which suffer from what Chinua Achebe calls a "cult of mediocrity." In Nigeria, he says, "it would be difficult to point to one important job held by the most competent person we have."[13]

South Africa, notoriously, has ethnic problems too. Under apartheid, the white tribe treated blacks so badly that the rest of the world was moved to sever trade links with South Africa. Since 1994, the country has been ruled by the African National Congress (ANC), the biggest of the parties of liberation, whose leaders see their task as righting the wrongs of apartheid by narrowing the wealth gap between black and white South Africans. They do this partly by taxing the rich and spending the proceeds on schools, clinics, and pensions in poor areas. But they also use more controversial methods, such as compelling companies to favor blacks in hiring and promotion and allowing black-owned firms to charge more and still win public works contracts.

Black executives and construction-firm owners do well out of this, but poor blacks suffer. Because the government pays a premium to black contractors, the budget for building houses for poor people stretches to fewer houses. Because employers are obliged to hire people on a basis other than ability, South African firms become less competitive, the economy grows more slowly and the jobless stay that way. Most worrying, the ANC's policy of positive discrimination, coupled with increasingly frequent appeals to black solidarity, has spoiled the harmony of the Mandela years and re-polarized South African politics along racial lines. This is unlikely to lead to violence; whites who don't like it can emigrate. But it is unlikely to promote prosperity either.

I devote the longest chapter in the book to these issues for two reasons. First, you cannot understand African politics without grasping the influence of tribal hucksters. Second, because my proposed solution is highly controversial. It is an article of faith among many in the West that governments should favor certain ethnic groups, especially those who have been discriminated against in the past. But after seeing what quotas and ethnically divisive laws have done in Africa, I have to disagree.

Smarter aid, more trade

Any discussion of Africa's poverty has to take into account its relations with the rest of the world. For half a century now, the continent has been deluged with aid, but this has failed to make Africans any less poor. The problem is that donors have opened their wallets with scant regard as to whether the money will be sensibly spent. They have bankrolled tyrants, such as Gnassingbé Eyadéma in Togo, or idealists with hopeless economic policies, such as Julius Nyerere in Tanzania. Both types of aid have been wasted.

Some people argue that aid to poor countries is always wasted and that we should cut it altogether. This is too simplistic. There is good evidence that aid works if directed to countries with sound economic polices and functioning institutions of government. Meanwhile, rich countries could do more good, more quickly, if they ripped down their trade barriers. Africa has terrific agricultural potential: fertile land, sun when the northern hemisphere is frosty, and cheap labor. The continent also has a comparative advantage in textiles, which are simple to make but require lots of labor. By exporting crops and shirts to rich countries, Africa could start on the path to growth. But imported food and textiles are precisely the things that rich countries most vigorously shut out of their markets.

Farm products face meager quotas and steep tariffs. Worse, rich countries subsidize their own farmers so lavishly that African producers cannot compete. The total value of agricultural subsidies in developed countries is almost a billion dollars a day: more than the GDP of sub-Saharan Africa. This wastes Western taxpayers' money and greases the ladder up which Africans are trying to clamber out of poverty.

That ladder is slippery enough in any case. Africa needs more successful businesses, but doing business in Africa can be tricky. Bad roads, punctuated by road blocks manned by bribe-hungry policemen, make it slow and costly to move goods even short distances. Frequent power and water cuts force Nigerian firms to resort to what local businessmen call BYOI ("Bring Your Own Infrastructure").

Surprisingly, foreign investors in Africa make better returns than on any other continent. But this is partly because the perceived risk of doing business in Africa is so high that firms only invest in projects that promise a quick reward. And a recent trend to demonize Western companies that operate in poor countries, encouraged by campaigning charities and protectionist Western trade unions, has deterred many from putting money into Africa.

Local firms, meanwhile, have been held back by arbitrary government, dysfunctional legal systems, and the difficulty, for those without political connections, of raising capital. Persistent and ingenious African businessfolk prosper despite all these obstacles, but many more would do so if the obstacles were removed.

If the examples of most developed countries are anything to go by, Africa's future prosperity will depend in part on the speed with which it adopts and adapts to new technologies. There are millions of wonderful ideas out there waiting to be borrowed, but so far Africa has been slow to train the necessary engineers and technicians to make use of them. As for original innovations, the continent produces depressingly few. But in several African countries, people recognize the need to embrace new technology. Even in backwaters such as Swaziland and Madagascar there are Internet cafés and pirated anti-malarial drugs.

Technology does not mean only high technology. Simple devices can also change people's lives. Take the rolling plastic water barrel, for example. Cheap but tough, the barrel is attached to an axle and frame, like a wheelbarrow. It can be filled with water and then pushed along the bumpiest of tracks. This enables women who previously had to carry water on their heads to transport much greater volumes of the precious liquid with less effort. Women who used to spend two hours a day fetching water are able to perform the same task in one hour a week.[14]

Several African countries are trying to leapfrog from the pre-industrial present into the information age. For example, most of the fixed-line telephone networks in Africa are awful, so many Africans are jumping straight to the latest mobile-telephone technology. Being largely privately owned, African mobile telephone firms have to satisfy their customers or go out of business. In theory, Africans could leapfrog to the latest technology in many areas. Having few factories, the continent has few factories with outdated technology that people might hesitate to close. The question is, how can Africa keep pace with a world that won't slow down?

The country with the best chance of catching up is South Africa, the most advanced industrial nation on the continent. Since the relatively peaceful passing of apartheid in 1994, anyone concerned about Africa's future has been watching South Africa carefully, for its success or failure will have a profound influence on its neighbors. A liberal, democratic South Africa would set an example for others to follow. A prosperous South Africa could provide the engine for the whole continent's economic growth, much as Japan did in East Asia.

South Africa's early years as a democracy have not been easy. The euphoria that most South Africans felt under the presidency of Nelson Mandela has given way to confusion and tension under his successor, Thabo Mbeki. The economy has failed to grow fast enough to create jobs for the third or more of the South African workforce who are unemployed. AIDS threatens to kill millions. Education for black South Africans, deliberately neglected under apartheid, has barely improved under the new order. Crime, once kept more or less in check through brutality, has flourished now that the police can no longer kick confessions out of suspects, but most have not yet learned other ways of securing convictions.

And yet there are reasons for optimism. In startling contrast to some of its neighbors, the new South Africa has enjoyed sound fiscal and monetary policies. Put simply, the government has not spent much more than it raises in taxes and has not printed money to pay its bills. A party that was once funded by the Soviet Union and determined to nationalize mines and to arrest speculators has made the hard transition to realism. South Africa still has the best roads, telephone lines, power stations, and restaurants in Africa. Its financial markets are more sophisticated than most of Latin America's. Many of its companies are advanced enough to list on the London stock exchange. A takeoff is possible. It needs only wise leadership to let it happen.

In the long run, I believe that Africa will prosper. Any country can make the transition from poverty to comfort. We know this because it has been done before, in countries as different as Italy and Japan. The technology that underpins prosperity already exists, and much of it is free. Want to know how to build a car, a microchip, or a factory for antibiotics? Walk into a library, or browse through old patent applications. The political, legal, and economic arrangements of rich countries are not exactly secret, either. When Japan's rulers decided, in the nineteenth century, that they had to modernize to avoid being colonized, they sent their brightest officials to Germany, Britain, and America to find out how industrial societies worked. They then copied the ideas that seemed most useful and rejected the Western habits that seemed unhelpful or distasteful; within a few decades Japan was advanced enough to win a war with Russia – the first non-white nation to defeat a European power in modern times.

Japan's example should be important for Africa, because it shows that modernization need not mean Westernization. Developing countries need to learn from developed ones, but they do not have to abandon their culture and traditions in the process. No one who has seen a Shinto priest blessing a new bullet train would argue that Japan is a Western country, but the engineering that went into the train is of universal applicability. Africans face the same challenge now that Japan faced in the nineteenth century: how to harness other people's ideas and technology to help them build the kind of society that they, the Africans, want.

Some readers may find my arguments too narrowly materialistic. Money is not everything. Despite their poverty, Africans are not obviously less happy than, say, Japanese salarymen. The man in a suit on the Tokyo subway earns far more than a Cameroonian peasant, but the peasant seems less stressed and has more time to sit in the shade eating papayas and enjoying the company of his family and friends. Which of the two is better off? There is no reliable means of measuring this.

Probably most Africans desire at least some of the material goods that are so abundant in industrialized societies. But are they prepared to undergo the wrenching changes necessary to industrialize? Some may not be, which is fair enough. Many subsistence farmers undoubtedly want to remain as they are. In their villages, they enjoy the familiarity that comes of living as their parents did and the warmth and security that comes from belonging to a community whose members look out for each other.

For the most part, peasants who wish to remain peasants are free to do so. The problem in Africa is that there are not enough opportunities for the large number of people who want something more. Economic growth brings not only greater material wealth but also greater choice. In peasant societies, children usually start work in the fields before they reach puberty and carry on planting and harvesting until shortly before they die. In industrialized societies, children start school young and continue their education into their twenties, broadening their minds and preparing themselves to pick one or more of a dizzying range of careers. Some pine for the days when life was simpler, but no one ever voluntarily goes back to being a peasant.

So the question is, how can African societies evolve so that more Africans have options other than growing yams? I think the answer is largely political: if Africa were better governed, it would be richer.

Politics matter, as can be shown by looking at Germany or Korea. South Korea shares 5,000 years of history and culture with North Korea. West Germany had almost as much in common with East Germany before the nation was divided. During the Cold War, both Germany and Korea were split into communist and capitalist parts. In Korea, the division remains. In Germany, half a century of separate government created a huge difference in wealth. By the time the Berlin Wall was knocked down, West Germany was freer, happier, and four times richer than East Germany. In their occasional humorous moods, West Germans ask: "How do we know that East Germans are not descended from apes?" The answer: "No ape could have gone forty years without bananas."

In Korea, the difference is greater still. Politics on the peninsula mean the difference between penury and excess, between fear and freedom. After fifty years of Stalinism, North Koreans are at least ten times poorer than their southern cousins. Power cuts leave northerners' homes dark at night and icy in winter. Famine killed hundreds of thousands of North Koreans in the 1990s and forced survivors to subsist on boiled grass and leaves. Dissidents are locked in labor camps or shot. Ordinary North Koreans are too scared of their rulers to talk openly to strangers. Contrast this with capitalist South Korea, a country where the only people who go hungry are fashion models, where manual laborers can afford foreign holidays, and where artists can lampoon the president in the crudest terms without provoking anything more frightening than a bored audience.[15]

Similar, if less extreme, comparisons can be made in Africa. Consider, for example, Zambia and Botswana. These two neighboring states may not be culturally identical, but they are certainly cousins. At independence in the 1960s, Zambia was Africa's second-richest country, whereas Botswana was what one British colonial official described as "a useless piece of territory."[16]

Zambia had a government determined to help the poor, rich copper mines, and a torrent of foreign aid. But the country's first president, Kenneth Kaunda, though well-meaning, was convinced that socialism was the route to prosperity. So he nationalized Zambia's copper mines, told peasants what to grow, and forced them to sell their crops to the government at artificially low prices.

Kaunda assumed that the mines would provide an inexhaustible flow of money, whether well-managed or not. He allowed the state mining firm to become bloated and corrupt. No serious effort was made to develop alternative sources of foreign currency. When the copper price plunged, Kaunda's costly policies suddenly became unaffordable. Kaunda was succeeded by a former trade unionist, Frederick Chiluba, who promised liberal reforms. But these reforms stalled as Chiluba's venal cronies began to loot the country. Corruption under Chiluba held Zambia back as surely as Kaunda's socialism. Despite huge infusions of foreign aid, Zambians are now poorer than they were at independence.

Contrast this with Botswana. The country's mineral wealth, in the form of one of the world's richest seams of diamonds, was discovered after independence. Unlike Zambia, Botswana spent the windfall wisely. Diamond dollars were ploughed into infrastructure, education, and health. Private business was allowed to grow; foreign investment was welcomed. Government was astoundingly clean. The budget is usually in surplus. The president, Festus Mogae, has been seen doing his own shopping. From 1966 to 2001, income per head in Botswana grew faster than in any other country in the world, from bare subsistence to well over $3,000.

Botswana is a wonderful success story, but it is tiny. Only a million and a half people live there, less than the population of a single slum in Lagos, Nigeria's commercial capital. For Africa to thrive, it needs more and bigger Botswanas. And for that, the continent needs saner politics.

1. THE VAMPIRE STATE

Africans are not yet free

All he did was to stuff envelopes for the opposition party, but in Robert Mugabe's Zimbabwe, it was a hazardous job. Deligent Marowa had joined the Movement for Democratic Change (MDC) because, he said, it was "time to throw the crooks out of office." But the crooks had other ideas.

Marowa was kidnapped after an MDC meeting in a township outside Harare, the Zimbabwean capital. As he walked home in the dark, two cars drew up beside him. A couple of heavy-set men stepped out and forced him, at gunpoint, to climb in. Marowa recognized one of his captors – the man had been pointed out to him before as an agent of Zimbabwe's Central Intelligence Organization (CIO).

Handcuffed to a door handle, Marowa was driven to a remote patch of waste land. There, his captors threw him to the ground and kicked him until he passed out. When he regained consciousness, they pushed a sharpened bicycle spoke into his rectum and up his urethra.

They left him for dead but, somehow, he made it to a hospital. A few days later, as he lay recuperating, they found him again. After dark, they slipped into the ward where he lay, flashed a gun, and said: "Let's go." Fortunately, another patient saw the pistol and screamed. Nurses came running, and the kidnappers fled. Marowa can now walk again, but he will never have children.

I met him in June 2000, a few days before a parliamentary

election in Zimbabwe. He was young, lean, and angry. His ordeal was intended to scare him into abandoning opposition politics but had had the opposite effect. He waved his X-rays at me like a banner of protest and promised not to rest until the ruling party, ZANU-PF, was turfed out of power – which would have happened that very week had the election not been rigged.

There is a connection, though it is not obvious, between Marowa's tragedy and the theme of this book. Africans are poor largely because they are not yet free. They live under predatory, incompetent governments, which they have great trouble shaking off. Their governments impoverish them in many ways: through corruption, through bad economic policies, and some-times, as in Zimbabwe, by creating an atmosphere of terror that scares off all but the most intrepid businessfolk. In theory most Africans have the freedom to vote their rulers out of office, but in practice they find it difficult to do so.

Zimbabwe's tragedy is especially poignant because the coun-try, which was once the British colony of Southern Rhodesia, has so much going for it. It enjoys a warm, gentle climate and is so beautiful that it should be choking with tourists. Besides the sun, wildlife, and waterfalls, it has music, art, flowers, and delicious food. In springtime, the jacaranda trees carpet the streets with blue petals. The wine may be lousy, but the beer is excellent and the beefsteaks in Bulawayo are the tastiest I have ever eaten.

The people of Zimbabwe are open, friendly, hospitable, and among the best-educated in Africa. They should be rich. There is plenty of land in Zimbabwe, much of it ideal for raising cattle or growing wheat, corn, and tobacco. Under the ground lie reefs of gold, platinum, and other precious ores. The country has a modern banking sector, skilled manufacturers, and adequate roads.

And yet Zimbabwe is a mess.

Two decades after independence, Zimbabweans are dramat-ically poorer and can expect to die more than a decade younger.

In 1980, the average annual income in Zimbabwe was $950, and a Zimbabwean dollar was worth more than an American one. By 2003, the average income was less than $400, a Zim dollar barely bought a fiftieth of an American cent, and the Zimbabwean economy was in freefall. AIDS was largely to blame for Zimbabweans' shorter lifespans, but the fact that they had, according to the World Health Organization, the least efficient health service in the world probably didn't help.

So what went wrong?

For an answer, look at the portrait that hangs on the wall of every government office, in every hotel lobby, and above the cash register in every shop. A grandfatherly figure gazes back, a man with big glasses and a tiny velcro-strip moustache in the middle of his top lip. Robert Mugabe, Zimbabwe's ageing president, is too subtle to foist a full-blown personality cult on his countrymen. But still, no one dares to remove his picture.

The hero of the *chimurenga*, the bush war for freedom from white rule, Mugabe has been in power without a break since that struggle ended in 1980. When he first took office, things went well. The world was glad of any alternative to the white supremacist regime of Ian Smith and showered Zimbabwe with aid. The civil war was over and sanctions had been lifted. Mugabe spoke of racial reconciliation. The rains were good and the national mood was optimistic. The first two years after independence saw startling economic growth of 28 percent. It did not last.

Though he calls himself a socialist, and even at one point invited North Korean officers to come and train his army, Mugabe never allowed Zimbabwe to become a Soviet satellite and never tried to erect a Soviet-style command economy. Even so, he has made it extremely hard for Zimbabweans outside his ruling party to prosper. The story of one local entrepreneur, Strive Masiyiwa, speaks for many.

In 1993, Masiyiwa decided that Zimbabwe needed a mobile telephone network. Zimbabweans, like most people, like to talk to each other. Back then, the only way they could do so at a distance was by using the fixed-line network operated by PTC, the state telephone monopoly, which was so inefficient that getting a line installed in your home could take ten years.

A skilled engineer and a charming salesman, Masiyiwa had no trouble raising the necessary finance. He suggested a joint venture with PTC, but its bosses refused, saying there was no call for mobile telephones in Zimbabwe. So Masiyiwa decided to go it alone.

Although PTC had no plans to provide a mobile service itself, the state-owned firm insisted that its monopoly barred anyone else from doing so. Masiyiwa hired lawyers to test the legality of PTC's obstruction. To many people's surprise, a judge found that there was no law that explicitly forbade Masiyiwa from going ahead. The government, which saw telephones as a means of spying on people rather than as a business, was unhappy. The Supreme Court overturned the ruling.

A faint-hearted entrepreneur would have given up at this point. Masiyiwa, who had returned to his homeland from Wales after the end of white rule, appealed to the constitution instead. He argued that PTC's behavior violated the constitutional right to free speech. At a time when most European countries still had equally obstructive telephone monopolies, this was a bold strategy. But it worked. In 1995, the Supreme Court ruled in Masiyiwa's favor, and Econet, his firm, started setting up base stations around Harare. At this point, the president took an interest, and life grew uncomfortable for Masiyiwa. In February 1996, Robert Mugabe issued a decree banning private cellphone operations and promising two-year jail terms for offenders. Econet's Swedish partners were forced to abandon their expensive equipment and retreat to their hotel rooms. But still Masiyiwa persevered.

He appealed to the Supreme Court on the ground that

Mugabe's decree was unconstitutional. The Supreme Court agreed. There was a tender for a private cellphone license. By this time, however, a number of political heavyweights were interested in the business. The license was awarded to Telecel, a consortium backed by, among others, Mugabe's nephew. Masiyiwa sued for the right to see the details of Telecel's bid, and sure enough, it met few of the technical specifications required in the tender.

Telecel's license was suspended, but the telecommunications minister, whose husband was an old business partner of one of the main Telecel shareholders, restored it. Two months later, there was a cabinet reshuffle, and suddenly Masiyiwa found his path cleared. He won his license in December 1997, while Telecel's was canceled. Go-betweens tried to bribe and then to intimidate Masiyiwa into sharing his business with Telecel's backers. Despite death threats, he refused.

Finally, his tormentors gave up and left him alone. Econet quickly became the most popular Zimbabwean mobile operator and expanded into other African markets, too.

Masiyiwa told me his story in 1998, in his office in Harare. He was only thirty-seven and looked boyish and dapper in his mauve socks and designer stubble. A devout man, Masiyiwa gave all the credit for his success to God. On a more earthly plane, it clearly helped that the Zimbabwean judiciary was still honest and independent enough in the mid-1990s to provide a check on the government's power. But the moral from this tale is that Zimbabwe would be a lot less poor if entrepreneurs like Masiyiwa did not have to fight the ruling party to stay in business.

Unfortunately for Zimbabwean businessfolk, many ruling-party bosses dislike them as a class. Like so many African liberators, Mugabe and his ZANU comrades grew up believing that, as Lenin argued, capitalism and colonialism were two sides of the same coin. At the time they were fighting for freedom, communist Russia had an empire that spanned eleven time zones, while America had Puerto Rico. But in colonial Africa, the idea seemed to make sense. Most of the big businesses were run by whites, so many African revolutionaries came to see business itself as a white occupation.

Like many African leaders, Mugabe thought that socialism fitted well with African traditions: land, for instance, was traditionally held in common in most African communities, with the chief deciding who could plough which patch.[1] Perhaps most important, the idea of a powerful central state was congenial to those, like Mugabe, who wanted to rule without too many cumbersome restraints.

When the Berlin Wall fell, Mugabe and his comrades were forced to reconsider their beliefs. Many former socialists decided that capitalism was all right, so long as the ruling party received a cut. A program of "affirmative action" to increase the number of black-owned businesses in Zimbabwe turned into a massive handout of public-works contracts and banking licenses to Mugabe's political allies. The old man himself never seemed interested in the nuts and bolts of commerce, but he hired a number of unsavory (and often white) managers and fixers to help run the business empire that ZANU built up using its political power.

Businessfolk without connections kept quiet in the hope of avoiding being shaken down. An Asian businessman in Bulawayo, over a lunch of hot and crispy peri-peri chicken, told me how he drove a rusty and dented old Datsun to avoid drawing attention to himself. "The government are a bunch of thieves. If I made it obvious that I have money, they'd try to steal it. So I keep my head down and act poor."

Zimbabwe is now one of the few countries where even miserably paid manual workers see eye to eye with their bosses about the source of their ills. In 1998, I interviewed a then little-known union leader called Morgan Tsvangirai, who is now head of the opposition party. It took time to get past the steel security grilles outside his office. A couple of months previously, some men he claimed were from the CIO had broken in and tried to throw him out of his tenth-floor window. When I finally sat face to face with him, he told me things that I had never heard a shop steward say before. Instead of arguing that workers were being squeezed by greedy bosses, he blamed the government for grabbing half their wages in taxes and then eroding the value of what was left by printing too much money and causing inflation.

Workers were fed up, he said, with continually being told they should be grateful to Mugabe for liberating them from colonial rule. Independence was eighteen years ago, he scoffed. The problem today was that wages were falling and life was getting harder. And it was Mugabe's fault. "The government needs to live within its means," he told me. "The government borrows money to spend on salaries – it should cut the number of its employees instead."

The regime was not merely crooked; it had lousy economic policies too. For example, Mugabe often sought to control prices, decreeing that some essential goods had to be sold at prices other than those voluntarily agreed upon by buyers and sellers. Several times, he decided that gasoline was "too expensive." Mugabe feared that rising bus fares might spark riots, so he fixed the price of gasoline at less than it cost to import the stuff. Inevitably, the pumps ran dry. Workers could not get to work, and factories crunched to a halt. Often when I visited Harare, there were long lines of stationary cars outside every gas station, blocking the road. Hawkers sold the angry motorists hot coffee and bananas, and the MDC recruited new members from their ranks.

When the prices of basic foodstuffs went up, Mugabe fixed them too. Several times, he ordered bakers to sell loaves for less than they cost to bake and wondered why the stores ran out of bread.[2] When the local currency collapsed, he tried to fix the exchange rate. Anyone swapping hard currency for Zimbabwe dollars was obliged to do so at a price that hugely overvalued the Zimbabwe dollar. Naturally, no one with hard currency wanted to be robbed, so the supply of American dollars dried up. Tractors seized up for want of imported spare parts, and a black market for greenbacks boomed.

In 2000, at the official exchange rate, an American dollar was worth fifty-five Zimbabwe dollars. But you could not possibly buy an American dollar at this rate. Black market dealers charged between eighty and one hundred Zim dollars for an American one. Two years later, the official rate was unchanged, but the black market rate had shot up to more than 1,000 to one. Only the government could buy real money at the official rate, and only by using the threat of force. Exporters were obliged to hand over a big chunk of their hard-currency revenues to the government at the official rate. In effect, the government was stealing their money, pushing some into bankruptcy, and forcing others to start smuggling.[3]

In a free market, prices are determined by haggling. The buyer wants to pay as little as possible; the seller wants to receive as much as possible. But if the buyer wants a pair of shoes more than he wants the $10 in his pocket, and the shoe-seller wants $10 more than he wants the shoes, they can agree on a price of $10. This is the principle by which African village markets have operated since the days when everyone was African. It's simple, it's voluntary, and both parties benefit. Marx called it "exploitation," and many of Africa's post-independence leaders agreed with him.

Mugabe's lingering socialist sympathies provided him with a moral justification for ruling the whole country in much the same way as he commanded his guerrillas during the liberation war. Rather than signing laws and letting Zimbabweans live freely under them, he issued orders and expected them to be obeyed. This is a sensible way of running an army, but not a modern economy.

Price-fixing is a bit like jumping off a tall building shouting "I abolish the law of gravity." You cannot simply decree that something is worth more than anyone will pay for it or less than sellers will accept for it. Mugabe's price controls never brought Zimbabwe's dreadful inflation under control, because they failed to address the real cause: the regime's habit of printing money to pay its bills.

Zimbabwe's public accounts came to look like a drug addict's credit-card statement. In 2000, for example, the government spent twice as much as it received in tax revenues.[4] To make up the shortfall, it borrowed money or printed it. Mugabe's ministers denied that this was what they were doing. The finance minister, Simba Makoni, told me that the government was "living within its means." But a quick visit to a cash machine in Harare suggested otherwise. The banknotes came out crisp and new, with consecutive serial numbers. Inflation was about 70 percent that year and had reached 526 percent by late 2003.

To be fair, when he first came to power, Mugabe spent a lot on worthwhile things such as schools and clinics. But he also lavished funds on an absurdly large bureaucracy and on his army and intelligence service. He doubtless thought this was money well spent, as it enabled him to put down an uprising in Matabeleland in the 1980s with relative ease, slaughtering 10,000–20,000 members of the dissident Ndebele tribe at much lighter cost to his own troops. But he could only maintain his big-spending ways as long as Zimbabwe received large amounts of foreign aid. The longer the Mugabe regime was in power, the more corrupt his cronies became, and the more erratic his policies became. Donors grew tired of handing over money and seeing it wasted or embezzled, so they became less generous.

From about 1997, public finances went haywire. Veterans of the liberation war rioted because a fund intended to compensate them had been looted by ZANU bigwigs. Mugabe calmed them with huge cash handouts, which pushed the budget into the red but bought the president some muscular support.

The same year, Mugabe promised to seize, without compensation, land belonging to white commercial farmers and give it to the landless poor. The Zim dollar plunged at the news. Then, even as the country was teetering on the edge of bankruptcy, he decided to send a quarter of his army to fight a pointless war in far-off Congo. The only way he could pay for all this was to print more banknotes.

It is hard to explain to someone who has never lived with massive inflation just how destructive it is. For the Mugabe regime, printing money provided one short-term benefit – it enabled the treasury to pay the army's wages at the end of the month. For ordinary Zimbabweans, however, high inflation spelled rapid impoverishment. For savers, it was like a huge additional tax. Anyone who left their money in the bank saw it munched to crumbs in a matter of months. Workers on fixed salaries saw their buying power waste away. By 2003, a laborer earning the minimum wage in Harare could not afford a typical bus fare into work each day even if he spent all his earnings on it. That was all. No clothes, fuel, medicine, or school fees. Since half of the workforce was unemployed, each wage earner usually supported a large extended family. Everyone ate less, and children dropped out of school to grow corn on patches of wasteland. Meanwhile, Mugabe's wife had the bits of her mansion that displeased her knocked down and rebuilt and went shopping in London, until she was banned from Britain.

Zimbabwe's inflation, on its own, would have made the country an unappealing place to do business – when prices are wildly unpredictable, it is hard to plan for the long term. But what spooked investors most was Mugabe's open scorn for property rights. When the government started confiscating commercial farms, every shopkeeper, factory boss, and homeowner in Zimbabwe started worrying that they might be next.[5]

A socialist might well say: "So what?" Shopkeepers, factory bosses, and homeowners are all pampered bourgeois types. Redistribution may hurt them, but it helps the poor and needy. Well, not necessarily. When pursued as chaotically as in Zimbabwe, it helps hardly anyone.

In August 2000, I visited a farm where fifty-one black families had been resettled. The handover had taken place two years before, amid raucous celebrations. Mugabe arrived in one of his helicopters. Cows were slaughtered, beer gushed, crowds danced and chanted, and television cameras recorded the event for posterity. The new smallholders had been selected by lot, so most of them knew little about farming. The government promised them seeds, fertilizer, and financial help to raise their crops but delivered none of these things.

A local white commercial farmer, Andrew Dawson, stepped in. He offered to plough his new neighbors' fields and to supply them with fertilizer. They could repay him, he said, at harvest time, interest-free, in corn. Twelve families took up his offer, but only two repaid their debts. The rest failed, for the most part, to raise any crops at all, despite ample rain. I drove around in a pick-up truck with Dawson, a stocky man in extra-short khaki shorts. We crossed from side to distant side of what had once been a productive tobacco farm, and he pointed out the resettled areas, which had almost all been reclaimed by wild grass, bushes, and baboons. Most of the resettlers had drifted away.

Some of those who had been given plots were not obviously poor or needy. One was a civil servant with a mobile phone, who rarely visited his land. When apes started eating his corn, he did not have time to do anything about it himself, so he asked Dawson to shoo them off.

Dawson told me that his farm was now earmarked for seizure, too. He had 300 employees, who each supported on average about five dependants. A band of self-proclaimed war veterans, who were acting as a private militia for President Mugabe, arrived before the June 2000 election and ordered him to sign over to them more land than he actually owned. They threatened his workers with death if they carried on working. They also threatened that if any MDC campaigners were seen in the area, they would kill Dawson and his family.

The tragedy is that land reform is necessary in Zimbabwe and has worked in the past. After independence, Britain forked out roughly $102 million to buy arable land and settle some 70,000 poor families on it. The land was bought on a willing-buyer, willing-seller basis. Recipients of land were selected, at least in theory, according to their agricultural skills: those likely to make the best use of the soil were given plots. There were problems in the implementation, but many small farmers took advantage of the opportunity to work for themselves and grew more prosperous. Before long, however, the process was corrupted. Donor support dried up when it was discovered that much of the land was being given or sold for woodshavings to wealthy cronies of the ruling party.[6] When Vice-President Joshua Nkomo died in 1999, he owned stakes in sixteen farms.

After 2000, the Zimbabwean economy started to contract at the sort of pace you might expect during a war. Farmers, who provided the largest portion of the country's exports, were paralyzed. No bank would lend them money because their collateral was liable to be confiscated at any moment. Nor was it easy to cultivate crops with hostile squatters vandalizing their irrigation pipes and breaking their workers' legs. Farmers' woes in turn affected their suppliers and customers, from tractor-repair shops to bakeries. Farm-related businesses, which accounted for perhaps half of Zimbabwean industry, were crippled. The country was undergoing an industrial revolution in reverse.

Mugabe's campaign of terror also – unsurprisingly – destroyed the tourist trade. Since the violence was not random but directed at the opposition, tourists were actually quite safe unless they visited farms or attended political rallies. My wife Emma and I, for example, went canoeing on the Zambezi River at the height of the troubles and suffered no frights except from the wildlife. While on foot in the bush, we interrupted two lions at an intimate moment. The male roared his annoyance. If we had run away, he would doubtless have chased, caught, and eaten us. But fortunately our guide stood his ground and roared back. The cats slunk off. In two weeks, we encountered no human hostil-ity at all. But our guide told us he had had no other customers for months and expected none.

The shortages of fuel and foreign currency hurt every firm in Zimbabwe. The lights stayed on only because South Africa supplied electricity on credit to avert an economic collapse and a flood of refugees across the border. (And perhaps on the assumption that, when the dust settled, South Africa would end up owning the Zimbabwean power grid.) Hundreds of companies went bust. Mugabe accused them of deliberately sabotaging the economy.

How to rig an election

The Mugabe regime has come to resemble a tapeworm infestation in Zimbabwe's stomach, feeding off the fruits of other people's labor, sapping the nation's strength. Unlike tapeworms, however, Mugabe and his cronies have proven fiendishly hard to flush out. At the election in June 2000, I saw at first hand the lengths to which they were prepared to go to stay in power.

It was a parliamentary election, not a presidential one, so Mugabe's job was not at stake. But the old man was worried, nonetheless. The MDC had only been around for a few months but looked set to wrest control of parliament from ZANU. Mugabe responded by offering free land to his supporters and bicycle spokes to his opponents.

It was a brilliant strategy. Many landless Zimbabweans dreamed of owning a plot to grow corn on. And many resented the fact that a handful of white commercial farmers owned about a third of the nation's farmland.[7] There was a genuine historical grievance: some white farmers were descended from British colonists who had stolen land from black Zimbabweans with official blessing.

In the run-up to the election, thousands of people calling themselves veterans of the liberation war (though many were too young to have fought) invaded white-owned farms. The invasions were portrayed in the state-owned media (which had a monopoly of radio and television) as a spontaneous expression of land hunger. But the invaders arrived in ruling-party pick-up trucks, were paid and fed by the security forces, and organized by CIO officials with cellphones. Zimbabwe's courts ruled the invasions illegal, but Mugabe told the police not to intervene.

In fiery speeches, Mugabe accused the MDC of being a front for racist whites, whom he blamed for all the country's ills. It was not a plausible story. White Zimbabweans may be richer than their black compatriots, but they account for less than 1 percent of the population and have little political power. There are, in fact, more elephants than whites in Zimbabwe.[8]

During the campaign, ZANU enjoyed the advantages of incumbency. State-owned newspapers applauded the party's unrealistic manifesto – free land, free houses, jobs for all, cheaper food, and so on – while "uncovering" MDC plots to bring back forced labor and colonialism. ZANU received state funding; the MDC did not. Constituencies were gerrymandered to favor Mugabe's ethnic group, the Shona. By one estimate, a quarter of the names on the electoral roll were of dead people, who usually voted for the ruling party.[9] Mugabe had the right to appoint a fifth of the members of parliament. A ZANU hack was in charge of the count. And the war veterans were shuttled at taxpayers' expense from one marginal constituency to the next, to beat up anyone suspected of supporting the MDC.

In the weeks before the vote, the terror grew systematic. Farm workers were a prime target. With their families, they numbered 2 million – almost a fifth of Zimbabwe's population. They had good reason to hate Mugabe, for his land policy threatened their jobs. So the war veterans were ordered to thrash them into line.

I visited several occupied farms and heard stories that spoke of meticulously planned thuggery. The veterans appeared to have been ordered to scare as many people as possible, without actually killing too many. They typically arrived at a farm armed with sticks, pangas, and a few guns. They claimed the land and divided it into plots but spent little time trying to cultivate it. Instead, they ordered the farm workers to stop work and forced them to attend political "re-education" sessions.

At one farm I visited, only one worker out of 300 was prepared to speak to me, and only on condition that I did not use his name. He said that the veterans had forced everyone to spend hours each day listening to revolutionary lectures and singing ZANU campaign songs. Those who sang with insufficient ardor were whipped until they fell unconscious. Several women were raped, and the veterans warned that worse would follow if ZANU lost the election.

There were only a few thousand so-called war veterans but they were better armed than the farm workers and had the tremendous advantage that no matter what they did, the police were under orders not to arrest them. However, if a farm worker so much as punched a veteran, he was immediately hauled off to the cells.

The veterans set up road blocks on rural roads. They waved down each passing bus and beat up passengers who failed to show ZANU membership cards. Teachers, nurses, and others who, because they could read and write, were assumed to be opposition supporters, had their identity cards shredded, their homes burned down, and their bodies beaten with hoes or seared with molten plastic.

At least thirty people were killed, thousands were forced to flee their homes, and the MDC was prevented from campaigning in large swathes of the country. In no-go areas, opposition activists pinned up MDC posters stealthily by night or dropped leaflets from light aircraft. The violence eased during the actual ballot-casting, but it did not stop everywhere.

I spent the election weekend in Mberengwa East, a rural constituency 400 kilometers south of Harare. The polling stations I visited seemed calm and orderly. Lines of people stood patiently outside, waiting their turn. Officials with official-looking badges matched voters' identity documents with names on the voters' roll, and voters marked their ballots behind wooden screens. A passing European election monitor glanced at one calm scene, concluded that all was well, and sped off in his Land Cruiser.

An MDC polling agent named Hlupo Nkomo pointed out to me a couple of details that the monitor had missed. Several "officials" standing outside the polling station were war veterans who had been terrorizing the area for months. The men handing over ballot papers to each voter were widely known as torturers. The war veterans had kidnapped dozens of local MDC activists, dragged them to a nearby occupied farm called Texas Ranch, and jolted their genitals with jumper cables. Small wonder that none of the people in the line wanted to talk to a stranger like me. When I asked them which party they favored, they looked away and gestured gently that they wanted to be left alone.

Nkomo took me to see the charred husk of his welding shop, which he said had been torched by ruling-party thugs three weeks previously, along with his house. As he stood amid the rubble, I crossed the dusty road and asked two neighbors if they knew anything about it. Flustered, they said they had seen nothing and denied even knowing who Nkomo was. As we drove away, Nkomo remarked that these two had been his neighbors for ten years. His wife and children were in hiding, he said, and he feared that he would never again be safe in his home town.

At a safe house, I met dozens of equally terrified MDC campaign staff. About 150 of them were living squashed into a three-bedroom bungalow, seeking safety in numbers. The fittest and least seriously injured young men stood guard. The owner's furniture stood outside to make way for all the extra people inside. They cooked communally and slept in shifts. One young woman had given birth there – she had been too afraid to go to hospital. Many of those huddled inside the safe house wore bandages, hastily applied to eye and leg wounds. Many had lost their homes. All spoke with fear of the local war veterans and their leader, a knife-juggling karate expert who went by the nom de guerre of Big Chitoro.

Some MDC people were so badly injured that they had to check into a hospital, despite the risk of being attacked again while in an open ward. One bed-bound man I spoke to was mourning his brother, who had been tortured to death a few days before. He was in no state to pursue the murderers because his buttocks had been slashed half away with a rhino-hide whip. It pained him to move, but he insisted on unwrapping his bandages to show me. Such injuries were common during the election campaign, but Zimbabwean journalists were discouraged from reporting on them. When one independent newspaper published a page of photographs of dissidents' mutilated behinds, the editor was arrested for "obscenity."

I snatched a beer, some grilled beef, and a chat at a pub with Sekai Holland, the MDC's candidate for Mberengwa East. She was a large, matronly woman with a red shawl wrapped around her shoulders and a voice that grew shrill when enraged. Six of her polling agents were missing, presumed dead, and 120 were in intensive care. She called the ruling party "parasites" and "barbarians." She reserved even more vitriolic epithets for Big Chitoro who, as it happened, was a distant relative of hers.

I met Big Chitoro outside a polling station. He was having a busy election day, driving around in a pick-up truck with a dozen youths in the back waving ZANU flags and iron bars. A massive man, resplendent in cowboy boots and combat trousers, he strutted into the hall where the ballots were being cast, brandishing a steel-tipped cane. He beamed at the line of people waiting to vote, shook hands with a few war veterans, and swapped jokes with the local policemen. The voters looked at the ground and avoided his gaze. Mercedes Sayagues, a small but feisty Uruguayan journalist I was traveling with, walked boldly up and asked for an interview. "There's no violence here," Big Chitoro said with a smile. "And of course anyone is free to support any party they like."

ZANU "won" the election, in Mberengwa East and nationwide. The MDC received more votes and swept the cities. But because the constituency boundaries were drawn in such a way that urban votes counted for less than rural ones, the ruling party won sixty-two seats to the opposition's fifty-seven. With thirty MPs picked by Mugabe, this gave ZANU a comfortable majority.

An exit poll commissioned by the Helen Suzman Foundation, a liberal South African think tank, found that 12 percent of voters voted not for the party they liked but in a way they thought might end the violence. In other words, the terror campaign worked. When Mugabe's men burned down peasants' houses and threatened to come back and kill them if ZANU lost, a lot of peasants took the threat seriously. Observers sent by other African governments, including South Africa's, declared the poll free and fair. No one else did. Two years later, Zimbabwe held a presidential election, which was even more violently rigged. Mugabe "won" by a wide margin, despite opinion polls suggesting that his opponent, Morgan Tsvangirai, enjoyed the support of 70 percent of Zimbabweans.

Wanted – a second, genuine liberation

Contrary to what many people assume, a change of government in Zimbabwe could mend matters. To stop Zimbabweans from drowning, the most important step is to remove Mugabe's foot from their heads. Investors, whether local or foreign, will never feel safe putting money into Zimbabwe while he is still in charge, but if a new government promised to stop the seizure of private property, many would be reassured.

Mugabe cannot rule forever, and though there is no guarantee that his successor will be any better, it would not be difficult to improve on the old man's record. A new government could end the shortages of fuel and hard currency at a stroke, simply by allowing the prices of fuel and hard currency to reflect what these things actually cost. To curb inflation, a new government would simply have to avoid spending beyond its means and printing money to fill the gap. A new government that did these things would attract torrents of aid and debt relief.

Zimbabwe still has a sizeable middle class, an independent press, a functioning civil society, and the most diversified African economy outside South Africa. If Mugabe's successor were to turn out not to be a despot, Zimbabweans could soon start farming, manufacturing, and entertaining tourists again. It would take years to repair the damage Mugabe has inflicted on his country, but Zimbabweans are up to the task. All they need is a less vampiric government.

The same is true of other Africans. Each country is different, but most African leaders since independence have shared at least some of Robert Mugabe's authoritarian instincts. Botswana has been consistently democratic and well run, but in most other countries, the revolutionaries who promised "liberation" replaced the old colonial shackles with even heavier ones. Some African countries fell under the rule of military dictators such as Mobutu Sese Seko of Zaire, who bluntly claimed that "democracy is not for Africa."[10] Other countries, such as Tanzania and Zambia, were subjected to one-party socialist rule, which was supposed to foster development but didn't.

In Tanzania, president Julius Nyerere tried to build a state-planned economy, a difficult task under any circumstances, but even more so in a country that had, at independence in 1961, only sixteen university graduates.[11] Nonetheless, Nyerere nationalized local industry, expropriated foreign businesses, shut down Indian and Arab traders, and tried to replace them all with bureaucrats. For some reason, the bureaucrats proved less adept at putting goods on shelves. Before long, it was hard to buy matches that lit properly in Tanzania.

Like Mugabe, Nyerere favored price controls. Peasants were obliged to sell grain to the government for as little as a fifth of its value, which was like a supertax on Tanzania's poorest citizens. Nyerere also forced two thirds of the rural population into collective farms. This was a policy that had caused millions of people to starve to death in China, Ukraine, and Cambodia, but in Tanzania it was less disastrous. Unlike Mao Zedong, Nyerere was not prepared to shoot peasants to make them stay on the collective farms, so many escaped and ran home to tend their own fields.[12] Ethiopian peasants were not so lucky. After their ruler, Mengistu Haile Mariam, forced them into collectives, a million died of hunger.

The World Bank describes African leaders' despotic urges in typically dry terms:

> By 1990, half of Africa's states had military or quasi-military governments. In parallel with authoritarian military govern- ments came a trend towards single-party rule under auto- cratic civilian leaders, largely pursuing interventionist economic policies, in some cases under the banners of socialism or Marxism. Especially when combined with external shocks, the resulting economic decline and politi- cization of the bureaucracy eroded much of what remained of institutional governance capacity and undermined many of the accomplishments of the 1960s.[13]

During the Cold War, outsiders often assumed that Africa's "socialist" and "capitalist" regimes were utterly different from each other, like their sponsors, America and the Soviet Union. African leaders, hungry for aid, energetically promoted this idea. "Pro-Western" leaders, such as Mobutu, Samuel Doe of Liberia, and Hastings Banda of Malawi, spoke earnestly of their loathing for their socialist neighbors. But the chief difference between them was that the pro-Western despots allowed Western firms to operate on their territory, whereas the socialists tended not to. Otherwise, as George Ayittey puts it, whether they claimed to be leftists or rightists, "the relevant ideology always has been statism."[14] Mobutu "indigenized" large firms, grabbing every shop and factory worth stealing, and sharing them out among his chums. Banda made whole industries off-limits to firms without permits, which he usually awarded to his political allies, or to himself.

When the Cold War ended, Africa became slightly more free. Despots could no longer count on American or Soviet aid in return for allying themselves with one side or the other. Soviet aid ceased, and Western donations started to become conditional on governments allowing their people more freedom. Hundreds of millions of Africans won the vote, and dozens of governments promised liberal economic reforms.

Sometimes these have been successful. In Mozambique, for example, the civil war ended in 1992 and the government decided to ditch socialism and start welcoming investors. The economy grew rapidly in the late 1990s, albeit from a low base. In South Africa, meanwhile, the collapse of the Soviet Union prompted the African National Congress, the main black liberation movement, to renounce Marxism. This reassured white South Africans that black rule would not mean having their shops and houses confiscated and so emboldened them to agree, in a referendum, to give blacks the vote. The apartheid regime was replaced, in 1994, by the more liberal ANC government.

During the 1990s, virtually every African state held elections of some sort. If one ignores countries that only became independent after 1990, such as Eritrea and (de facto) Somaliland, the sole laggard was the inaptly named Democratic Republic of Congo.

All this is admirable, but there is more to liberty than voting. Few African elections are truly free or fair. In Togo, for example, the main opposition parties boycotted the 2002 parliamentary election largely because of the government's habit of locking up their candidates. In Swaziland, elected members of the *tinkundla* (parliament) have no powers other than the right to advise the unelected and absolutely powerful king. With few exceptions, African ruling parties still use the apparatus of the state to keep themselves in power. Public radio spouts their propaganda, public money pays for bags of grain to hand out on polling day, and the police arrest their opponents for jaywalking. Few African governments are peacefully voted out of office.

Term limits, enshrined in several African constitutions since the 1980s, are helping to change that. As their terms have run out, bad presidents, such as Zambia's Frederick Chiluba and Kenya's Daniel arap Moi, have been forced out. And a couple of reformists, such as John Kufuor in Ghana and (one hopes) Mwai Kibaki in Kenya, have been ushered in. Term limits can be scrapped, as happened in Namibia. But changing constitutions is harder than changing laws, so they do act as a check on the big man's power.

Liberal economic reforms (known as "structural adjustment"), however, have been hugely controversial. Critics point out that African countries that have attempted to embrace the free market at the behest of the World Bank have not grown much less poor, if at all.

This is true, and rather depressing. The problem is not the policies themselves, which are largely sound. Donors offer soft loans to distressed governments, which in return are supposed to spend within their means, abolish price controls, stop tethering entrepreneurs with red tape, and come up with plans for easing the plight of the poorest. The difficulty is that although many African leaders promise to do all these things in return for a cash injection, they rarely follow through. Donors are in effect asking vampire governments to give up the very powers that enable them to feed on their fellow citizens. Or, as one author put it: "In most cases in Africa, [structural adjustment] amounted to reorganising a bankrupt company and placing it, together with a massive infusion of new capital, in the hands of the same incompetent managers who ruined it in the first place."[15]

Good policies cannot be imposed on unwilling governments. Several African leaders have grown skilled at enacting the letter of reform while sabotaging its spirit. State firms are "privatized," but too often this means being sold for a trifle to cronies of the ruling party. Red tape is slashed but re-imposed informally. Sound budgets are passed but not adhered to. Belt-tightening measures hurt schools and hospitals, but ministers still get their Mercedes limousines, and the military budget is never cut. Sensible laws are passed but repealed or overridden once the aid check has been cashed. Robert Mugabe has broken countless promises to donors. Daniel arap Moi, Kenya's president for twenty-four years, grew adept at "selling" the same package of reforms several times.

The African vampire state is hard to reform because most necessary reforms would reduce the power and wealth of the people in charge. And the people in charge do not, on the whole, want to lose their privileges. Even business leaders, who you might expect to favor market reforms, are often so reliant on state patronage that they actively oppose them.

In most African countries, the best chance of proper reform comes with a change of government. New leaders are not always better. Even Mobutu's successor, to everyone's surprise, wasn't. But when people can freely ditch their rulers, it gives those rulers an incentive to govern a bit better. Sadly, men like Robert Mugabe fight fiercely and cunningly to resist the popular will.

As I write, Zimbabwe is undergoing a severe food shortage. President Mugabe blames the weather, which has indeed been dry. But drought is turning to famine largely because commercial farmers, who saw the country safely through all previous droughts, have mostly been driven off their land.

Half the people of Zimbabwe are dependent on grain

donated by foreigners to survive. To punish those who dared to vote against him, Mugabe has barred aid agencies from operating in areas where opposition support is highest and used the government's legal monopoly on grain distribution to make sure that ruling-party members are fed, while the MDC are not. Some of his cronies do not even bother to hide what they are doing. Abednico Ncube, the deputy foreign minister, told villagers in Matabeleland: "As long as you value the government of the day, you will not starve, but we do not want people who vote for colonialists and then come to us when they want food. You cannot vote for the MDC and expect ZANU-PF to help you. . . . You have to vote for ZANU-PF candidates . . . before government starts rethinking your entitlement to this food aid."[16]

Most chilling of all, Didymus Mutasa, the ZANU-PF organizing secretary, mused that "We would be better off with only six million people, with our own people who support the liberation struggle. We don't want all these extra people."[17]

The population of Zimbabwe is about twelve million.

2. DIGGING DIAMONDS, DIGGING GRAVES

How mineral wealth has impoverished Africa

What scared me most about Congo was not the shouting, stone-throwing crowds, nor the rattle of gunfire, nor the occasional dead body slumped by the side of the road. It was the sight of a boy soldier – he looked no more than twelve, but he might have been a malnourished fifteen – sitting on a step, resting his chin on the barrel of his AK-47.

Teenagers with guns are always terrifying. An older soldier is more likely to ask himself, before shooting you, whether there is any point in doing so. Children are more unpredictable and harder to reason with, especially when drunk or drugged. All this I knew. But the sight of the boy idly pointing an automatic weapon at his own brain made me gasp with anxiety. If he is so careless of his own life, I thought, how careful will he be of mine?

I was in Kinshasa, the bougainvillea-garlanded capital of the Democratic Republic of Congo, in August 1998. A great war was breaking out, one that would soon suck in most of the countries in central Africa. A rebel army was advancing on the city, and everyone expected them to capture it, probably within days. The Congolese government was in a panic. The regular army was in disarray, and Congo's president, Laurent Kabila, was recruiting a militia of jobless youths to defend his regime. Thousands of these militiamen were gathered in Kinshasa's main soccer stadium, drinking beer all day, waving knives, and loudly spoiling for a fight.

Congo's state radio had told them to kill members of the Tutsi tribe because the rebels were backed by Rwanda, where the government was dominated by Tutsis. "Wherever you see a Rwandan Tutsi, regard him as your enemy," went one broadcast. It then urged loyal Congolese citizens to "bring a machete, a spear, an arrow, a hoe, spades, rakes, nails, truncheons, electric irons, barbed wire, stones, and the like, in order, dear listeners, to kill the Rwandan Tutsis." In the prevailing atmosphere of alarm neither mobs nor soldiers made much distinction between Rwandan Tutsis, Congolese Tutsis, and anyone else suspected of supporting the rebels.

The government also accused foreign journalists of "spreading dismay," of being "less than human" and of somehow being partly responsible for the war. A mob gathered outside the Hotel Memling in the center of Kinshasa, baying for a French radio reporter inside to come out and be lynched. The security forces dragged some BBC journalists from their hotel room and roughed them up for filming from the balcony. A French television crew was put through a mock execution in front of the information ministry. A Reuters cameraman was stripped, beaten, thrown into a cell for several hours, and threatened with death.

I stayed out of trouble, more or less. If I moved around after curfew, I did so only with government permission and in a large armed convoy. During the day, I hired a rusty old car and a driver who knew Kinshasa well. The Belgians had thought the city so picturesque, with its wide boulevards and white walls, that they called it *Kinshasa la belle* – "Kinshasa the beautiful." But after four decades of decay, the boulevards were scarred with potholes and strewn with garbage and dead dogs. Locals now referred to their city as *Kinshasa la poubelle* – "Kinshasa the trash can." The only new and shiny objects on display were huge posters showing President Kabila's bowling-ball-shaped head, with the doubtful caption *Voici l'homme qu'il faut* – "Here is the man we need."

I had entered Kinshasa by boat, across the Congo River, and

was regretting it. I am not a war correspondent. I get no thrill from being shot at. This sets me apart, I suppose, from the large number of foreign correspondents in Africa who spend half their working lives wooing death. The photographers and camera-men, particularly, have to stick up their heads when the bullets are whizzing, or they won't get good pictures. If the pictures are poor, as the snappers say, you aren't close enough.

My employer, on the other hand, requires no heroics. Articles in the *Economist* are anonymous. *Economist* writers are supposed to aim for objectivity, which means, among other things, not dwelling on our personal experiences. If I spend the night in a ditch ducking shrapnel, there is no chance that the *Economist* will feature the incident on the front page, so I have no profes-sional incentive to do it. While the real war reporters try to find out *where* the action is, so they can snap it, I prefer to hang back and talk to people – in the hope of figuring out *why* they are fighting.

The impression I've gained from talking to combatants is that a lot of wars are about economics. Poverty seems to breed war, especially civil war. Rich democracies occasionally use force to settle foreign disputes, but they almost never suffer armed conflict at home. The same is true, albeit to a lesser extent, of middle-income countries. But the poorest one sixth of humanity endures four fifths of the world's civil wars.[1]

Africa is worse afflicted than any other continent. In 1999, one African in five lived in a country racked by civil or cross-border war. Ninety percent of the casualties were civilians. Nineteen million Africans were forced to flee their homes. And an estimated 20 million landmines lurked beneath African soil.[2]

Why is this? The available evidence tends to support the idea that there is a strong link between war and poverty. Researchers at the World Bank, after looking at all the world's civil wars since 1960 to try to figure out what they had in common, found that poverty and economic stagnation were two of the main risk factors. When income per person doubles, they calculated that the risk of civil war halves. For each percentage point by which the growth rate rises, the risk of conflict falls by a point.[3]

Poverty and low growth are often symptoms of corrupt, incompetent government, which can give people a reason to rebel. They are also common in immature societies, where people have not yet learned to live together in peace. And it is not hard, as the saying goes, to give a poor man a cause. Neither regular armies nor rebel ones have much trouble recruiting in Africa. For young men with few prospects, a soldier's pay, or the opportunity to loot a neighboring village, can seem appealing.

A thin young veteran of the Congo war, who said his name was Kaseleka Wabo, explained to me why he fought. I met him in a refugee camp in Tanzania, a 170-kilometer ferry trip from eastern Congo. He mumbled and scratched his face nervously as he spoke. He said he had joined Kabila's army for the wages and deserted when he stopped receiving them. He switched to fighting with the rebels, who did not pay him at all. He survived by "living off the land." I don't think he meant gathering roots and fruit. The United Nations, which ran the camp, kept Wabo apart from other refugees for fear that someone might take revenge on him. He admitted that, while in uniform, he had killed several of his fellow Congolese. "It's normal," he said defiantly. "I'd do it again."

Not only does poverty breed war, but war exacerbates poverty, too. The World Bank estimates that a typical civil war reduces average incomes by 2.2 percent each year.[4] In laymen's terms: if soldiers steal your cows, you have nothing to sell on market day. War even affects African countries that are at peace. Many investors regard the continent as an undifferentiated whole. If Burundi is in flames, they may be wary of setting up safari lodges in neighboring Tanzania, even if Tanzania has been tranquil for decades.

African wars start for all sorts of reasons. During the Cold War, Soviet-backed Marxist regimes fought equally vicious American-backed rebels who claimed to be pro-capitalist, and vice versa. But since the collapse of the Soviet Union, ideology has more or less ceased to be a motive for war in Africa. New conflicts are more likely to spring from ethnic antagonism or from a tyrant's desire to distract attention from troubles at home.

However conflicts begin, they are more likely to continue if they are fought on mineral-rich soil, and Africa is fabulously rich in minerals. Diamond mines, for example, give warlords a lucrative reason to keep fighting and often pay for their weapons, too. This makes many African wars particularly intractable. In the 1990s, at least eleven African nations fought over natural resources or the prospect of them. Among these were Angola, Chad, Congo-Brazzaville, and Sudan, whose civil wars were all fueled by oil. Rebels fought for control of diamond mines in Sierra Leone, phosphates in Western Sahara, and iron, timber, diamonds, and drugs in Liberia.

Some mineral-rich African countries – South Africa, Botswana, and Namibia, for example – remain peaceful enough for ordinary citizens to benefit from their buried treasure. But on balance Africa's natural resources have proven more of a curse than a blessing.[5]

Congo's war was typical. It began as an aftershock from the genocide in neighboring Rwanda but quickly degenerated into a scramble for loot. The country is huge, weak, and naturally rich. Congolese soil is studded with diamonds and streaked with ores of gold, cobalt, and tantalum. So there is much to steal, and it is easy for any semi-professional fighting force to steal it. Unfortunately for Congo, it is surrounded by smaller, more aggressive countries, which from the mid-1990s set about tearing it apart like jackals around a sick buffalo.

Congo is two-thirds the size of Western Europe and thinly populated. Only about 50 million people live there, although this is a guess. Communication between different regions is tricky. Telephones rarely work, and the bush has swallowed the old colonial roads, although some of the milestones remain, poking out of the undergrowth. Only the Congo river links the western half of the country to the east. The central government in Kinshasa lost control of Congo's provinces long ago, and the trackless rainforest is lawless.

Congo has a long history of being badly governed. The approximate area we now call Congo was roped together into one state in the nineteenth century by King Leopold II of the Belgians. Leopold never visited Congo but ruled it as his personal fiefdom from his chateau in Laeken. His men enslaved the locals to tap rubber and collect ivory and sliced off slackers' hands. Leopold's misrule became such an embarrassment that the Belgian government took Congo off his hands in 1908 and ruled it somewhat less harshly until independence in 1960. Soon after, a young military commander named Joseph-Désiré Mobutu seized power. During a dictatorship that spanned four decades, Mobutu looted the state into paralysis. He was overthrown in 1997, but the story of Congo's current war begins three years earlier.

In 1994, in tiny neighboring Rwanda, some of the more bloodthirsty leaders of the Hutu tribe tried to exterminate the Tutsis, with whom they lived cheek by jowl. The genocide ended when an army of Tutsis from Uganda seized control of Rwanda and drove the *génocidaires* away. Thousands fled into Zaire (as Congo was then called) and hid in the jungle.

From there, they mounted frequent raids on Rwanda. The new Tutsi-led Rwandan government appealed to Mobutu to stop them. Mobutu, who had been friendly with the old Hutu regime, armed and encouraged them instead. In 1996, the Rwandan army invaded eastern Congo, hoping to scatter or kill the *génocidaires* and set up a buffer zone against future attacks. It was easier than they expected. Congo's defenses crumbled so quickly that the Rwandans figured they could overthrow Mobutu and replace him with someone more pliable. Uganda, Rwanda's ally, agreed to help.

They picked Laurent Kabila, a Congolese guerrilla leader whose curriculum vitae included a spell running a brothel in

Tanzania. At first, the alliance went smoothly. With Rwandan support, Kabila raised a rebel army in eastern Congo and sent it marching in rubber boots toward Kinshasa. The scruffy rebels and their Rwandan backers met almost no resistance. Only the lack of roads slowed their advance. Some villagers actually paid for transport to help Mobutu's men flee so that they would go quickly instead of hanging around to loot. In May 1997, Kabila marched into the capital. Joyous crowds greeted his troops, waving palm fronds. Shots were fired, but only in celebration. Few people knew much about Kabila, but they figured that he could not possibly be worse than Mobutu.

They were wrong. Kabila was, if anything, more cruel than Mobutu but lacked his predecessor's intelligence. He promised elections but never held them. He jailed and tortured suspected opponents. He tried to fine businessmen for breaking unpublished rules and to levy taxes on as yet unrealized profits. He printed money with reckless abandon, and when the governor of Congo's central bank tried to explain to him why this was a bad idea, he had him locked up. Western governments offered aid, but he treated them with suspicion. Western mining firms came scouting for business but soon wearied of Kabila's habit of dishonoring contracts.

A toad tries to swallow an elephant

Perhaps Kabila's greatest mistake, however, was to betray his Rwandan backers. After only a year in power, he allied himself with their enemies, the genocidal Hutu militias who still lurked in eastern Congo. Furious, the Rwandans decided to overthrow their former protégé. They struck with the speed of a coiled cobra, flying troops almost 2,000 kilometers across the jungle in old Soviet transport planes and setting up bases at Kitona and Matadi, not far from Kinshasa. Within days, they had captured the hydroelectric dam that powered the capital and were threatening, with their Congolese rebel allies, to take the capital itself.

That was the situation when I was cowering in Kinshasa. The city would certainly have fallen but for the arrival, at the last minute, of some powerful allies. The armies of Zimbabwe, Angola, and Namibia arrived with fighter-bombers and relatively well-trained troops. They quickly repelled the rebels and Rwandans and secured the city. The insurgents dispersed, hiding in bushes and backyards. The ill-disciplined Congolese army was given the task of mopping them up. The resultant killings were more or less random.

Anyone with thin features or a long nose, traits associated with Tutsis, was at risk. After decades of intermarriage between Tutsis and other tribes, a long nose was not a reliable indicator of anything, but it was enough to condemn many to death. Young men with dust in their hair were assumed to have acquired it marching through the bush. In a city that had had little or no running water for a month, such reasoning was hardly foolproof, but it was good enough for Kabila's troops. Those unfortunate enough to be caught looking disheveled were beaten or shot. I saw corpses lying on the crumbling pavement, blackened and charred after being doused with gasoline and set ablaze. One suspected rebel was hurled from a bridge in front of a television camera and machine-gunned as he bobbed in the river below.

After the relief of Kinshasa, the war grew more complex. At one time or another, nine national armies were involved, in alliance with several local rebel groups and militias.

The four armies that mattered were those of Rwanda, Uganda, Angola, and Zimbabwe. The Rwandans and Ugandans fought against Kabila because, they said, he was helping Rwandan and Ugandan rebels. The Angolans supported Kabila because they thought that was the best way of crushing their own rebels. The Zimbabweans had no obvious reason to be involved but said they wanted to defend the legitimate government of Congo against external aggression.

There were other, smaller players: Namibia, Chad, and Burundi all sent troops at one time or another, and Sudan briefly sent some transport planes. Hutu militias fought against the Rwandans. The Mai-Mai, a Congolese warrior cult whose members sometimes charge into battle naked, started off supporting the rebels but then switched sides and started slaughtering Tutsis. Both Rwanda and Uganda backed their own puppet rebel movements. Uganda backed at least two.

Finally, there were mercenaries, the rough and reckless types who show up in every African war. The government hired a small number of eastern Europeans to fly planes and operate complex military hardware. On their days off, they could be seen relaxing by the pool at the Grand Hotel in Kinshasa "wearing nothing but the Y-fronts of their native Ukraine."[6]

Confused? So was everyone else. All but the bravest aid workers fled Congo in terror. Outsiders despaired of restoring peace. In 2000, when South Africa first considered sending peacekeepers to Congo, a cartoonist summed up why this might be tricky. A peacekeeper at a road block in Congo sees the tip of a rocket-propelled grenade launcher poking out of a bush. "Halt," he cries: "Who goes there?" "Congolese Rally for Democracy," comes the reply. "Hang on a minute," says the peacekeeper, and he turns to consult a chart of parties to the war, of which seven are listed as "friend," eight are listed as "foe," and ten are listed as "not sure."[7]

Pillage delays peace

The war reached a stalemate in 1999. Talks in Lusaka, the Zambian capital, produced a peace pact that no one honored. The main stumbling block was that most of the commanders in the field were making fortunes by looting Congo's mineral wealth.

In the east, the Rwandan and Ugandan armies dug diamonds

and cobalt, chopped down trees, slaughtered apes for bushmeat, harvested ivory, and grabbed everything else they could carry away. A bustling diamond market sprang up in Kigali, the Rwandan capital, although Rwanda produced no stones of its own.

In June 2000, Ugandan and Rwandan troops, supposedly allies, came to blows over the spoils. For six days, they blasted each other in the city of Kisangani, destroying much of the town center. In April 2001, a UN report accused Rwanda and Uganda of "the systematic and systemic" exploitation of Congo's natural wealth, in particular diamonds, copper, cobalt, gold, and coltan, a rare and costly mineral used in the manufacture of mobile telephones and computer-game consoles.

The report alleged that presidents Yoweri Museveni of Uganda and Paul Kagame of Rwanda were "on the verge of becoming the godfathers of the illegal exploitation of natural resources and the continuation of the conflict in the Democratic Republic of the Congo." It did not claim that the presidents were looting Congo themselves but accused them of failing to prevent their associates – including Museveni's younger brother – from doing so. It called for sanctions on both countries.[8] Both presidents denied the allegations.

Kabila's allies did well out of the war, too. Zimbabwean and Angolan commanders demanded, and were granted, the rights to mine precious minerals in areas they defended. Angola formed a joint oil venture with the Congolese government. South of the town of Mbuji Mayi, Zimbabwean troops guarded a diamond concession worth an estimated $1 billion, which was awarded in 2000 to a firm partly owned by the Zimbabwean ruling party. The costs of Zimbabwe's military adventure in Congo were borne by Zimbabwean taxpayers. The profits went largely to President Mugabe's cronies. A UN report in 2002 accused top Zimbabwean officers of the "organised theft" of Congolese assets.[9]

Senior officers in all armies ran small patches of Congo as

their own private estates. Ordinary soldiers and guerrillas eked out their rations, if they received any, by robbing Congolese villages. Life grew so frightening for Congolese peasants that millions of them abandoned their cassava crops and hid in the bush, subsisting on wild fruit and insects. In the first four years the Congo war caused an estimated 2 million premature deaths, mostly through starvation and disease.[10]

In January 2001, Laurent Kabila was assassinated. A body-guard named Rashidi Kasereka, one of whose jobs was to announce new visitors and to whisper messages in the president's ear, entered Kabila's office and asked to speak to him. As Kabila lent forward to listen, Kasereka shot him once through the neck and twice through the stomach. Why he did it, or who put him up to it, is not known: Kasereka was himself killed within minutes.[11]

Kabila was replaced by his twenty-nine-year-old son Joseph, who showed signs of being less truculent than his father. In July 2002, he signed a peace deal with most of his adversaries, which led to the majority of foreign troops being pulled out of Congo. Even the Rwandans left, although no one would be surprised if they came back. Joseph Kabila created a transitional government and promised eventually to hold elections. Peace, of a sort, returned to about two thirds of the country, but not to eastern Congo, where a confusion of militia groups continued to rape, rob, and occasionally eat hapless villagers.

I visited Bukavu, a stunning lakeside town in eastern Congo, in September 2003. The town itself was quiet, as there was a force of UN peacekeepers encamped by the water's edge, and the rebel group that ran Bukavu was nominally at peace with the central government in Kinshasa. But in the surrounding hills armed bands plundered unchecked.

I spoke to peasants in nearby villages and heard a hundred variations on the same story. Charlotte, a petite lady with chunky earrings, told me how men with guns had broken into her home and forced her to carry all her belongings – her clothes, her children's clothes, her cooking pots, her mattress – to their forest hideout. When she protested, one of them broke her wrist. Then two of them raped her. She struggled home, but, she said, "For a long time after that, I felt pain everywhere, in my back, all over. And after two months, another group of armed men came, and stole everything that the first group had missed."

To avoid a similar fate, most of the villagers I met said they abandoned their huts at night and slept in the forest or in crevices below river banks. But, according to Barhingenga Mujijima, a small farmer, "now that the bandits no longer find anyone to rob in the villages, they've started looking in the fields and round about." Mujijima said he now walked six kilometers from his home to the nearest garrison town every night, where he slept in the street, and then six kilometers back to his fields every morning. This daily trudge left less time and energy for growing food, he said, so he never had enough to eat.

Riches without effort – for the few

Throughout the world, mineral wealth tends to corrupt. Part of the problem is that mines cannot move. If the Chinese government tried to plunder Hong Kong's financial district, the bankers would simply move to Singapore. Gold and diamonds, by contrast, must be extracted where they are found – meaning that politicians can grab a big slice of miners' profits without fear that the miners will emigrate.

Governments that depend on natural resources for most of their income are usually venal and despotic. Most oil-rich Gulf states are, and African oligarchies, such as Nigeria, Gabon, and Equatorial Guinea, have a wretched record, too. But perhaps the country where oil has proven most destructive is Angola.

Angola is the world's ninth-largest oil producer, but most Angolans are poorer than they were when the stuff was first discovered off the country's Atlantic coast. Oil fueled a civil war that left Angola scorched and starving, while allowing a tiny elite to grow fantastically rich.

I caught a glimpse of how Angola's Big Men live in 1999, on a veranda outside the Hotel Panorama in Luanda, the capital. It was the scene of the Miss Luanda beauty contest. On a smooth white stage, a procession of gorgeous women twirled and posed, first in ball gowns, then in swimsuits. Most had big hair, all wore explosively loud make-up. Against a backdrop of softly lit palm trees, they sashayed past the judges in a whirl of pink and blue silk. On a dais to the left stood the prize: a shiny new car.

The audience sported emerald necklaces, Prada handbags, and fat fistfuls of gold rings. One man wore a red crushed-velvet suit over his paunch. There was some excellent fresh lobster on the buffet and as much Cutty Sark whisky as the crowd could drink.

It was night-time, so when I looked past the stage and across the bay below, I could see only a few lights winking in the distance. The air was pleasantly warm, and since I could not see the city, with its sagging shacks and mounds of uncollected trash, it felt as if I were in some gilded resort: Saint Tropez, say, or Mauritius. Daylight spoiled the illusion.

I visited some of Angola's less fortunate citizens in a nearby refugee camp. I smelt the place before I saw it. Children squatted by the dusty track that led there, tattered shorts around their ankles, faces wincing from diarrhea. When the car I was riding in rounded a dune, I saw ahead a village of drab, khaki tents nestling in the sand.

Twenty-five hundred souls were squeezed into Campo Malanje, a haven for Angolans who had fled from fighting in the hinterland. Most refugees were peasants. UNITA, Angola's rebel movement, had deliberately driven them off their land and into the cities in the hope that they would become a burden on the government. They arrived with heavy iron hoes and centuries of agricultural know-how. But the camp was crowded, so each family typically had only enough land to grow a few dozen stalks of corn or cassava. Everyone in the camp was hungry, and the sick lay limply on filthy mats outside their tents.

Angola's civil war started in 1961 as a struggle against Portuguese colonialism. In 1975, the Portuguese left in a hurry, and Angola became a Cold War battlefield. A Marxist group, the Popular Movement for the Liberation of Angola (MPLA), seized power but was challenged by the National Union for the Total Independence of Angola (UNITA). Apartheid South Africa, terrified of having a Soviet satellite on its doorstep, sent an army to help UNITA. The United States, equally keen to block Soviet expansion, sent weapons and cash. The MPLA, meanwhile, was supported by thousands of Cuban troops and supplied with arms by the Soviet Union.

When the Cold War ended, Angola should have found peace but did not. A ceasefire was reached in 1991, followed by elections. But when UNITA lost, its leader, Jonas Savimbi, cried foul. The fighting continued, almost without pause, until February 2002, when Savimbi was shot dead. More than a million Angolans died out of a population estimated at 13 million in the late 1990s. An estimated 1.7 million were forced to flee their homes. Many found themselves living for years in places like Campo Malanje.

Why did Angola's war last so long? A clue can be found by looking at Portugal's other large African colony, Mozambique. Like Angola, Mozambique endured a bloody anti-colonial war and then, when the Portuguese left, an even bloodier civil war. The country was blasted back into the bronze age as its Soviet-backed government fought anti-communist rebels, armed first by white supremacists from Rhodesia, then by similar folks from South Africa. But unlike Angola's civil war, Mozambique's ended shortly after the Cold War did.

Why the difference? It doubtless helped that as apartheid crumbled South Africa, the regional giant, put pressure on both Mozambican parties to make peace. (South African diplomats tried the same in Angola but failed.) It also helped that the Mozambican leaders were more reasonable people than their Angolan counterparts. Savimbi, particularly, was determined not to share power with anyone else. This was a man who had his own lieutenants burned alive, along with their families, if he suspected them of disloyalty.

When he failed to win the presidency of Angola, Savimbi went back to war. A story from his youth, which may be apocryphal but has the ring of truth, casts light on why. Fred Bridgland, a biographer who once admired him, tells how when Savimbi was a boy, he owned a football. The missionaries at his school arranged a match between their students and some white boys from a neighboring town. Savimbi provided the ball, and the white boys brought a Portuguese referee. The white team surged ahead. Savimbi accused the referee of bias, picked up the ball, and stomped off with it, spoiling the match.[12]

Savimbi's personality was not, however, the only force that prevented peace from breaking out. The crucial difference between Mozambique and Angola was that Mozambique had nothing much worth stealing.

Angola's precious curse

A few miles off Angola's Atlantic coast, oil rigs rise above the waves. Unlike most other structures in Angola, they are in good repair. Smooth steel spars fit neatly into concrete bases. Engineers in hard hats walk briskly about their business. Everything works.

Angola's oil industry has so little connection to the mainland that it might as well be in another country. Most of the oil is under the sea, so most of the action takes place offshore. The industry accounts for over 90 percent of Angola's exports but employs only 10,000 people. Western oil firms provide most of the capital and expertise. Expatriate technicians arrive in Luanda and fly straight out to the rigs in helicopters, rarely stopping for long on Angolan soil.

Angola's offshore wells disgorged 800,000 barrels a day in 2000, and production was expected to double by 2004. Oil accounts for half of GDP and provides the Angolan government with almost all of its taxes. But many ordinary Angolans do not even know that their country has oil. They never see the rigs, and they never see any benefits from the petrodollars, either.

On the contrary, oil kept Angola's civil war blazing long after the original reasons for fighting were forgotten. Both sides wanted the oil. Ultimately, the government won the war because it already controlled the oil wells and therefore had more money to pay its troops and buy guns. But it did not exactly hurry towards victory, not least because so many politicians grew so wealthy from prolonging the fighting. The war gave them an excuse ("national security") for secrecy, which made it easy to pocket huge kickbacks on arms deals or simply to funnel oil receipts into offshore accounts. By one estimate, in the late 1990s between a third and a half of public spending in Angola was not properly accounted for.[13]

UNITA, meanwhile, bought its supplies with diamonds, mined by virtual slaves in areas the rebels controlled. For a while, UNITA grew rich from diamond smuggling, earning an estimated $300 million to $500 million annually. But after the turn of the millennium, a global ban on buying UNITA's gems began to bite. At the same time, the Angolan army forcibly evacuated peasants from areas where UNITA operated, so that the rebels would have no one to steal food from. By the time the government found and killed Savimbi, his followers were starving. Even the UNITA leaders who negotiated a ceasefire in 2002 were so malnourished that their belts were threaded twice around their waists.

Chasing the spoils of peace

If peace holds, Angola has a chance to recover. But it will not be easy. The country needs honest and benevolent government, but war has allowed a rather different type of leader to rise to the top. Corruption blights almost everything that the state does. New businesses cannot start without paying bribes, nor can goods move through Angolan ports without pay-offs. Even the supply of subsidized textbooks to schoolchildren has been tarnished. Officials have reportedly pocketed the subsidy and sold the books to parents at ten times what they were supposed to charge.[14] An anti-corruption commission, established in 1996, has done nothing.

Because the government has no need to raise money from sources other than oil, it has done little or nothing to nurture other parts of the economy. Angola's coffee plantations withered long ago. So did Angolan industry, apart from oil, diamonds, and the firms that supply oilmen and diamond miners with equipment, hotel beds, and so on.

Since nothing much is made in Angola, everything of value has to be imported. When I first boarded a flight from South Africa to Angola, I had trouble reaching my seat. The big wives of Angola's Big Men were blocking the aisles with microwave ovens and cramming television sets into the overhead luggage compartments.

Doing business in Angola is tough. Miners and oil firms have to import everything from mechanical diggers to fresh vegetables to keep their expatriate managers happy. If machinery breaks down, it often has to be sent 2,000 kilometers to South Africa to be fixed. Firms have popped up that specialize in moving supplies through Angola's ports without losing too much to thieves or crooked officials. I visited one such firm, called Global Mining Support Services, run by a hard bunch of former officers of the South African army. The manager, Cobus Viljoen, told me that his diamond-digger clients even wanted their guard dogs flown in from Johannesburg. The local pooches were too scrawny and timid, he said, to be of use.

Despite all these troubles, there were signs, immediately after the ceasefire, that things might be getting better in Angola. Exhausted and hungry rebels surrendered and handed in their weapons. Angola's roads suddenly became safe from ambushes, which allowed families separated by the war to hop onto rusty minibuses and reunite. Commerce started to flow again. Trucks began carrying corn and peppers from rural areas to coastal cities and fish and electrical goods in the opposite direction. Prices in some towns halved. In Luanda, carjackings suddenly increased, a sign that there was now somewhere to drive the stolen vehicles.

African wars usually end for much the same reasons that wars elsewhere do. Either one side wins, as happened in Angola, or the two sides tire of fighting and try to resolve their differences through dialogue, as happened in Mozambique.

Outsiders can play a useful role. Nelson Mandela, the former South African president, and Ketumile Masire, the former president of Botswana, have both worked tirelessly as neutral intermediaries between warring groups in Burundi and Congo. Western countries sometimes provide an incentive for peace by withholding aid from governments that fight and showering it on those that stop. Such tactics may have helped to persuade Ethiopia and Eritrea to cease shooting in 2000 and Rwanda and Uganda not to go to war with each other in 2001. Campaigners against "blood diamonds" may also have helped by prompting the more reputable parts of the global diamond industry to adopt, in 2003, a system of certificates to keep stones from war zones out of Western jewelery shops.

If they really wanted to, Western governments could probably stop most African wars simply by sending in their own vastly superior armed forces. But they don't, because however much they may deny it, since the Cold War ended they have had no big strategic interest in Africa. The continent produces little that foreigners cannot buy elsewhere. Voters in rich countries may feel compassion for the starving, but they rarely have strong views about which side deserves their support in any given African war.

Occasionally, when television cameras publicize some particularly awful tragedy, Western consciences are pricked and Western troops are sent to Africa on what are called "humanitarian" missions. President Bill Clinton sent American soldiers to protect food-aid deliveries to Somalia in 1993, but when eighteen were killed and their naked corpses dragged through the streets of Mogadishu, the Somali capital, the rest were pulled out. The experience probably helped to persuade the Clinton administration not to dispatch troops to stop the genocide in Rwanda the following year.

With more political will, humanitarian interventions can work. In 2000, a mere 800 British troops turned the tide of Sierra Leone's ghastly civil war in a matter of days. The Revolutionary United Front, a band of rebels notorious for cutting off hands and slapping their owners' faces with them, looked set to overrun Sierra Leone's capital, Freetown. The British stopped them and, with the help of a larger number of UN peacekeepers, pacified the country. Two years later, Sierra Leone was calm enough to hold an election. But that calm is enforced by up to 17,500 blue helmets, and no one knows what will happen if they leave, which they are bound to do eventually.

For the cold, hard truth is that the world's great powers no longer want colonies. Although a few controversialists advocate it and a few conspiracy theorists think it is already happening, there is not the slightest chance that Britain or any other Western country will try once more to rule Africa. Western governments are reluctant to sacrifice even a single soldier to resolve the continent's feuds.

So Africans will have to solve their own problems. Many African leaders realize this, and some have sent troops to try to keep the peace in other African states. Nigeria dispatched soldiers to Sierra Leone and Liberia; South Africa sent some to Burundi. But no African country is powerful enough to impose peace on any but the tiniest neighbor.

To stay peaceful in the long term, countries need governments that serve their citizens instead of robbing them and that can be removed without violence. Not only must these governments be elected; they must be elected under rules that more or less everyone agrees to be fair. Countries need constitutions that provide reasonable protection for all citizens, regardless of whether they support the ruling party. Governments must respect the constitutions under the terms of which they govern and should stand down when they are voted out.

This may sound like a tall order, but it is not impossible. South Africa managed it. In 1991, the last white government, under the presidency of F. W. de Klerk, organized a "Convention for a Democratic South Africa" (CODESA), at which representatives of twenty-five political parties and various anti-apartheid groups hammered out the framework for a new constitution and set a date for all-race elections. No party was excluded – though some ultra-nationalist white parties boycotted the discussions. CODESA's decisions were binding on government, and de Klerk bowed to them. The intermittent fighting between anti-apartheid guerrillas and the government ceased, and full-scale civil war, which many predicted, was averted.

A similar procedure could help resolve other conflicts, too. Ghanaian scholar George Ayittey argues that big, inclusive national conferences ought to succeed in Africa because they mesh with pre-colonial tradition.

> When a crisis erupted in an African village, the chief and the elders would summon a village meeting. There, the issue was debated by the people until a consensus was reached. During the debate, the chief usually made no effort to manipulate the outcome or sway public opinion. Nor were

71

there bazooka-wielding rogues intimidating or instructing people on what they should say. People expressed their ideas openly and freely without fear of arrest.[15]

Such nation-building conferences can only work, however, if the men with the bazookas agree to participate and to be bound by the decisions that emerge.

And even if rebel leaders agree to make peace, their foot-soldiers are sometimes reluctant to disarm. A freelance photographer called Sven Torfinn once sent me a snap from eastern Congo that encapsulated the difficulty of peace-making. It shows a young Mai-Mai warrior with a Kalashnikov over his shoulder. Lashed to the magazine is his only inoffensive possession: a yellow toothbrush. A boy whose only livelihood is his gun may be slow to lay it down.

3. NO TITLE

Why Africans need property rights

When I asked the nomad how much his house cost, he had no idea what I was talking about. He looked at me quizzically and explained, as if to a fool, that he had built it himself, with materials he had at hand. The walls were of sticks, woven together and curved into a dome. For added protection against rain and sandstorms, he had laid animal hides over the top and skillfully lashed them in place. He could not put a price on the place, because it would never have occurred to him to sell it. When he moved away in search of better pasture for his cows, he simply dismantled his house, loaded it on to a camel's back, and took it with him. I had asked a stupid question, perhaps because I had house prices on the brain. My wife and I were trying to buy a place in London that month, which was such a huge undertaking that it was hard to think of anything else.

In the midst of this domestic maelstrom, I was dispatched to cover a peace conference in Addis Ababa, the Ethiopian capital. None of the important delegates (all parties to Congo's civil war) showed up, so I abandoned the conference and flew off into the desert to write a story about food shortages instead. I went to Gode, a small town in the Ogaden, the arid space that separates Ethiopia from Somalia. The people there were mainly ethnic Somalis: statuesque nomads in brilliant purple, green, and orange shawls. They were as courteous as they were proud. When Askar Ahmed, the acting provincial governor, and his entourage came to dinner with me and some UN workers, they arrived on the dot at 7 p.m., chatted seriously over the chicken and rice, said "thank you," and left by 8:30.

For all their dignity, however, the nomads were not doing well. A drought the previous year had killed perhaps 5,000 of them. A swift airlift of food aid saved thousands more. But the governor told me that the crisis was far from over. Most people's cattle and goats had died during the drought, so they had no way of coping if the rains failed again. With no beasts to herd, the nomads clustered around the town in their portable shacks, hoping to grow enough corn to sell, buy some more cattle, and resume their wandering, pastoral way of life. For this they needed water, of which there was little to be had. Just to get enough to drink people took potentially mortal risks.

Standing on the shore of the murky brown river that flowed past Gode, I saw a young woman throwing stones vigorously into the water. I could not figure out what she was doing until my guide explained that there was a crocodile lurking beneath the ripples. The young woman needed to scare it off before she could fill her plastic jerry can. Then she turned and started to walk home. It was so hot that I could barely stand up, but she seemed unruffled as she put the heavy jerry can on her head and turned her feet towards the horizon. Her home was too far off to be visible. In fact, nothing was visible in the direction she was heading, nothing but miles of searing sand.

The nomadic lifestyle is probably doomed. Itinerant pastoralists need a lot of space to keep their livestock alive. Crop-growing societies can feed a much denser population on the same patch of territory, which is why sedentary folk outnumber nomadic herders everywhere on earth. Sheer weight of numbers has allowed tribes of farmers, over the last few thousand years, to grab the best land from nomads and push them into the driest, least fertile quarters of the planet.[1] The process is almost complete. Nomadic hunter-gatherers are almost extinct, and nomadic herders have been squashed into such harsh patches of terrain that they are increasingly forced to mix their traditional livelihood of cattle-rearing with a bit of sowing and reaping. It keeps them alive, but many find the idea of putting down permanent roots repellent. Hence the nomad's bewilderment when I asked him, in my intrusive journalistic way, how much his house was worth.

Intrusive though it was, the question was important. One of the reasons that Africa is so poor is that most Africans are unable to turn their assets into liquid capital. In the West, the most common way to do this is to borrow money using a house as security. This is how most American entrepreneurs get started, and without such loans America would be much less dynamic and rich than it is. But most Africans cannot do the same thing because even if they own their homes they usually do not have the title deeds to prove it. And since they cannot prove it, banks will not accept their homes as collateral for a loan. Africans are thus deprived of capital – the lifeblood of capitalism.

Somali nomads are an extreme example, but even the most settled people in Africa, as in much of the developing world, do not usually own the land they live on, at least not in the formal, documented way that Emma and I own our home in London. Indeed, most economic activity in Africa is unrecorded. The man selling fruit at the traffic lights in Lusaka is not registered as a grocer. The minibus driver who brakes suddenly in your path and nearly causes you to crash takes his fares in cash and files no tax returns. Subsistence farmers grow most of the starchy food in Africa but eat most of it themselves, barter much of the rest, and make no impression on the continent's fledgling stock exchanges.

Economists tend to think of the informal economy as a marginal phenomenon, of interest only to missionaries, aid workers, and the police. But in most African countries, the informal economy is larger than the formal one. Barely one African in ten lives in a formal house with title deeds, and only one African worker in ten holds a formal job. The remaining nine tenths are usually ignored.

This is a mistake. The poor have assets – plenty of them. In towns, houses as flimsy and biodegradable as a nomad's are the exception, not the rule. Many Africans toil for years to save enough to build brick-and-timber homes in the shanty towns of Nairobi or Cotonou. Since there are so many of them, their houses are collectively worth a great deal of money. But since they do not formally own them, they cannot use them as collateral.

According to Hernando de Soto, a Peruvian economist, the total value of Africans' informal urban dwellings in 1997 was $580 billion. The value of rural land which African farmers ploughed or grazed their cattle on, but did not formally own, he estimated at $390 billion. This is a phenomenal sum. It adds up to almost a trillion dollars. To put this in perspective, a trillion dollars is roughly three times the continent's entire annual gross domestic product. In 1998, Africa attracted net foreign direct investment equivalent to less than a hundredth of this.

The failure to extend formal property rights to the bulk of the population is not a uniquely African problem. It is a feature of all poor countries. Include the rest of the developing world, and the total value of dead capital is over $9 trillion, according to de Soto. Third World leaders wander rich-country capitals begging for aid and investment. All the while, they fail to notice a much larger source of potential wealth at home. "In the midst of their own poorest neighborhoods and shanty towns," writes de Soto, "there are trillions of dollars, all ready to be put to use if only the mystery of how assets are transformed into live capital can be unravelled."[2]

To investigate these ideas, I went to Malawi, a country I picked because it is peaceful, stable, off the beaten track, and fearfully poor. The capital, Lilongwe, is leafy and sleepy. By day, sunlight bounces off a million palm fronds. By night, the city is so dark you would not believe you were in a city. I don't think I saw a single working street lamp, although a couple of restaurants cast a faint light on the crater-ridden sidewalk.

Lilongwe's grander buildings were largely paid for by the old South African regime, to reward the late Malawian dictator, Hastings Banda, for not supporting sanctions. Banda was unusual among African leaders in that he refused to condemn apartheid. But in other respects he was a typical dictator. He murdered his opponents, grabbed whole industries for himself, and started a youth movement that was somewhere between the Boy Scouts and Mussolini's Blackshirts. As he entered his nineties, he started to lose control. In 1994, he succumbed to pressure to allow elections. Malawi is now more democratic – but not much richer.

My first destination was a shanty town called Mtandire, not far from the capital. I hired a big Toyota with plenty of clearance, cajoled a civil servant to skip out of work and act as interpreter, and set off bright and early. The roads in Mtandire were unpaved, bumpy, and wet. Corn sprouted in every backyard. Cars were so rare that children waved excitedly as we drove by, and chickens fearlessly blocked our path. A slum in one of the poorest countries on the world's poorest continent: you would expect the people who live there to be very poor indeed. You certainly would not expect to find a large store of hidden wealth in Mtandire.

Killing two goats with one loan

The meaty scent of goat stew hung in the air. This delicacy, with its rich gravy mopped up with handfuls of *nshima* (a kind of sticky corn paste), is served at Malawian weddings, or indeed almost any other celebration. The lumps of goat-on-the-bone are chewy but worth the effort. Malawians love goat stew, which is why Grace and John Tarera's goat-slaughtering business was thriving.

The Tareras bought goats from farmers, chopped them up, and sold chunks at the nearest market. Demand was brisk, and they wanted to expand the business. But they lacked capital. Grace Tarera told me she thought they needed about 20,000 kwacha ($250). This may not sound like much, but in Malawi, where the average annual income is only about $200, it can take years to raise such a sum.

I asked Grace Tarera how much her house was worth. The question meant something: Malawian slum-dwellers do buy and sell houses. The Tareras had bought a piece of land five years before and thrown up a sturdy brick bungalow, fussily furnished with lacy tablecloths and painted a restful shade of light blue. This pleasant structure was worth about 25,000 kwacha, she reckoned – a figure which tallied with what other people in Mtandire told me their places were worth. Since this was more than the sum the Tareras wanted to expand their goat-slaughtering business, surely they could use the house as security to raise the necessary cash? No, they couldn't, because they had no formal title deed.

The Tareras' house, like all the others in Mtandire, is built on "customary" land, which means that the plot's previous owners had no formal title to it. The land was simply part of a field their family had cultivated for generations. About two thirds of the land in Malawi is owned this way. People usually till the land their parents did. If there is a dispute about boundaries, the village chief adjudicates. If a family offends gravely against the rules of the tribe, the chief can take their land away and give it to someone else. In effect, the chief holds all the land in trust for the tribe, as kings did in feudal Europe.

The system worked well enough when Malawians were all farmers and there was plenty of land to go around. But it is ill-suited to a crowded urban setting. As people flock to Lilongwe in search of jobs, they increasingly settle on the farmland that surrounds the city. Peasants are happy to sell them plots, but informally. Would-be buyers and sellers approach the local chief, who confirms that the seller owns the land he is selling and gives him permission to sell it. The contract may be oral, or it may be written in one of the local languages and signed by the chief. The chief often takes a cut – anything from a modest 5 percent to an exorbitant 40 percent.

This was how John and Grace Tarera bought the land beneath their house. They have a contract signed by the local chief, but no bank will accept it as collateral because it is not enforceable in a court of law. Rather, it is an expression of traditional law, which is usually unwritten, unpredictable, and dependent on the chief's whim. The chief may be a wise, just, and consistent fellow. But the bank does not know this. So the Tareras' house is dead capital. They own it, but they cannot make its value work for them.

Tied to the land

Informal ownership hurts rural folk, too. Take Nashon Zimba, a twenty-five-year-old peasant I met in Chiponde, a small village in Kasungu district, north-west of Lilongwe. Zimba is poor even by Malawian standards. He grows corn, beans, cassava, and tobacco on a couple of hectares which he inherited from his parents. He rarely has much left over to sell: he told me that his cash income in 2000 was $40. He lives with his wife and baby daughter in a tiny mud shack with plastic bags for window panes.

We sat on a reed mat under the shade of a mango tree. It was midday and too hot to work, so Zimba was happy to talk. He was barefoot, and his T-shirt was streaked with soil stains. He cradled his baby daughter, who was chewing on a bicycle spoke.

"I've got enough land," said Zimba, "but I can't afford enough seeds or fertilizer to make good use of it." Borrowing, he lamented, was out of the question. Loan sharks – "caterpillars," as they are known in Malawi – charge impossible rates of interest. A few farmers in Zimba's village raise small loans from a donor-supported microlender called the Malawi Rural Finance Corporation, but only those who are organized into groups to cross-guarantee each other's borrowings are eligible. Such groups are exclusive: the most productive farmers do not want less able neighbors to spoil their collective credit history. "I wanted to join one of those groups," said Zimba, "but it was full." One of his neighbors told me that the village elite did not think Zimba quite made the grade.

For those who cannot join credit circles, there is charity. The government hands out free "starter packs" of seeds and fertilizer, intended for the poorest farmers. Only thirty-two such packs arrived in Zimba's village the previous year, for a population of about 900. They were not sent directly to the intended recipients; the poor do not have addresses. Instead, the chief doled them out as he saw fit. Zimba did not receive one.

Almost 90 percent of Malawi's 11 million people live off the land. Their average plot size is tiny: less than a hectare. Productivity is woeful. The population is expected to double by 2020. Unless a lot of people move to the cities, plots will continue to be sliced ever smaller. Smaller plots mean smaller harvests for each family, which is one reason why Malawi suffered deadly food shortages in 2002.

Zimba sensed that there was little future in farming. His ambition, he said, was to be a hawker. He envisaged buying soap and paraffin in the nearest town and selling it in the village. It would be wonderful, he supposed, if he could one day earn enough to buy a bicycle. But, he said: "I haven't got the money to get started."

Some people in Zimba's position move to the city, find jobs, and save to start a small business. But this is hard. A Malawian peasant cannot usually sell his land without agreement from his family and the village chief. If he leaves his property unattended, there is a danger that the chief will give his land to someone else or that a sibling will grab it.

When he arrives in the city, there will be no cheap shelter. Without mortgage lending, there are never enough houses in shanty towns. A landlord in Mtandire cannot borrow money to build and then recoup it from rental income. He has to pay cash in advance and then try to get it back. So a typical slum rent is much higher, relative to the value of the house, than it would be in a more affluent area where landlords have title deeds. In Mtandire, ten months' rent will buy you the house.

Capitalism needs rules

The advantages of sound property rights are so taken for granted in the West that it is worth spelling them out. First, secure title makes assets fungible. In a country with good property laws, almost anyone can use a house or a piece of land as collateral to raise a loan. It is also easy to divide assets between multiple owners. Ownership of a factory, for example, can be shared out among hundreds of people, any of whom can sell all or part of his share without the need take the factory physically apart. If a French farmer dies, his children can sell the farm, or retain equal shares in it, or the more agriculturally inclined sibling can buy the others out. The possibilities are legion. African small-holders, by contrast, have much less flexibility: plots tend to be divided into ever-smaller parcels with each generation.

A uniform property system is also a way of sharing know-ledge. When information about the ownership and value of houses, companies, and other assets is centrally recorded and freely available, it makes it easier for people to see economic opportunities outside their own neighborhood. In other words, formal property law enables people to do business with strangers. Those who are part of the formal property system have addresses, credit records, and identifiable assets. A Westerner who does not honor his debts is blacklisted. The debt collectors know where to find him and what to seize. So he has a powerful incentive to play by the rules. Millions of Third-World squatters, by contrast, cannot obtain telephone or electricity lines because no one trusts them to pay their bills.

Western property laws protect not merely ownership but transactions, too. People in poor countries can usually prevent their assets from being stolen by forming self-defense groups or hiring the protection of local mobsters. But they cannot confidently buy anything they cannot see. Poor people carry their pigs and tobacco bales physically to market. The prohibitive cost of carrying them back means that they have to sell them right away, whether prices are good or not. American farmers sell paper representations of their crops, which is easier. To smooth their cash flow, they can sell the rights to purchase crops which have not yet been sown. If a Malawian farmer wants cash in advance, he must grow marijuana.

The house that Nashon built

When you cannot do business with strangers, you have to do everything yourself. This is inefficient. Imagine building your own house. Some Westerners do, of course, build their own houses, but not in the way rural Africans do. An American who wants to do it himself buys industrially produced bricks, cement, glass, nails, screws, drills, pipes, window frames, and so on. All these parts have been made cheaply and well by a company that specializes in making them and that has in turn bought its machine tools and accounting services from other specialists.

Compare this with Nashon Zimba's experiences. He digs up mud, shapes it into cuboids, and dries it in the sun to make bricks. He mixes his own cement, also from mud. He cuts branches to make beams and thatches the roof with sisal or grass. His only industrial input is the metal blade on his axe. Working on his own while at the same time growing food for his family, Zimba has erected a house that is dark, cramped, cold in winter, and steamy in summer and that has running water only when tropical storms come through the roof. He kindly invited me in, and I found that I could not stand up straight inside it. He told me that it would probably fall down within five years.

I thought of my own home, with its sturdy walls and modern kitchen. Zimba is a skilled builder; I barely know which way is up on a brick. Yet he lives in a hovel, while I, like most Westerners, live in a relative palace, built by a network of millions of people I have never met. In all my travels, I have never seen a more poignant illustration of why the world's poor people need capitalism.

How to be formal

Since the demise of the Soviet Union, few people still argue that property is theft. It is a rare despot – Robert Mugabe springs to mind – who openly urges his followers to grab other people's land. In theory, property rights are available to all in most poor countries. But in practice, most poor people do not take advantage of these rights.

It is often assumed that informal homes and businesses stay that way because their owners do not wish to pay taxes. This is doubtful. Taxes are of course burdensome, but the costs of extra-legality are often more so. The informal entrepreneur pays gangsters for protection and bribes officials to ignore him. His operations are often geographically dispersed to hide them from the authorities, which stops him from achieving economies of scale. He cannot declare limited liability or obtain insurance or cheap credit. In short, informality is uncomfortable.

The reason that extra-legal businesses and landowners in poor countries do not become legal is that it is absurdly hard to do so. In some parts of Africa, such as Ethiopia and Mozambique, freehold land ownership is simply not allowed. In others, bureaucracy blocks the way to formal ownership. In Egypt, to obtain permission to build a house on land zoned for agriculture takes six to eleven years. If you build first and then try to become legal, you risk having your home demolished and spending up to ten years in jail. In Angola, the deeds registry is so chaotic that even tower blocks in the capital city are sometimes subject to overlapping claims. You can rent an apartment from one ministry and be evicted the next month by another.

In Malawi, the bureaucracy that administers property law is, in the words of an official commission of inquiry into the subject, "riddled with jurisdictional overlaps and internal conflicts" and "often the cause of delays, errors of judgement, lack of coordination, rampant corruption and dereliction of duty."[3]

Such obstacles are not a purely African problem. In Peru, Hernando de Soto's researchers set up a one-man garment workshop and tried to register it. The team worked for six hours a day, filling out forms, traveling by bus into central Lima, and standing in line in front of the relevant bureaucratic desks. It took them 289 days to make their micro-enterprise legal and cost $1,231 – thirty-one times the monthly minimum wage in Peru.[4]

All rich industrialized countries have secure property rights, accessible to more or less all citizens. No poor country has. Better property laws are not the only reason that some countries are richer than others, but they clearly make a difference. Many poor countries recognize this and are trying to devise ways to make their property systems more inclusive. But the hurdles are high.

Lawyers often oppose attempts to simplify the law. Tribal chiefs resist changes that may reduce their power. And cultures, though they evolve quite rapidly, cannot be changed by fiat. People who live in traditional rural communities are often wary of alien ways of doing things. Stanley Ngwira, for example, chairman of an association of small farmers from Nashon Zimba's district, finds the idea of selling land abhorrent. "There would be nothing for our children," he told me with a frown.

Tony Hawkins, a professor of business studies at the University of Zimbabwe, argues that it is relatively simple to institute sound property rules in cities but much harder in rural societies. While he admires de Soto's work, he thinks the Peruvian has "glossed over" the difficulties of switching from communal to individual ownership in Africa, where most people are peasants, and most peasants are unfamiliar with written contracts.[5]

Today's rich countries took hundreds of years to forge uniform property codes. Until the last century (or more recently, in the case of Japan) they were shackled with multiple and contradictory sets of property laws. The early American colonists were mostly squatters. The country was so vast and sparsely populated that the land-hungry simply fenced and ploughed without worrying about title. Big landowners, such as George Washington, tried to evict and prosecute squatters, but they tended to resist violently, and juries seldom convicted them.

Powerless to stop them, some legislators tried instead to bring squatters inside the law. As early as 1642, the state of Virginia passed a law that allowed for squatters to be compensated for improvements they had made to land they occupied. If the rightful owner was unwilling to pay, the squatters were given the right to buy the land from him at a price set by a jury. This helped many squatters to become legal.

In the nineteenth century, when the pioneers rushed west to stake out claims to farms and gold mines, they made their own local rules to determine who owned what. Several states passed laws allowing those who occupied and improved idle land to claim title to it. Federal law followed behind. There was a heroic effort to tie all local property systems together into a single code. The Homestead Act of 1862 and the mining law of 1866 essentially formalized the arrangements that extra-legal farmers and prospectors had already worked out for themselves hundreds of miles from Washington.

For poor countries today, the lesson is not in the details of American history but in the general principles. For property law to be respected, it has to reflect what is actually happening on the ground, and it has to try to include as many people as possible.

Poor countries' efforts at reforming property law have rarely succeeded. Middle-class reformers have too often assumed that their ideals could be imposed on the poor. In Peru, for example, numerous attempts to give indigenous people title to their land failed because the mechanisms by which they could assert this right were too complex and costly.

In Malawi, laws allowing freehold and leasehold were introduced by the British in colonial times but were never widely trusted because they were the means by which settlers hoodwinked the locals into surrendering their ancestral lands. The despot Banda also tried to encourage formal ownership. But his habit of grabbing large tracts of land for his cronies undermined the rule of law. Banks were forced to lend for political rather than commercial reasons, which prevented the evolution of property-backed lending.

The Malawian government said, in 2001, that it wanted to make it easier for holders of customary land to upgrade to formal leasehold. But it has yet to persuade people that formality offers concrete advantages and that it does not conflict too much with their traditions. All this will take time, especially since not all Malawian politicians are exactly passionate about property rights. In 2002, the government took a retrograde step by declaring that leaseholds held by foreigners, including Malawi's sizeable Asian minority, would not confer the same rights as those held by native Malawians.

Africa, like Malawi, has a long way to go before its people can unlock the wealth trapped in informal property. But it can be done. In every poor village, anywhere in the world, people know who owns what. De Soto tells a story. On farms in Bali there are few fences to mark the boundaries between properties. But the dogs know. Cross from one farmer's land to his neighbor's, and a different dog barks. The challenge for governments in poor countries is to take the information contained in those yelps and fashion from it a clear and enforceable set of laws. The alternative, in Africa and elsewhere, is to stay poor.

4. SEX AND DEATH

The calamity of AIDS

I was staying in a vile hotel in Port Harcourt, in Nigeria's oil-rich Niger delta. The sheets on my bed were ragged and torn, the breakfast bacon was leathery and lukewarm, and there was a sign on the door warning me not to steal things from the room. This being an oil town, my fellow guests all had something to do with the business. All were involved either in pumping the black stuff or protesting about its environmental impact. Burly drilling engineers from Texas mixed with earnest greens from London in the execrable Chinese restaurant on the ground floor.

Port Harcourt is humid, malarial, and prone to riots. No one comes here for fun. But a risky kind of entertainment was rather obviously available. A crowd of prostitutes dawdled in the lobby, between the Chinese restaurant and the elevators. Any male guest who had finished his glutinous chicken-with-tinned-mixed-vegetables and wanted to go to bed had first to dodge some forceful sales pitches. On my first night in the hotel I was outnumbered by about forty to one. The shyer ladies merely beckoned; the more aggressive ones seized handfuls of sleeve or trouser-leg and tugged. One lady grabbed my wrist, declared that she had fallen in love, and pulled me towards the toilets.

After several embarrassed no thank yous, I reached the elevator. But before I could close the door, one of the largest prostitutes squeezed in too and started to tear at my shirt buttons. Then the power failed, the elevator groaned to a halt between floors, and the lights went out. I'm not sure how long it was before the back-up generator kicked in. But time does not hurry when you are trapped in a steel box with a sex worker who weighs more than you and won't take no for an answer. Every time I pushed her away, she offered to lower the price. She was down to $5 before I convinced her that it wasn't a question of money.

"So you're worried about disease?" she asked. I repeated that I was married and simply not interested in her services. She began to explain various ways in which she could enliven my evening without swapping body fluids. "I can give you a massage," she said. And then, gesturing between her legs, she added: "You don't have to touch me here."

As a man who travels alone in Africa and stays in reasonably expensive hotels, I have been propositioned rather a lot. In bars, ladies with long purple fingernails and brittle perms often sit beside me and smile. In most African cities I visit, hopeful girls wave from under broken streetlights or tap on the windows of my taxis and rental cars. Sometimes they are desperately pushy. A waitress in a hotel in Brazzaville memorized my room number when I signed a bill, knocked on my door at midnight, shoved her foot in to stop me shutting it, and wriggled inside. She then refused to leave until I took her by the shoulders and pushed her gently but firmly outside.

A barbershop I used to visit in Zimbabwe mirrored that country's decline over the years I've reported from it. It was a friendly place with pink walls in a smart part of Harare, the Zimbabwean capital. In 1998, when I first walked in, it was just a barbershop: bustling, thriving, and businesslike. The young women working there were mildly flirtatious, but they never offered to do more than just cut my hair. They did it cheaply and well, so whenever I later found myself in Harare with a fringe flopping into my eyes and an hour to kill, I went back.

Each time I returned, the barbershop had grown emptier and sleazier. The government's terror campaign against whites and dissidents had driven off all the tourists, and the collapse of Zimbabwean industry had drastically reduced the number of locals who could afford to pay someone else to cut their hair. The lines of customers vanished, and the hairdressers gradually switched from light-hearted flirting to insistent hustling. The last time I went there, in 2001, I was the only customer. Before I even sat down in the barber's chair, the lady I had asked to cut my hair offered instead to take me upstairs for a shower and a body-rub. When I said no, she asked if I preferred one of the other women working there. Two of her colleagues appeared from nowhere and started pulling my wrists. I left a bigger-than-usual tip for the haircut and never returned.

All these encounters sadden me. When an African woman offers to sleep with me for money, I know I am talking to some-one who will probably be dead in a few years. Most African prostitutes contract the human immuno-deficiency virus (HIV), which leads to AIDS. They die emaciated and ravaged by fungal infections, and they take many of their clients with them.

In rich countries, AIDS is no longer a death sentence. Costly drug cocktails can keep HIV-positive patients alive and healthy for a long time. After being bombarded with warnings in the 1980s, most Westerners know how the disease is transmitted and are fairly cautious about swapping body fluids. HIV prevalence is low throughout the developed world, and only a handful of people actually die of it.

In most African countries, by contrast, only tycoons and cabinet ministers can afford AIDS drugs. By 2002, about 17 million Africans had died of AIDS, and 29 million were HIV positive.[1] Pause for a moment to ponder it: 46 million Africans either dead or doomed. It's more than seven times the number of Jews, Gypsies, and homosexuals murdered by Hitler. It's one and a half times the 30 million Chinese who died of starvation under Mao Zedong.[2] It's three quarters of the death toll during the whole of the Second World War, and by the time AIDS has claimed its last African victim, it may outnumber even that.

In several countries in southern and eastern Africa, a fifth or more of adults carry the virus. That does not mean that a fifth of the population of these countries will die of AIDS. It is worse than that. Almost all those who are now infected will die in the next ten years, but before they die they will infect others. In Botswana, the worst-hit nation, more than a third of adults carry the virus. The president of Botswana, Festus Mogae, lamented in 2001 that unless the epidemic was reversed, his country faced "blank extinction."[3] He was not exaggerating.

Nowhere has the AIDS epidemic run its course, so any predictions about its long-term effects are speculative. But even on the most optimistic assumptions, Africa faces an unprecedented catastrophe. Everywhere I travel south of the Sahara, I see signs of the silent havoc wrought by AIDS. I have visited hospitals where virtually every bed was occupied by an AIDS patient, some so thin that their skin sagged and their arms looked like broken broom handles. I have flipped through the obituary columns in dozens of African newspapers: all are filled with photos of young faces: thirty- and forty-year-olds who died "after a long illness." I have visited schools that lack teachers because of AIDS and companies whose managers have started to limit the number of funerals employees may take time off to attend.

When my wife and I lived in South Africa, our housekeeper's boyfriend, a long-distance taxi driver, grew thin and died. The doctor wrote "tuberculosis" on the death certificate, which was accurate enough, but probably only part of the story.

Why is this happening? Why has Africa suffered so much more than anywhere else from AIDS? What can be done to curb the epidemic? I've spent years pondering these questions. I still don't know the answers, but I've found some clues. I've spoken to doctors, to charity workers, and to politicians. I've swapped stories with my wife, a former charity worker, who has written a book about AIDS orphans. While researching it, she used to come home from visits to orphanages with her clothes flecked with tears and spit where dozens of lonely children had clung to her.

In 1998, I went to Uganda, where a taxi driver inadvertently helped me frame the question. His name was Charles, and he drove me along the unlit road from Entebbe airport to Kampala, the capital, after dark. Long-horned cattle blundered onto the asphalt, but we could not see them until the headlights bounced off their eyes. Cars coming in the other direction sometimes had no lights at all. But Charles hit the gas pedal and swerved when necessary. He coaxed more speed out of an old Toyota than I would have thought possible. He overtook on blind corners. I looked the other way.

As we drove, he told me his life story. He had lost his mother, his father, two brothers, and their wives to AIDS. Everyone in his family knew how the virus was transmitted and that it was deadly. But they still failed to take precautions. And the thought struck me, as we sped and weaved through the dimly visible traffic. Anyone who wants to curb the devastation that AIDS is wreaking in Africa must answer this: how do you promote safer sex on a continent where no one wears a seat belt?

We Westerners have grown accustomed to caution. We wear crash helmets when we cycle, we expect our governments to ensure that every last molecule of any chemical that even sounds scary is removed from our tap water, and we buy bags of nuts with the words "Warning: contains nuts" on the packet. All this is quite recent. Our great-grandparents did not expect all their children to survive to adulthood. Premature death doubtless upset them as much as it upsets us, but it did not surprise or anger them so much. It was too common for that.

In this respect, Africa resembles Europe at the turn of the twentieth century. Poverty fosters a kind of fatalism. Life is hard when you are poor and death could come at any time. Malarial mosquitoes swarm at night, but you can't afford mefloquine. You take the cheapest, most crowded minibus to work, which is cheap because it's old and the brakes are dodgy.

You take things one day at a time and seize passing pleasures when you can.

How the virus spreads

Most scientists think that HIV originated in the rainforests of central Africa in the 1920s or 30s and then eventually spread around the world. Some Africans are insulted by the assertion that AIDS began in Africa and feel that they are somehow being blamed for the disease. They are not. A deadly virus evolved and jumped from apes to humans, perhaps when a woman with a cut on her finger prepared chimp meat for the pot. No one could have foreseen this, and no reasonable person could believe that it was anyone's fault. The question of exactly when and how HIV first found its way into a human bloodstream is of great scientific interest. But of more immediate concern for anyone interested in keeping the death toll down is the question of how it spreads today.

Unlike in the West, HIV in Africa is contracted mainly through heterosexual sex. Men and women infect each other when they make love without condoms. The virus then travels from town to town along the old colonial highways, in crowded minibuses and lorries. Its staging posts are bus stations and truck stops, where travelers meet locals and the virus finds new hosts.

I visited a truck stop at Beitbridge, on the border between Zimbabwe and South Africa. It was hot and dusty, and there was not much to do. A little kiosk sold cold Cokes and beef jerky, but that was about it. Truck drivers waiting to cross the border parked their eighteen-wheelers on any vacant patch of dirt and opened cans of Castle beer. As dusk fell, they sat in their cabs, watching a parade of young women in tight tops saunter by. When they saw one they liked, they called out to her.

"Sister, come and cook for me," was the most common

come-on. It was meant literally. Cooking was part of the package. Every trucker had a pot, a stove, and a chicken or some fish in a plastic bag. For a few rand, a truck-stop prostitute would cook a tasty stew with whatever ingredients the trucker had on his dashboard. And then they drew the curtains across the windscreen.

"I fuck thirty bitches a month," boasted John Masara, a twenty-nine-year-old trucker. He slammed his fist into the palm of his left hand to emphasize the point. He was wiry and strong, with a thin gauze of facial hair and enough beer in his bloodstream to loosen his tongue. Fucking was the only entertainment in Beitbridge, he explained. It could take a week to process the paperwork required to move a load over the border. Rumor had it that customs officials owned shares in local hotels. Most truckers shunned hotels, however. It was cheaper to sleep where they parked or to pay a prostitute for a share of her mattress.

Did Masara know about AIDS? Sure, he said, a colleague died of it two days before. He knew how the virus spread, too. "You get it from women." He knew how to protect himself too, but did he use condoms? "Sometimes," he said. His friends laughed: "When you're not drunk."

He ignored them and said that he "condomized" with most women but not the most beautiful ones. A trucker's life is dangerous, he explained. He'd been hijacked by men with guns. Any day, he said, he could fall asleep at the wheel and die in a ditch. But the job paid well by local standards, so he had some spare cash. He figured he might as well have some fun while he could.

His relaxed attitude to risk extended to his two wives, whom he said he saw about once a month. They didn't ask him to use condoms, so he didn't. "There's nothing I can do about it." He shrugged. "I'm a trucker."

Masara's wives probably didn't know how much danger they were in. Most of the prostitutes he slept with, by contrast, understood the risks but carried on as if they didn't.

Chipo Muchero, for example, who sold sex on the Zimbabwean side of the border at Beitbridge, insisted that "if a client won't use a condom, then I refuse sex." But she was lying.

Her black hair was bleached yellow at the front. Her denim dungarees were cut off above the knee, to expose bruised calves. She was suspicious of questions but had nothing better to do than answer them. Business was slow: there were too many women in the same line of work in the crowded slum where she lived and not enough clients to keep them busy.

Muchero hung out with half a dozen other women of varying ages outside a dark, one-roomed house with mud-brick walls. There was no sign outside to indicate that it was a makeshift brothel. It was no different from hundreds of neighboring homes: mostly mud and wood, occasionally reinforced or waterproofed with sheets of corrugated iron or black plastic. Dirty water ran past in an open ditch. Children dashed around playfully shrieking, while their mothers built fires or scrubbed clothes.

Muchero and her friends all did other kinds of work, too. They fetched water and firewood, sewed and cooked, and tended small patches of corn. But no one paid them for any of this. To earn cash, they brought men home. Inside the house, blankets hanging from the ceiling subdivided the room and created a bit of privacy.

After a while, Muchero admitted: "OK, I'll have sex with any man – trucker, tourist, or local guy – with or without a condom. I need the money. I don't have a job or education. I have no other option."[4]

If she had a passport, she said, she would cross into South Africa and trade things other than her body. She knew others who had done this. South African shops are cheaper and better-stocked than those in Zimbabwe, so there is money to be made buying toasters and televisions on the South African side and bringing them home to sell. One store in Messina, the nearest sizeable South African town, had a big red sign outside proclaiming that "Zimbabweans and hawkers are welcome for one-stop shopping."

But Muchero could not afford a passport. To get by, she entertained about four clients a week. The price was fixed by haggling; she usually made between one and two dollars per trick. Eventually, her job was bound to kill her. But in the short term she could think of no other way to support herself.

How AIDS keeps Africa poor

After the Black Death wiped out a third of the population of medieval Europe, many of the survivors were better off. Because so many died there was a sudden labor shortage, and land-owners were forced to pay their workers better.

Africans who survive AIDS will not be so lucky. AIDS takes longer to kill than the plague did, so the cost of caring for the sick will be much greater. Modern governments, unlike medieval ones, tax the healthy to help look after the ailing, so the burden of AIDS will fall on everyone. And because AIDS is sexually transmitted, it tends to hit people in their most productive years.

AIDS is making Africans poorer. But since the epidemic has not yet run its course anywhere, any prediction as to how much poorer it will make them involves a lot of guesswork. For what it's worth, researchers at ING Baring, a bank, forecast that the South African economy will be 17 percent smaller in 2010 than it would have been without the virus. They could be wrong. But there is no doubt that AIDS will make a lot of things worse.

Africa's already painful skills shortage will grow more acute. Skilled workers who die will be hard to replace, not least because so many teachers are dying too. Zambia is suffering power shortages because so many engineers have succumbed. Farmers in Zimbabwe are finding it hard to irrigate their fields because the brass fittings on their water pipes have been stolen for coffin handles. All over Africa, AIDS is making employees sicker and therefore more expensive and less productive. Costly and unproductive employees tend to get sacked.

At a national level, the effect of AIDS is felt gradually. But at a household level, the impact is sudden and catastrophic. When a breadwinner falls ill, his (or her) family is impoverished twice over. Their main source of income vanishes, and they must somehow find extra money for medicine. Daughters drop out of school to help nurse their ailing fathers. Because husbands infect wives and wives infect babies, AIDS often strikes several times in the same family.

A study in urban Côte d'Ivoire found that households afflicted by AIDS subsequently spent only half as much on education. Family members ate two-fifths less and were forced to spend four times as much on health care. Another survey in Tanzania found that a woman whose husband was sick with AIDS spent 60 percent less time growing food than before. And in Zimbabwe the disease so weakened peasant farmers that the ones tilling communal land produced half as much in 1998 as they had five years previously.

Orphans of the virus

I went to Ndola, in the copper-mining region of northern Zambia, where I had heard that the virus was wreaking particular havoc. The local cemeteries bore grim witness to the truth of this rumor. It wasn't just that they were so huge or that so many of the headstones were new. What struck me was how unkempt the places were. There was a shortage of survivors, I was told, with the energy to tend the graves. Those whom the virus missed were often too busy battling hunger to waste time and burn calories hacking back the long grass that had swallowed their relatives' tombs. Many graves were lost in the undergrowth. And some had been dug up: local thieves were so desperate, a local charity worker told me, that they stripped fresh corpses of the smart suits in which they were buried.

AIDS is wiping out whole families: the Zambian health ministry estimated that half of Zambia's population would eventually die of it. Those who die are mostly breadwinners or mothers. Estimates of the proportion of Zambian children who have lost one or both parents (usually, but not always, from AIDS) range from 13 percent to 50 percent.[5] If the difference between these two numbers seems absurdly large, remember that accurate statistics are rare in countries as poor as Zambia. Personally, I don't believe that the higher figure can be true. But even at the lowest estimate Zambian children are a dozen times more likely to be orphaned than children in rich countries.

It is not only children who are hit. Elderly Africans usually expect their adult children to look after them in their twilight years. But because AIDS is causing many middle-aged people to die before their parents, the elderly are being "orphaned" at an alarming rate. Not only do they lose their main means of support, but they suddenly find themselves caring for their orphaned grandchildren as well.

I met one such elderly orphan in a "compound" (shanty town) near Ndola. Faides Zulu, a small and slender grandmother with gentle eyes, was old enough to have no idea when she was born. We spoke, through an interpreter, sitting on a rush mat on a concrete floor in a schoolhouse, where she came about once a month to receive a bag of corn from a local Catholic charity. Both her daughter and her daughter's husband died in the same year "after being sick for a long time," leaving her to look after five small children.

Faides Zulu's "second motherhood" was not easy, she said. She grew vegetables in her backyard and then walked several miles on frail legs to sell them. One child was often ill, with bloody diarrhea, fever, and headaches. She preferred not to talk about the likelihood that this child had contracted HIV from his mother, either during birth or while breastfeeding.

Zulu fretted about the future. "I am old," she said. "In ten years' time I will not be able to work in my garden. What will happen to my children then?" Probably, she guessed, her eldest granddaughter would land the responsibility of looking after her younger siblings.

In 2002, there were an estimated 11 million AIDS orphans living in Africa. Extended families have adapted heroically to the crisis. In Zambia, one study, conducted in the parts of the country worst hit by AIDS, found that 72 percent of households had taken in one or more orphans.[6] The national average is probably lower than this, but there is no doubt that such generosity is common.

Throughout Africa, families have opened their arms and homes to orphaned siblings and nephews. No matter how poor they are, they have welcomed them without hesitation, fuss, or a hint of resentment. There are millions of Faides Zulus, most of whom show a warm selflessness that leaves me stunned with admiration.

AIDS has put these families under a huge strain, of course. Extra mouths mean less food to go around, so many fostered children are made to work for their keep. The unluckiest can slip through the family safety net entirely. For example, if a mother dies of AIDS, her relatives sometimes wrongly assume that her baby too is doomed and so don't waste scarce food delaying the inevitable.[7] For the most part, however, Africans have lavished their orphaned kin with love and pumpkin-leaf stew. Not even AIDS can break the African extended family.

Why AIDS is hard to curb

The best hope for halting AIDS would be a cheap vaccine. Scientists are trying to find one, but it could take years. HIV mutates rapidly, so it is hard to teach the body's immune system to recognize and attack it. In the short term, the only way to curb the epidemic in Africa is to persuade people to shun risky sex. This is also hard, for several reasons.

Sex is fun. And many people feel that condoms make it less so. Zimbabweans ask: "Would you eat a sweet with the wrapper on?"

Talking about sex is often taboo. Many traditional parents think it shameful to discuss the subject with their children. Some conspiracy theorists even argue that the whole hoo-ha about AIDS is a bizarre plot to make blacks appear immoral. When my wife's book on AIDS orphans was published, a South African reviewer accused her of trying "to advance a racist ideology that portrays African people as promiscuous and reckless" simply because she repeated the conventional view that HIV originated in Africa.[8]

Myths abound. Some young African women believe that without regular infusions of sperm, they will not grow up to be beautiful. Ugandan men have been known to use this myth to seduce schoolgirls. In much of southern Africa, HIV-infected men believe that they can cleanse themselves of the virus by passing it on to a virgin. This is an old myth. Nineteenth-century Brazilian slave-owners thought they could cure themselves of syphilis in the same way. The result is the same in Africa now as it was on Amazonian rubber plantations a century and a half ago.

Poverty. Those who cannot afford television find other ways of passing the evening. Poor people often cannot afford antibiotics to treat other sexually transmitted diseases (STDs). STDs can open sores on the genitals, which provide easy openings for HIV to enter a new host.

Migration. When people are mobile, the virus spreads. Migrant traders and bricklayers flock to South Africa, where wages are much higher than in neighboring countries. Gold miners spend eleven months of the year apart from their families, often living in single-sex dormitories surrounded by prostitutes. Living with a one in forty chance of being killed in a rockfall, they are inured to risk. When they go home for Christmas, they often infect their wives.

War. Refugees spread HIV as they flee. Soldiers, with their regular wages and disdain for risk, are more likely to be infected than civilians. They are also able, in the chaos of battle, to rape with impunity. A friend and colleague of mine, James Astill, the *Economist*'s former Nairobi correspondent, spent time with the Mai-Mai, a ragged militia band notorious for gang-raping peasant women in eastern Congo. They offered him a chance to ingest a charm they said would make him invulnerable: a paste made from the severed penises of their enemies, the Rwandan soldiers who had invaded Congo. The spell worked, they said, if you opened a cut in your arm and rubbed in the paste. They all used the same rusty knife. James said thanks but no thanks.

Sexism. Many African women find it hard to ask their partners to use condoms. In one survey in Zambia, less than a quarter of women believed they had the right to refuse sex with their husbands even if they knew he was unfaithful and HIV-positive. And only one in ten thought she could ask him to use a condom in this situation. Women who try to insist on condom use risk being punched. In two districts in Uganda, 41 percent of men admitted to researchers that they beat their partners. Another study found that sexual violence was "widespread" in South African schools.[9] Forced sex is an unusually effective means of HIV transmission because the victim usually bleeds.

Alcohol. African beers are, by and large, delicious. Drunken lovers are less likely to remember to use condoms. A survey of women in an area frequented by sex workers in Carletonville, a mining town in South Africa, found that 65 percent of those who drank were HIV-positive, compared with only 30 percent of non-drinkers.

Finally, there is the question of foreskins. Several studies suggest that African men who are circumcised before puberty are less likely to contract HIV. Even allowing for cultural differences between groups that snip and groups that don't, circumcision appears to offer limited protection. Possibly this is because the tip of the penis grows tougher if not cushioned by a foreskin. Unfortunately, the discovery that circumcision makes sex safer has led some people to believe that it makes sex safe and so they neglect to use condoms.

None of these problems is unique to Africa. But nowhere else has them all in such abundance. Of all the factors driving the epidemic, promiscuity is the hardest to discuss without upsetting people. Sexual mores clearly differ between cultures. Premarital sex carries less of a social stigma in Holland or Japan than in, say, Saudi Arabia. But it is hard to determine how promiscuous societies are, because people lie about sex. Ask a young British man how many women he has slept with, and he may exaggerate the number to make himself seem more virile. Or, if he is religious, he may downplay it.

We don't know how much sex Africans have, or how many partners they have it with. But a couple of generalizations are possible. First, many sub-Saharan societies are relatively permissive. Polygamy is quite common. Sex may not be discussed openly, but many men flaunt mistresses, and unmarried urban women do not seem embarrassed when a boyfriend stays the night.

What may be as important as the number of partners is what is called the "pattern of sexual networking." Consider the way AIDS spreads in Thailand. Thai women are expected to be virgins when they marry, but men can fool around without being thought immoral. Extramarital sex usually means a trip to a brothel. If a Thai man contracts HIV, it will probably be from a prostitute. He may then pass the virus on to his wife, who may infect her unborn child. The family is destroyed. But the chain usually stops there.

In Africa, the pattern is often different. A married man may have sex with prostitutes, but he may also have casual affairs with teenage girls. Girls who contract HIV from a "sugar daddy" often survive long enough to get married and pass the virus on to their husbands. Those husbands may then have affairs with younger women. And so on. Sex between people of different generations helps keep the virus circulating.

In eastern and southern Africa, HIV prevalence is far higher among teenage girls than boys. The only plausible explanation is that young girls are having sex with older men who have been sexually active for long enough to contract the virus.[10] Anecdotal evidence is plentiful, too. Anyone standing outside a high-school gate in Kenya or Zambia will sooner or later see girls get into cars with middle-aged men who are not their fathers. These girls then usually go on to marry men of approximately their own age.

How to fight it

There is hope. Two African countries – Uganda and Senegal – have shown that AIDS can be curbed. Uganda's example is especially heartening because it shows what can be done with almost no money.

Uganda is poor by any standards. When Yoweri Museveni seized power in 1986, the country was one of the poorest and most violent in the world. In the 1970s and 80s, under the tyrants Milton Obote and Idi Amin, perhaps 800,000 Ugandans were shot or bludgeoned to death or starved when soldiers stole their harvests. Average annual income in Uganda was a meagre $150 or so. Half of the population was illiterate. Years of chaos and civil war had allowed HIV to spread unchecked, although no one knew this at the time because the doctors who might have tested people had mostly fled the country.

President Museveni has his faults, but he quickly recognized the threat that AIDS posed. In 1984, he recalls, while listening to the BBC he heard an Italian professor talking about the situation in Zambia. He explained that HIV could be spread through heterosexual as well as homosexual intercourse. "I thought this was very dangerous, given the habits of our people – it would finish them," Museveni told the *Times*. Shortly afterward, he sent sixty of his soldiers to train in Cuba, where the government tested them for HIV. Museveni was shocked to discover that eighteen of them were infected.[11]

He acted swiftly, forcing every government department to draw up a plan suggesting what it could do to tackle AIDS. The budget was tiny, but they coped. Accurate surveys of sexual behavior were conducted for only $20,000–30,000 each. Posters discouraging risky sex were erected by busy roads. A rise in literacy, from 51 percent in 1980 to 65 percent in 1998, allowed more Ugandans to read them.[12]

To fill the gaps that the state could not, non-governmental organizations (NGOs) were given free rein to do whatever it took to educate people about HIV. Scores of charities, many foreign-financed, took up the challenge. I visited a few, including the Straight Talk Foundation, which publishes newsletters that teach adolescents and pre-teens about sex in a straightforward, unpreachy way. Rather than seeking to scold or scare, they probe the complexities of puberty, relationships, and sex.

Talking about relationships is often more important than talking about the mechanics of how HIV is transmitted. For many young people, the problem is not that they are ignorant about AIDS but that they are unsure how to deal with romantic situations. So Straight Talk's volunteers do not merely issue warnings; they run romantic role-playing sessions in Ugandan schools. These help girls learn how to insist on condoms, for example, or how to persuade their boyfriends that they are not yet ready for sex. Convincing teenage boys that remaining a virgin is cool has proven more difficult. One reason, according to Cathy Watson, the foundation's director, is the popularity of pirated Western porn videos, which some viewers think reflect the way rich and sophisticated people behave.

Straight Talk's newsletters, handed out free in schools, cover everything from nocturnal emissions to what to do if raped. Visiting AIDS workers from Zimbabwe and South Africa asked Watson how she won government permission to distribute such explicit material. They were astonished to hear that she had not felt the need to ask.

The climate of free debate has led young Ugandans to delay losing their virginity, to have fewer partners, and to use more condoms. Among fifteen-year-old girls, the proportion who said they had never had sex rose from 20 percent in 1989 to 50 percent in 1995. Between 1994 and 1997, the proportion of teenage girls who reported ever having used a condom tripled.

And the epidemic was rolled back. Between 1992 and 2002, HIV prevalence among women attending urban antenatal clinics fell from almost 30 percent to about 5 percent.[13]

If Uganda shows how a poor country can roll back an epidemic that is already raging, Senegal shows how to stop it taking off in the first place. West of the Sahara, this mainly Muslim country is fortunate to be several thousand miles from HIV's origin in central Africa. In the mid-1980s, when other parts of the continent were already blighted, Senegal was still relatively HIV-free. In concert with NGOs and the media, the government set up a national AIDS-control program to keep it that way.

In Senegal's brothels, which had been regulated since the 1970s, condom use was firmly encouraged. The country's blood supply was screened early and effectively. Vigorous education resulted in 95 percent of Senegalese adults knowing how to avoid the virus. Condom sales jumped from 800,000 in 1988 to 7 million in 1997. Senegalese levels of infection have remained stable and low for a decade – at under 2 percent.

How to dither and die

Other governments have been less alert. South Africa, for example, has resources and skills that Uganda and Senegal can only marvel at. But AIDS-prevention efforts in South Africa have been, to put it kindly, confused.

The government had plenty of warning. AIDS came late to South Africa. In 1990, it was a relatively small problem. Fewer than 1 percent of South African women in antenatal clinics tested positive for HIV that year. The African National Congress had ample opportunity to observe the epidemic devastating South Africa's northern neighbors. But perhaps because negotiating an end to apartheid was such an all-consuming task, they did not pay it much attention.

During its first five years in government, 1994–9, the party did practically nothing. Nelson Mandela, South Africa's first black president, rarely mentioned the disease. When I arrived in South Africa in 1998, I was amazed to see no anti-AIDS posters at all. In my first year in the country the only two I noticed were both in a small office used by the United Nations anti-AIDS program in Pretoria. The only senior member of Mandela's government who tried to do much about AIDS was the health minister, Nkosazana Dlamini-Zuma. Her contribution was to sponsor a costly flop of an anti-AIDS musical, to promote a toxic "cure" based on an industrial solvent, and to purge South Africa's drug-control agency when its members objected.

By 2002, HIV prevalence had risen fifteenfold, making South Africa the country with the most infected people anywhere in the world. Roughly 4.5 million South Africans carried the virus.[14] By way of comparison, this is more than 200 times the number of people who died in political violence during the turbulent decade before liberation.

Many people hoped that Thabo Mbeki, who succeeded Nelson Mandela as president in 1999, would take the catastrophe more seriously. He did, but not in the way anyone expected. After long nights researching the subject on the Internet, he began to question whether HIV really caused AIDS. He appointed a panel of experts to look into the matter, including some American AIDS "dissidents" (who denied that HIV caused AIDS) and excluding anyone from African countries that had actually succeeded in tackling the epidemic. His health minister, Manto Tshabalala-Msimang, circulated chapters from a book claiming that HIV was concocted by a secret organization called the Illuminati as part of a conspiracy to wipe out homosexuals, blacks, and Hispanics. All this nonsense baffled ordinary South Africans. Some thought that their president was telling them that AIDS didn't exist and concluded that it was therefore OK not to wear condoms.

Despite all the strange goings-on in the presidential mansion, many young South Africans seem to have realized that unprotected sex is risky. The media have treated the issue far more responsibly than the government has. NGOs have paid for a lot of gaudy posters on city billboards and pamphlets suggesting how to have fun without penetration. The main targets of these warnings are teenagers. Those who are not yet having sex are rarely infected. If campaigners can catch them while they are still virgins and persuade them either to stay that way or to use condoms, a generation could be saved. It might yet be. A survey of young women in 1998 found that only 16 percent said they had used a condom the last time they had sex with someone they weren't married to. By 2000, another survey found that a more encouraging 55 percent of young South Africans said they always used condoms. One hopes most were telling the truth.

Thabo Mbeki attracted so much criticism for his attitude to AIDS that he eventually said he would "withdraw" from the debate. His government's policies then started to improve. In November 2003, the South African government unveiled a serious, well-funded, and long-term plan for treating its sick citizens with the anti-retroviral drugs that have worked so well in rich countries – which would make no sense if HIV did not cause AIDS. Such drugs are not a solution; they suppress the disease, but they do not cure it. But if the plan is competently implemented, they should keep millions of South Africans alive long enough to raise their children to adulthood. Other African countries still find it hard to afford such drugs, but the prices are falling fast, and foreign donors are increasingly willing to pay for them.

A speck of hope

Looking at the carnage AIDS has wrought in Africa, it is easy to despair. Some Africans do. Chenjerai Hove, a Zimbabwean novelist, put it like this: "Since our women dress to kill, we are all going to die."[15] But if the sexual urge is basic, so is the will to live. If enough Africans wake up to the fact that unprotected sex is Russian roulette, Hove could yet be proved wrong.

5. THE SON OF A SNAKE IS A SNAKE

Why tribe and state should separate

Nestor Nebigira fell in love. But because he fell in love with the wrong woman, tribal politics ruined both their lives and left their children forever at risk of being murdered.

Nebigira is a Hutu married to a member of the Tutsi tribe. I met him in a refugee camp in Tanzania, where he was selling matches, combs, and other essentials to his fellow fugitives. It was hardly a lucrative business: refugees have little money, and there was, in any case, only enough room for one customer at a time to browse in Nebigira's tiny shop. When I spoke to him he had no customers at all; a storm was pounding the camp, and the other refugees were sheltering in their huts.

"I was a successful businessman once," he told me. Born in Burundi, he lived well until 1994, when, after months of ethnic massacres, he decided that there was nowhere in his homeland safe for a "mixed" family.

He was terrified that Tutsi soldiers might kill him, or that angry Hutus might kill his wife, or that zealots of either hue might kill the whole family for not being bigoted enough. So they packed as many possessions as they could carry and fled to Zaire, as Congo was then called. I gulped when he told me this. You have to be desperate to seek refuge in Congo. But that was not the end of the story. After two years, another war forced them to flee again. This time, they took a ferry across Lake

Tanganyika and ended up in the camp where I met Nebigira, standing on the mud floor of his comb shop.

Burundi has roughly the same ethnic make-up as its more notorious equatorial twin, Rwanda. The Hutus form a large majority of the population of both countries, while the Tutsis are a minority. Burundi was ruled by a succession of Tutsi despots from independence until 1993, when a brief experiment with democracy went wrong. The reigning Tutsi strongman, Pierre Buyoya, called a free-ish election and then stood aside for the Hutu victor, Melchior Ndadaye. President Ndadaye lasted for less than five months before he was kidnapped and murdered by Tutsi army officers. Hutu mobs retaliated by killing their Tutsi neighbors, which in turn prompted the Tutsi-dominated army to seize power. In the ensuing civil war, 300,000 people died and 1.2 million fled their homes. In other words, Nebigira's tale is not unusual.

He said he would love to return home but saw little hope that he ever could. "My children," he sighed, "will always be in danger. Hutus hate them because they have a Tutsi mother. Tutsis hate them because they have a Hutu father." There is a local saying: "The son of a snake is a snake."

The perils of tribalism

Other people's tribal quarrels never make much sense. Can you recall why the Tamils and the Sinhalese of Sri Lanka don't get along? Me neither. I once tried to explain to a Japanese friend what the troubles in Northern Ireland were about, and I remember thinking how fatuous it sounded. What's the difference between a Catholic and a Protestant? Well, 500 years ago, there was a split in the Christian church, with some people arguing that you could find salvation through faith alone, while others maintained that you had to submit to the authority of the Pope in Rome. . . . My friend nodded politely and said: "Ah . . . I see" from time to time, but I could see that she had no idea what I was talking about.

European history in the first half of the twentieth century is largely a story of tribal bloodletting, and recent years have seen carnage in the Balkans. Asia and the Americas have had also their troubles, from the Pacific War to the periodic pogroms of Chinese people in modern Indonesia. But these days it is in Africa that ethnic strife seems most acute. Memories of the Rwandan genocide of 1994 are still fresh, and Burundi's civil war shows few signs of ending. Ethnic or religious differences have been the pretext for violence in Sudan, Nigeria, South Africa, Zimbabwe, Namibia, Kenya, Liberia, Côte d'Ivoire, Uganda, Somalia, Ethiopia, Eritrea, both Congoes – the list goes on.

Africa's ethnic conflicts are often imagined to be the spontaneous expression of ancient hatreds. Tribal animosity certainly exists, but it rarely erupts into large-scale bloodshed unless deliberately inflamed by unscrupulous leaders. In pre-colonial times, tribes often fought over such things as pasture and water, but their battles were usually brief, local, and not especially bloody. Today, tribes fight for control of a much larger prize: the nation-state. And many more die in the struggle.

The historian Basil Davidson has written a whole book on "Africa and the curse of the nation-state." He argues that because post-colonial states were alien transplants, based usually on British or French models rather than old indigenous institutions, they "failed to achieve legitimacy in the eyes of a majority of African citizens, and soon proved unable to protect and promote the interests of those citizens, save for a privileged few." Against this illegitimate state, he says, "the majority have sought ways of defending themselves. The principal way they have found of doing this is through 'tribalism', perhaps more accurately, clientelism: a kind of Tammany Hall-style patronage, dependent on personal, family and similar networks of local interest. Insofar as it is a 'system', clientelism has become the way politics in Africa largely operates. Its rivalries naturally sow chaos."[1]

It is not tribal feelings themselves that cause trouble; it is their politicization. Most of Africa's ethnic strife has its roots in the manipulation of tribal loyalties by the colonial authorities. And most of today's conflicts owe their persistence to modern politics, not primordial passions.

In attempting to analyze the interplay between politics and tribalism in Africa, it helps to use a broader definition of tribalism than most dictionaries would allow, one that amalgamates tribalism, racism, and sectarianism. I know they are not the same, but I think the similarities matter more than the differences. The theme is bigotry: treating individuals badly, not because of something they have done, but because they belong to a particular group. People find all sorts of unjust reasons to hate, and unjust governments exploit them all.

To illustrate this argument, I am going to concentrate on the modern histories of Rwanda, Nigeria, and South Africa. Knowledgeable readers may object that these three countries are so different that it makes no sense to squash them all into the same chapter. It is a reasonable objection. They are indeed very different, and there is not enough space in a single chapter to do justice to the complexities of culture, tradition, and colonial experience that make them what they are today.

But I would like to argue that what these places have in common is both interesting and important. In all three countries politicians have at times sought to stir up, rather than soothe, ethnic passions. In all three, governments have made laws that explicitly discriminate against their own citizens on tribal or ethnic grounds. And in all three, the results have been either woeful or, in Rwanda's case, catastrophic.

Rwanda's holocaust

From 6 April 1994, a government dominated by Hutus tried to exterminate the Tutsis. The killings were carried out mainly with

111

simple tools: machetes and clubs studded with nails. To be chopped or bludgeoned to death takes time; some Tutsis paid to be shot instead. Sometimes the task of killing all the Tutsis on a particular hillside took several days. The executioners had to rest each evening, and so victims had their Achilles tendons cut to prevent them from running away. The killers drank gallons of beer to cool their throats and dull their consciences. At night, they feasted on the cows they stole from the dead.

The piles of bodies grew so large that city councils had to remove them in garbage trucks to avert the spread of disease. Many corpses were simply thrown in rivers: about 40,000 were fished out of Lake Victoria by the authorities downstream in Uganda. In all, about 800,000 people – a tenth of the population – were killed in six weeks. This was a rate of slaughter roughly five times that of the Nazi extermination camps.

Visitors to Kigali, the Rwandan capital, in late 1994 were struck by the fact that there were no dogs in the streets. Most African cities teem with dogs, so the lack of barking made Kigali seem eerie. Why were there no dogs in Kigali? The gruesome answer is that after the genocide, when there were piles of human bodies everywhere, Rwanda's dogs started gnawing on the corpses. Soldiers grew so sick of the sight that they shot them all.[2]

There is a common assumption that Rwanda's holocaust was simply an explosion of bigotry. The Hutus hated the Tutsis, so they tried to kill them all. The Hutus have always hated the Tutsis, and vice versa. That's just the way it is in central Africa. But this explanation simply won't do. Many Hutus do indeed hate Tutsis, but this is not an ancient, immutable fact of nature. It was only in the last forty years that large-scale ethnic killing began in Rwanda and Burundi. Hutus and Tutsis have only thrown themselves at each other's throats since their political leaders started urging them to. The genocide was carefully planned by a small clique of criminals to maintain their grip on power.[3] They were not forced to carry it out by passions beyond their control or by the irresistible tide of history. They had a choice. And they chose to try to create an ethnically pure Rwanda, ruled by themselves. They nearly succeeded, too.

The roots of the Hutu–Tutsi conflict can be traced back to colonial times. (The same is true of most aspects of modern Rwandan society, as few problems spring from nowhere, and the colonial period was when written records began.) When Europeans first arrived in Rwanda and Burundi in the nineteenth century, they found two large tribes and one small one. The Hutus were mostly peasant farmers, the less numerous Tutsis largely tended cows, and the Twa, a group of pygmies who were only 1 percent of the population, lived mainly as hunter-gatherers.

They all seem to have gotten along reasonably well. They lived on the same hills, spoke the same language, and intermarried freely. When a Tutsi woman married a Hutu man, their children were considered Hutu. Hutus could sometimes become Tutsis, too. There were tensions: Tutsi chiefs sometimes forbade Hutus from owning cows, and small wars were common. But these wars were not terribly bloody because there were traditional mechanisms for ending them. And Hutus, Tutsis, and Twa often fought side by side to repel invaders or steal cattle from neighbors.[4]

Rwanda and Burundi were German colonies for a couple of decades until the First World War, when Belgium seized them. In keeping with the nineteenth-century European obsession with race, the colonists saw great significance in the divide between Hutu and Tutsi. They surmised that the Tutsis were a Nilotic people, immigrants from the north, more intelligent than the native Hutus and a "natural" ruling caste. They toppled Hutu chiefs, replaced them with Tutsis, and turned a blind eye when these Tutsis stole large tracts of Hutu land. They favored Tutsis in admission to colonial schools and set Hutus forcibly to work digging ditches, planting trees, and building roads, often under the cruel eye of a Tutsi overseer. They even introduced ethnic identity cards. Where it was not possible to determine someone's tribe, the Belgians counted his cows. Those with ten or more were classified as Tutsi; those with fewer were condemned to be Hutu.[5]

The Europeans' tribal policies had two effects. First, the Hutus grew to resent their Tutsi overlords as never before. Second, both tribes came to believe the myth that they were utterly distinct. Tutsis, even the poor ones, took pride in their alleged racial superiority. Hutus began to see all Tutsis as "feudal exploiters," even the ones who lived in the same rags and ate the same scraps as they did.

After independence, politics split along ethnic lines. The main Hutu party in Rwanda easily won an election in 1960, organized by the Belgians as they prepared to leave. The first Hutu government tried to enforce ethnic quotas: since Tutsis were estimated to be 9 percent of the population, no more than 9 percent of school places were to be held by Tutsis, and no more than 9 percent of salaried jobs, whether in the civil service or in private companies. Businesses did their best to ignore the rules because they needed skilled workers and the Tutsis were, on average, better educated. But occasional purges kept the civil service strongly Hutu.

In 1973, a Hutu major general called Juvenal Habyarimana seized power and established a police state. He banned all opposition and set up his own party, the National Revolutionary Movement for Development (MRND), which all Rwandans were obliged to join, including babies. Party spies watched every hilltop village, moving house required official permission, and "loose women," such as the Tutsi girlfriends of European aid workers, were arrested.

Habyarimana's only claim to democratic legitimacy was that he was a Hutu. He often repeated the slogan *"rubanda nyamwinshi"* (literally, "the majority people"), implying that any government dominated by the ethnic majority was ipso facto democratic. Many Hutu peasants swallowed this ludicrous idea.

French author Gérard Prunier observed that just as poor Tutsis under the old order "felt proud of belonging to the 'ethnic aristocracy', although it brought them very little beyond [a] sense of superiority," so now the Hutus "fell prey to the same error and mostly persuaded themselves that because the government was Hutu, they, the humble peasants from the hills, somehow shared in that power."[6]

Habyarimana did his best to exclude Tutsis from public life. From the time of the coup until his assassination in 1994, he allowed only one Tutsi officer in the army and forbade Hutu soldiers from marrying Tutsis. Local governors, called *bourgmestres* and *prefets*, were all Hutu, with one exception, who was killed in the genocide. There were only two Tutsi members of parliament and only one Tutsi cabinet minister.[7]

The Tutsis did not like living under Habyarimana's dictatorship, and by 1990 about 600,000 or 700,000 of them had fled the country. In October that year, some of these Tutsi exiles, calling themselves the Rwandese Patriotic Front (RPF), invaded Rwanda but were beaten back. There followed four years of sporadic fighting, during which neither side prevailed. France provided Habyarimana with money and weapons because although odious he did at least speak French.[8]

To begin with, Habyarimana used the war as an excuse to lock up and torture his opponents, but French diplomats pressed him to stop embarrassing them, and he was eventually persuaded to unban opposition parties. The slighty less dictatorial atmosphere allowed many groups to flourish, but unfortunately some of the most influential were even more bigoted than Habyarimana. A new party called the Coalition for the Defence of the Republic lambasted the government for being too soft on the Tutsis and indeed on Hutus who favored ethnic tolerance. A bold and chillingly well-written paper called *Kangura* demonized Tutsis, and Radio Mille Collines mixed funky music with incitement to murder.

The editor of *Kangura* published ten "Hutu commandments."

Hutu men, said the paper, should never marry or befriend Tutsi women, for they were all Tutsi agents. Every Tutsi, the paper continued, was a cheat, so any Hutu doing business with Tutsis was a traitor. It was essential that "all strategic positions, political, administrative, economic, military and security," be controlled by Hutus. The eighth commandment was "Hutus must stop having mercy on the Tutsis." These commandments were widely copied and frequently read aloud by Hutu headmen at village meetings.

Throughout the early 1990s, there were signs that something was brewing. Army officers started diverting weapons to the Interahamwe, an anti-Tutsi militia. Hutu officials started firing up peasants for the task ahead, portraying the Tutsis of the RPF as demonic creatures with tails, hooves, horns, and red eyes that glowed in the dark. After RPF attacks, they organized small retaliatory massacres in which peasants were encouraged to take part. Hacking men to death was referred to as "bush clearing"; killing women and children was "pulling out the roots of the bad weeds." Tutsis were called "cockroaches," and those who helped exterminate them were sometimes rewarded with the victims' land or cows.

Meanwhile, pushed by the French, President Habyarimana was talking peace with the Tutsi rebels, the RPF. On 6 April 1994, he was assassinated. His private plane was hit by two missiles as it approached the runway at Kigali airport and crashed, killing all aboard.

"Hutu power" apologists blamed the RPF. The RPF blamed the Hutu power fanatics. Whatever the truth, within forty-five minutes of the crash, Interahamwe road blocks were thrown up all around Kigali. The killings began almost immediately.

That the genocide was premeditated is not in doubt. On 3 April, Radio Mille Collines broadcast that "On the third, fourth, and fifth, heads will get heated up. On the sixth of April, there will be a respite, but 'a little thing' might happen. Then on the seventh and eighth and the other days in April, you will see something."[9]

The first to die were those on pre-prepared lists of "enemies": politicians, journalists, lawyers, and businessmen who held liberal views. To begin with, the killing was carried out mainly by the presidential guard, a 1,500-strong elite corps based in Kigali, and the Interahamwe and other militiamen, who numbered perhaps 50,000. Jobless urban Hutus soon joined in. The most senior army leaders hesitated for a couple of days but then went along with the bloody flow.

From the capital, orders were swiftly sent to officials in the countryside. In almost every village peasants were called together to murder their Tutsi neighbors. Since Tutsis were only a small fraction of Rwanda's population and both tribes lived intermingled, most Tutsi peasants had Hutu neighbors on all sides. This made it nearly impossible to escape.

All the while, Radio Mille Collines called for more blood, shrieking that "the graves are not yet quite full" and asking, "Who is going to do the good work and help us fill them completely?"[10]

Anyone stopped at a road block who could not produce an ethnic identity card was assumed to be a Tutsi and killed. Those who had cards identifying them as Hutus but who looked too pale or long-nosed were often killed, too. Hutus who refused to take part in the slaughter were denounced as allies of the enemy and killed. Professionals, students, and anyone who looked educated or prosperous was at risk. In the words of one survivor, "the people whose children had to walk barefoot to school killed the people who could buy shoes for theirs."[11]

The outside world did almost nothing to help. The genocide only stopped when the Tutsi rebels of the RPF won the war and stopped it. They found it unusually easy to march across the country, largely because the Rwandan army was distracted by the business of killing civilians. In July, the RPF took Kigali. As they gained control of the countryside, which they did with considerable brutality, the *génocidaires* lost heart and fled into Zaire, along with nearly a million other Hutus who feared reprisals.

The rebels were victorious, but the land they had conquered was shattered. Tutsis who had survived the genocide emerged from church vaults and septic tanks to find their huts burned, their cows eaten, and their villages deserted. Hutus who had risked death by resisting the genocide were sometimes killed by the RPF; in the confusion no one knew for sure who was guilty and who was not.

Rwanda has regained a measure of stability under a Tutsi strongman, Paul Kagame. With help from foreign donors, Kagame's government has done a good job of rebuilding the country. Average incomes are now all but back to their pre-genocide level, but the psychological wounds of the genocide are, unsurprisingly, far from healed.

When I visited Rwanda in August 2003, I was struck by how frightened everyone was. The people were afraid of their government, and the government, despite its strenuous denials, was afraid of the people.

I was there to watch the first presidential election since the genocide. Kagame was already president but had decided, under pressure from donors, that he wanted to be a directly elected one.

On the night before the polls, I spoke to the main challenger, Faustin Twagiramungu, a moderate Hutu, in the little flat that served as his campaign headquarters. He was in despair. His party had been banned for promoting ethnic "divisionism" – an odd charge to level at a man who had lost thirty-two relatives during the genocide, but one Kagame seemed to aim at all serious rivals. Twagiramungu had barely been allowed to campaign: his pamphlets had been confiscated; his supporters threatened. As we spoke, some of his provincial campaign managers, all twelve of whom had been arrested the previous day, were paraded on the television news, denouncing their former leader. Twagiramungu showed me a letter which he said was from one of them. The message, he said, was: "I'm so sorry, but I have to stay alive."

I drove out into the countryside, where most Rwandans eke out a living growing beans and bananas, to find out what people thought of Kagame. No one wanted to talk. Asked what they thought about the way the country was being run, villagers told me they had no opinion. At one point, two policemen drew up in a car and demanded to know what was going on. My traveling companion, an American freelancer called Carter Dougherty, told them we were journalists reporting on the election. They suggested that we should redirect our enquiries to the Bureau of Elections.

Kagame's party, the RPF, has made sure that its people control all the institutions that matter in Rwanda: the army, the police, the bureaucracy, the judiciary, banks, universities, and state-owned companies. Few Rwandans believe that the party will surrender power in the foreseeable future. (Among other safeguards, the law allows for an election to be annulled if the winner campaigns on a "divisionist" platform.) Most Tutsis are grateful for this. Many see Kagame as their savior and their only protection against a repeat of the slaughter of 1994.

Kagame's regime has many fine qualities. It is more efficient than you would expect; its policemen almost never ask for bribes. But it is ruthless. During the war against the *génocidaires* in Rwanda, the RPF killed between 25,000 and 45,000 people. When the *génocidaires* regrouped in Congo, Kagame's men invaded, twice, and with their local allies killed perhaps 200,000 refugees.[12]

Back in Rwanda, life is now calm and orderly, but even some of Kagame's supporters wish there was a bit more freedom. A group of well-off, RPF-voting students in Kigali grumbled to me about the censorship that made it hard for them to know what was going on in their own country.

Those who dislike the regime, meanwhile, have no outlet for their grievances. One Hutu told me he had spent eight years in jail before being found innocent of abetting the genocide. Someone lost his case file, he said, perhaps because "those who came from abroad" – i.e., the Tutsi exiles who now rule Rwanda – wanted his plum government job. Since his release, he said he had been unable to find work, but he did not dare complain. "I've seen men beaten to death in prison," he told me. "I don't want to go back."

Kagame won the election, of course, with 95 percent of the vote. Twagiramungu managed 3.7 percent.

African disunity

Nowhere else in Africa compares with Rwanda. But politicians in most African countries play on tribal grievances to a greater or lesser extent, and the results, while never as disastrous as in Rwanda, are usually harmful. The Nigerian example is illuminating.

Africa's most populous country is home to some 250 ethnic groups and is also split along religious lines, with the north mainly Muslim and the south mainly Christian or animist. Tribal sniping is common. Nigerian comedians play endlessly on ethnic stereotypes: that Yorubas are noisy, Ibos are miserly, Hausas are dim, and so on. Nigeria's many newspapers are full of columnists who complain that their own tribe has contributed more to the country than any other but never gets its fair portion of pepper soup. Ordinary Nigerians spend hours mouthing similar complaints. The only time this great nation cheers with one voice is when its football team scores.

This matters, because ethnic solidarity is used to justify Nigeria's great vice: corruption. Since the discovery of oil in Nigeria, politics have been largely a scramble for petrodollars. Politicians want money for themselves, of course, and they also want to grab a fistful for their supporters, to make sure they keep getting re-elected.

Nigerians almost all say they disapprove of corruption, but they tend to forgive or even applaud the perpetrator if he is one of their own tribe. Most Nigerians feel far stronger loyalty to their tribe than to the state. Big Men are therefore expected to use their power to help their kith and kin. Eghosa Osaghae, a political historian, puts it like this: "It is a popular Nigerian saying, which took root under colonial rule, that 'government business is no man's business'. There was thus nothing seriously wrong with stealing state funds, especially if they were used to benefit not only the individual but also members of his community."[13]

For most of the time since independence, Nigeria has been ruled by northern Muslim military strongmen. They and their hangers-on grew fabulously wealthy, as a short wander around Kaduna, a northern town where several of the military elite hail from, reveals. I visited in 1999, not long after Nigeria reverted to civilian, democratic rule, and marveled at the palaces these fortunate officers had built for themselves. There were marble follies with mirrored gates and satellite dishes the size of ordinary people's houses, estates with private mosques, and one unbelievably tacky mansion shaped like a ship. The cars parked outside the Kaduna polo club were impressive, too.

The king of crooks was Sani Abacha, the northern Muslim dictator who ruled from 1993 until 1998. He used to send trucks round to the central bank with orders that they be filled with banknotes. When he died, reportedly of Viagra-fueled overexertion with three prostitutes, the records showed that he and his associates had stolen over $2 billion – more than a million dollars for every day he was in office, including weekends. According to his successor, Olusegun Obasanjo, he also awarded $1 billion in contracts to front companies and accepted another $1 billion in bribes from foreign contractors. That kind of money bought him a lot of support while he was alive, and his surviving relatives remain influential.

*

Inevitably, one can trace Nigeria's tribal troubles back to colonial times. The country's borders were drawn by the British, who, in 1914, lumped the whole melange of tribes and religions into a single unit. Nigerians sometimes refer to this as "the mistake of 1914." The British were not completely blind to the rifts within their new colony. They did seek to avert religious strife by discouraging Christian missionaries from preaching in the Muslim north, but while this seemed wise at the time, it stored up problems for the future.

Because the missionaries were effectively barred from northern Nigeria, they built all their schools in the south. By 1950, there were thousands of university graduates in the south but only one in the north.[14] Southerners dominated all the jobs in the civil service that required numeracy or literacy. Members of the south-eastern Ibo tribe, owing to a long tradition of trading, dominated commerce in the north as well as in their own region. The Hausas and Fulanis of the north felt left out. But they had the upper hand in the army because the British thought them good soldiers, which was to prove important later on.

As independence approached, northern leaders realized that the better-educated southerners would dominate Nigeria unless they did something drastic. So they began a program of "northernization" within their own region. Initially, it was presented as a policy of training native Nigerians to replace British expatriates in the civil service. But the northern leaders felt less threatened by British experts than by Yorubas and Ibos. In 1957, the Public Service Commission of the Northern Region stated: "It is the policy of the Regional Government to Northernize the Public Service: if a qualified Northerner is available, he is given priority in recruitment; if no qualified Northerner is available, an Expatriate may be recruited or a non-Northerner on contract terms" (i.e., not as a permanent employee).[15] The northern regional government tried to bar southerners from winning public works contracts, running shops, or owning land in the north. This bias swiftly spread to the federal government after independence, or at least to the parts controlled by northerners.

Southerners resented being discriminated against, which was one reason why a group of mainly Ibo officers tried to mount a coup in 1966. The coup leaders promised, among other things, to establish national norms that all applicants for civil service jobs would have to meet. To northerners, this sounded like a promise that all the best jobs would go to southerners. Horrified at the prospect, a group of mainly Hausa-Fulani officers led a counter-coup and seized control of the state.

A chain reaction of violence followed, culminating in an attempt by south-easterners to secede from Nigeria, taking most of its newly discovered oil with them. The northern-dominated army ferociously put down the rebellion. It took three years and cost a million lives. To many people's surprise, the northerners then treated their vanquished enemies with restraint and even repealed some of the more extreme regulations that discriminated against southerners.

But the government did not become tribe-blind. Instead of favoring only northerners, it decided that civil service jobs and university admissions should be decided by tribal quotas. This policy has remained ever since and has set every ethnic group in Nigeria bickering over whether they have received their rightful share.

When the price of oil jumped in the early 1970s, the Nigerian government suddenly had billions of dollars to dole out. Politicians discovered that the most effective way to win the support of their fellow tribespeople was to promise them more roads, schools, and handouts, to be paid for with petrodollars. And the most effective way to parlay tribal support into political office was to carve out a new state in which one's own tribe was a majority.

Nigeria started to fragment. From three regions at independence, it has splintered into thirty-six states today. This has caused endless complexity. For example, state governments hoping to privatize state-owned firms often find that the state which originally set up the firm has split into several smaller ones, none of whose leaders can agree on how to proceed. Worse, civil service jobs have come to be seen as gifts that Big Men bestow on their grateful ethnic cousins.

Between the early 1970s and Abacha's heart attack, Nigeria received some $280 billion in oil revenues. Through corruption, waste, and foolish investments, successive governments squandered the lot. In fact, since they borrowed billions against future oil revenues and squandered that money too, it is fair to say that Nigeria blew more than all of its windfall. By 1998, Nigerians were poorer than when the oil boom began in 1974, and the country was saddled with debts of some $30 billion.

The scale of Nigeria's failure is simply staggering. Contrast the place with Indonesia, another huge, populous, ethnically diverse, and oil-rich nation. Both countries have suffered military rule and, at times, massive bloodshed. Both were, at independence, nations of subsistence farmers. Both struck oil and were deluged with petrodollars. But here the parallels cease. Indonesia has not exactly been a model of good governance, but average incomes rose nonetheless, from under $200 in 1974 to $680 in 2001, despite the Asian financial crash of 1997. Today, Nigerians are more than twice as likely as Indonesians to be illiterate or to die before the age of forty.[16]

Tribalism is not the only reason why Nigeria is so dysfunctional, but it clearly doesn't help. In Lagos, I have seen piles of rubbish, some of them twenty feet high and three blocks long, festering in the middle of the road. Electricity comes, as novelist Wole Soyinka puts it, in "periodic vengeful surges . . . as if the god of lightning has . . . taken personal charge."[17] All this is at least partly because someone has looted the rubbish collection budget, and the state electricity firm has been stuffed with various managers' incompetent kinsfolk.

After Abacha died, Nigeria held reasonably fair elections. The winner was Olusegun Obasanjo, a Yoruba and a born-again

Christian, but also a former general and a friend of several northern Muslim leaders.

To his credit, Obasanjo has not abused his power to pamper his own ethnic group. He has tried to divide federal funds more equally between the states, while at the same time reducing the incentives for the states to continue splitting into even smaller ones. His bloated cabinet usually contains at least one representative from each of the thirty-six states. He has promised to increase the share of oil revenues that go to the states where the oil is actually drilled from a wretched 3 percent to 13 percent. But it is impossible to please everyone.

Since federal money is, at least in theory, allocated to the states in amounts proportional to their populations, Nigerian censuses are usually marred by fraud and mayhem, as each tribe seeks to inflate its numbers. As a result, no one really knows how many Nigerians there are. A census in 1991 put the number at 88.5 million. In 1998, the government's estimate was 108.5 million, and the United Nations' was 121.8 million. Most tribes claim to have been undercounted and underpaid. Obasanjo has discovered that using federal money to bribe the tribes to behave only whets their appetite for more.

Ethnic bloodletting has actually increased since democracy was restored, perhaps because the police no longer suppress it so brutally. Yoruba youths hurl "magic bombs" – eggshells filled with sulphuric acid – at members of other tribes in Lagos. And in the Niger delta, where most of Nigeria's oil is pumped, a feud has arisen between the Ijaws and the Itsekiris.

I went to investigate this feud in April 2003, at the height of an election campaign when the spoils of office were up for grabs and tempers were accordingly hot. The trouble centered on Warri, a busy, smoggy town surrounded by swampy forest. When I arrived, Warri was under curfew. Soldiers manned road blocks at every major intersection, stopping cars and searching them for arms.

The soldiers were in a bad mood and made a point of

humiliating motorists who spoke disrespectfully to them. At one road block, I saw them force a young man to hop down the street in a squatting position, with his hands behind his head: a petty punishment known as the "frog jump."

The town was tense because Ijaw youths had been burning Itsekiri villages. Eric Igban, a local Itsekiri activist, told me of a recent attack.

"They wore red bandannas," he said, "and they arrived in speedboats, with mounted machine-guns. They opened fire indiscriminately, at men, women, and children. Then they burned the village down. More than a hundred bodies were found, and there must be more lost in the bush."

Why was this happening?

Igban told me that the Ijaws and the Itsekiris used to live in peace. But when the new democratic regime promised the people of the delta a greater share of oil revenues, top jobs in local government suddenly became more lucrative and worth fighting for.

Ijaw leaders realized that they would win more governorships, and more seats in state parliaments and local councils, if electoral boundaries were re-drawn in such a way that there were more constituencies where Ijaws were in a majority. Before long, Ijaw youth militias were conducting a terror campaign to force the government to re-draw the electoral map in their favor.

"They think that with guns they can get anything they want," said Igban. "They want to control all the wealth of the Niger delta. And they want to wipe us out."

An Ijaw leader gave me a different perspective. He did not want to be named as he was a local government official and did not want to be quoted expressing support for the Ijaw militias. "The Ijawman is peaceful," he said, "but it is better to be dead than to live with injustice."

The injustice that upset him most was that Ijaws were 63 percent of the population of the Warri electoral district but were a majority in only four out of ten wards. Ijaw youths, he said, were determined to prevent any elections taking place until this anomaly was corrected. "The person in power controls the economy of the area," he said, "and we just want our fair share." He then told me that the best thing would be "separate local government areas for each ethnic group – homogenous districts with no minorities."

As I left Warri, I noticed, near the burnt-out husks of Itsekiri shops, a campaign poster urging voters to re-elect the governor, one James Ibori. Beneath a smiling picture were the words: "Ibori's healing hands have brought peace to Delta state."

The call of Islam

In northern Nigeria, meanwhile, relations between Christians and Muslims have been fraught. After the Christian Obasanjo became president, a dozen northern states asserted their independence by adopting *sharia* (Islamic law) for criminal cases. In other words, a third of the country's state legislatures decided to start whipping those who drank alcohol, cutting off thieves' hands, and stoning adulterers. Some of the governors who introduced these laws may have done so for reasons other than simple piety. Some were on bad terms with the new president and may have figured that if they posed as the champions of Islam, no Christian president could attack them without appearing to attack the faith.

Whatever the truth of this, *sharia* was initially very popular among Nigerian Muslims. Nigeria's courts are slow and corrupt, and many Muslims hoped that *sharia* courts would be swift and fair. But Christians who lived in the north were not so happy; many feared that the new religious laws would be used to persecute them. Since *sharia* was introduced, northern states have seen a wave of street battles between Christians and Muslims in which thousands have been killed.

President Obasanjo has used considerable tact to try to defuse the situation. He has quietly tried to persuade northern governors not to let *sharia* be used to persecute Christians, and he has resisted southern calls to seek a court ruling as to whether *sharia* is constitutional (which it probably is not), reasoning that any decision is likely to spark more riots. (His hand may be forced on this issue, however, as lawyers for one woman who was condemned to be stoned to death are seeking to have the sentence overturned on constitutional grounds.)

Some observers predict that Nigeria will break up. It is hardly reassuring that, at a presidential election in 2003, more than four decades after independence, the three main candidates were all retired generals. Two were former military heads of state (Obasanjo and Muhammadu Buhari), and one was the officer who led Biafra's catastrophic attempt at secession, Emeka Ojukwu. Lurking behind the scenes was yet another former military ruler, Ibrahim Babangida, reputedly the richest man in Nigeria, whose support was keenly courted by almost everyone. A general election, indeed.

Ken Saro-Wiwa, a leader of the Ogoni tribe who was hanged by the old military government in 1995, once warned that "you must not think that there is this thing called Nigeria and it's untouchable, no matter what happens. The Soviet Union was set up about the same time [as] Nigeria. It's gone. Yugoslavia is gone. Therefore, you have to be very careful."[18]

But most Nigerians trust that the country will somehow muddle through. A story I chanced upon in Kaduna augurs well. In the early 1990s, two religious terrorists, Muhammad Ashafa and James Wuye, tried to have each other killed. It was during a burst of religious rioting for which Ashafa blamed the Christian paramilitary group led by Wuye, and Wuye blamed Ashafa's Muslim youth organization. Christian assassins knocked on Ashafa's door and killed the man who answered it. Their victim, as it happened, was Muhammed Ashafa's uncle. But they did not realize this.

Meanwhile, Muslim assassins attacked James Wuye, hacked his arm off, and left him for dead.

Both men believed they had killed the other. When they later discovered that they had not, they took it as a sign from God that they should make peace. So they set up a joint charity to promote dialogue between Muslims and Christians. Ashafa told me this story over hot tea in his small but elegantly carpeted flat. A tall and slightly overbearing man, he greeted me with a big hug and a long sermon on the need for people of faith to live in harmony. Wuye and he are now, he said, the best of friends.[19]

From apartheid to affirmative action

Under apartheid, there was only one black employee at the Koeberg nuclear power station. It was one of South Africa's most secret sites, and since any black South African was considered a security risk, the management strained to avoid hiring any. But there was one job that could not be done by a white. Koeberg's lone black worker was paid to run away from the guard dogs, to train them to bite blacks.[20]

For centuries, white settlers in South Africa burned black people's houses and stole their land. From 1948 until 1994, the country was ruled by the National Party, an organization that sought to advance only the interests of South Africa's "European" tribe. White "superiority" was codified in law. At the height of apartheid, blacks were not allowed to vote, hold desirable jobs, or own land in "white areas" (about 87 percent of the country). When an area inhabited by blacks was designated white, the inhabitants were sometimes forced onto trucks at gunpoint, driven away as bulldozers crushed their homes, and dumped on distant patches of waste land.

With such a history, no one would have been surprised if South Africa had disintegrated into civil war. In the 1980s, when black protesters were daily showered with tear gas and sometimes shot dead by white policemen, a bloodbath seemed inevitable. Several thousand people were killed, but South Africa somehow held back from the precipice.

There were several reasons for this. The collapse of the Soviet Union forced the leaders of the African National Congress to reconsider their socialist beliefs. This reassured whites, who were nervous that if they surrendered power, their country would become another Marxist basket case. The ANC, meanwhile, realized that it was never going to win power by force. After years of "armed struggle," it had won no battles. But in the propaganda war, it had triumphed. The world ostracized the apartheid regime. Sanctions gnawed at South African business. South African sports teams were barred from international contests. White South Africans traveling abroad were met with hostility, and British satirists composed a catchy song with the refrain "I've never met a nice South African." With the world spitting on their shadows, white South Africans, even leaders of the National Party, began to lose the courage of their apartheid convictions.

Both sides were drawn to talk to each other. After the first secret, tentative contacts in the mid-1980s, serious negotiations began in 1990. Slowly and fitfully, a political settlement was thrashed out that more or less satisfied both sides.[21] Black-on-black political violence grew worse in the run-up to the first all-race election in 1994, as the two main parties, the ANC and the Zulu nationalist Inkatha Freedom Party, fought for local dominance. But the election itself passed relatively smoothly. The ANC won easily, with almost two-thirds of the vote. The National Party accepted defeat. A rumored armed revolt by white hardliners never materialized, and black-on-black political killings dropped dramatically.

In 1996, South Africa adopted a new constitution, one of the world's most liberal. Besides guaranteeing all sorts of freedoms, it forbids discrimination on the grounds of "race, gender, sex, pregnancy, marital status, ethnic or social origin, colour, sexual orientation, age, disability, religion, conscience, belief, culture, language and birth."

The surprisingly peaceful transition was the work of many South Africans, but one stands out. Having acquired titanic moral stature after twenty-seven years in jail, Nelson Mandela, the ANC leader, was able both to soothe white fears and to curb the violent inclinations of some of his followers. As the country's first black president, he preached reconciliation. He spoke of a "rainbow nation" in which people of all colors might live together in harmony. By including the Inkatha leader, Mangosuthu Buthelezi, in his cabinet, he helped bring peace to the province of KwaZulu-Natal, where the ANC and Inkatha had been fighting each other most fiercely with the tacit encouragement of the apartheid security forces.

In his gestures, Mandela showed generosity of spirit. He addressed Afrikaner audiences in Afrikaans. He took tea with Betsie Verwoerd, the frail widow of the architect of apartheid. He even donned the colors of the traditionally white national rugby team, the Springboks, during the world cup in 1995. When South Africa won the tournament, blacks and whites celebrated together. That day, the nation probably felt more united than ever before or since.

Mandela's message was one of forgiveness but not of forgetting. Under his presidency, a "Truth and Reconciliation Commission" recorded testimony from some 21,000 victims of apartheid-era crimes. The commission was criticized both for being too soft on the perpetrators – who were offered amnesty in return for confessions – and for an alleged pro-ANC bias. But whatever its faults it gave thousands of unhappy people their only chance of a day in court and made it impossible for white South Africans to pretend that apartheid was anything but vile.

Walk through a South African city today, and you still do not see anything like as many mixed-race couples as you would in, say, London. But you do see a few. Given that romance across the color line was recently illegal, this is encouraging. Ugly incidents of racial violence are reported in South African newspapers with depressing frequency, but these headlines tell of exceptions, not the norm. For the most part, South Africans of all races tolerate each other. No one now finds it odd that black pupils study alongside whites at formerly whites-only schools or that white waiters grovel to black diners at restaurants that until recently excluded them.

Few black South Africans now cite racism as the greatest problem facing the country; unemployment, crime, housing, and water supplies worry them far more.[22] But President Mandela's successor, Thabo Mbeki, thinks they are wrong. In speech after wordy speech, he insists that South Africa is "a country of two nations,"[23] that "wealth, income, opportunity, and skills continue to be distributed according to racial patterns," and that there can be no rest until the ruling party has achieved the "fundamental transformation of our society."[24] President Mbeki has increasingly sought to divert attention from his government's shortcomings by blaming whites for blocking this "transformation." The ANC remains a multiracial party, but the trend is nonetheless worrying.

Before the mid-1970s, blacks, no matter how enterprising or intelligent, were barred from the best jobs. Whites, no matter how lazy or stupid, were all but guaranteed an adequate wage working on the railroads or at some other state-owned firm. The most offensive apartheid rules were gradually dismantled in the 1980s and early 1990s, but it was not until 1994 that white legal privileges were wholly abolished. Apartheid was not, however, replaced by a simple ban on racial discrimination. Instead, the ANC passed laws mandating preferential treatment for members of "previously disadvantaged" groups, in hiring, promotion, university admissions, and the award of government contracts. These preferences apply not only to blacks but also to women and the disabled. The system is inspired by America's "affirmative action" programs, but there is a difference. Whereas in America the intended beneficiaries of affirmative action are a minority, in South Africa they are 95 percent of the population.

On the face of it, the case for corrective laws to make up for the injustices of the past is unanswerable. Because black education was neglected under apartheid, many blacks feel they cannot compete in the job market. Under the old regime, spending per white pupil was roughly seven times as much as was spent on blacks. Hendrik Verwoerd, prime minister from 1958 until his assassination in 1966, argued that there was no point in educating blacks well, for this might create "people trained for professions not open to them."[25]

ANC leaders believe, like the late Lyndon Johnson, American president in the 1960s, that you do not take a person who for years has been hobbled by chains and liberate him, bring him up to the starting line in a race, and then say "You are free to compete with all the others." Emotionally, this is persuasive. But the important question about corrective discrimination is not "Is it justified?" but "Does it work?"

A boost for the black middle class

For black professionals, the answer may be yes. Partly because the old anti-black laws were abolished, and partly because of the new pro-black laws, the black middle class expanded swiftly in the 1990s. Progress has been fastest in the civil service, where the proportion of managerial jobs filled by blacks has soared. In 1994, more than 95 percent of public-service managers were white; now more than 60 percent are black.[26] Whites are rarely sacked. But when they retire or resign because their chances of promotion are slim, they are usually replaced by blacks.

In private business, figures are harder to come by, but the proportion of managers who are black appears to have risen rapidly from hardly any in 1994 to about half in 2003. The reason the transformation has not been faster, according to business-men, is that the supply of appropriately skilled blacks has run dry. This is mainly the legacy of the apartheid government's deliberate neglect of black education. In 2001, of the 884,000 South Africans of working age who had university degrees, 55 percent were white and only 31 percent were black.[27] This imbalance is being reduced, but not in the most commercially useful disciplines. Although whites are only a tenth of the population, three times more whites than blacks gained degrees or diplomas in computer science in 1998. In engineering and business studies, the ratio was two to one. White high-school pupils were fifty times more likely to pass higher-grade science and math than black pupils.[28]

The education budget is quite generous, and some state schools achieve excellent results. But many are no better than they were under apartheid: awash with guns and drugs, lacking textbooks and discipline, and with teachers who show up to work drunk or not at all.

In 1999, I visited the Morris Isaacson high school, best known as the starting point of the Soweto uprising of 1976, when students protesting against apartheid education were cut down by the police. In those days, the school was a hotbed not only of radicalism but also of academic excellence. The headmaster, Elias Mashile, told me that its former pupils included many doctors and South Africa's only black nuclear physicist. The pupils I saw, however, did not seem single-mindedly studious. Many were wandering aimlessly around the courtyard, when they should have been in class. Mashile admitted that three-quarters of his students failed to graduate and that only one in fifty made it to university.

The school was not short of money: the buildings were sturdy and comfortable, and there were enough teachers. The problem was unruliness. Students in their twenties who had repeatedly failed their exams mixed with teenagers, sometimes impregnating them. School equipment was often stolen. The previous month an entire school in Port Elizabeth had been pinched, its prefabricated walls used to make houses in nearby squatter camps. During the struggle against apartheid, school-children used to chant "Liberation before education." Despite liberation, the rowdiness persists. "We are trying to revive the culture of learning," said Mashile, "but it takes time."

Nationwide, the number of students with good enough grades to qualify for university entrance actually fell after liberation, from 88,000 (18 percent of the total) in 1994 to 68,000 (15 percent) in 2001. Kader Asmal, an able ex-academic who was appointed education minister in 1999, has promised to sort out the mess. His efforts are starting to bear fruit, but the results will not be felt in the labor market for several years.

In the meantime, since blacks with commercially useful skills are scarce, they command high salaries. For instance, in 1999, Barloworld, a large industrial conglomerate, offered newly qualified black accountants about 20 percent more than their white colleagues plus an "entry-level BMW," pension, health benefits, in-house training, and excellent prospects for promotion. Despite this, Tony Phillips, Barloworld's chief executive, sighed to me: "After a few months, they are mercilessly head-hunted."

More laws, more justice?

If firms are paying a premium for black skills, this suggests that the supply of these skills is not matching demand. In other words, firms are searching hard for black talent but not finding enough to reach their racial targets. But the South African government believes that black advancement is being blocked by racist white bosses. Its response has been to pass ever-tougher new racial laws.

The Employment Equity Act, which came into force in 1999, obliges firms above a certain size to submit annual reports on their efforts to make their workforces "demographically representative" from the factory floor to the boardroom. That is, roughly 75 percent black, 52 percent female, 5 percent disabled, and so on. Some allowance is made for the size of the pool of "suitably qualified" individuals. But employers must not refuse to hire a black applicant simply because she lacks the necessary qualifications. Rather, they must show that she could not have acquired the relevant skills in a reasonable time. If someone alleges racism, it is up to the employer to prove his innocence. The normal burden of proof, in other words, has been reversed, and employers face fat fines if found guilty.

In 2000, the government passed an even broader law. The Promotion of Equality and Prevention of Unfair Discrimination Act affects all firms, no matter how small, as well as individuals, private clubs, professional bodies, and so on. It forbids discrimination on grounds of race, sex, pregnancy, age, disability, belief, culture, or language. Discrimination is only allowed if it is intended to uplift the previously disadvantaged. That is, you can discriminate in favor of blacks and women but not in favor of white men.

A case from 1997 gives some idea how hard it is to be racially correct. Sarita van Coller, a white woman, applied for a job at Eskom, the state-owned electricity provider. She scored top marks on an aptitude test, but the job was given to a "colored" (the South African term for mixed-race) applicant. She protested to a labor arbitrator and won. The arbitrator ruled that there was nothing wrong with giving preference to blacks or coloreds but that the firm should not discriminate unfairly against whites. It is, of course, impossible to do both.

Mampuru Maseke, a black employee at the same firm, has observed that affirmative action makes white engineers reluctant to pass their skills on to inexperienced black colleagues, because a well-taught black colleague will soon be promoted over their heads. He goes on: "When an affirmative action appointee does not perform well, Eskom usually hires the white former incumbent of that post to act as a consultant to help the appointee. He has generally retired with a nice package and when recalled as a consultant – now earning an extra salary on top – has no incentive to help the black appointee become fully competent, for then his role will end."[29]

White bosses are reluctant to complain about the new racial laws because of the utter certainty that they will be branded racist. On the record, they tend to sound like Chris Thompson, the head of Gold Fields, a big mining firm, who growled tersely to me that "it [affirmative action] is good for the country" and credited the government with showing a "spirit of pragmatism." Other bosses, talking on condition that their names should never appear in print, have told me that the laws are a burden, and would be a crushing one if they were vigorously enforced, but that they hope they will not be.

Perhaps they are right. The ANC does not want to strangle business: it just wants private firms to do some of its social engineering for it. But government inspectors are not the only ones who may enforce affirmative action, nor are disgruntled present, former, and would-be employees the only ones who can sue for racial discrimination. Any party acting "in the public interest" can initiate an action against an allegedly discriminatory employer, and lawyers can accept cases on a no-win, no-fee basis.

The assumption behind all these laws is that white employers will never treat blacks fairly uncoerced. This is questionable. Doubtless, many white bosses are bigots. But discrimination has costs. A rational employer hires staff on merit: he employs those who will do the best job for the best price. An employer who discriminates on the basis of an unproductive quality such as skin color will be at a disadvantage relative to competitors who hire on merit.

How many businessmen care more about race than they do about money? In 2001, the *Sunday Times*, a South African newspaper, sent a team of twenty reporters to forty-eight restaurants to find out how racist they were. Black journalists and white journalists entered each restaurant separately and waited for staff to treat them differently. To their editors' surprise, black reporters reported that they were treated well almost everywhere. The only ugly incident was when a black waiter told a black reporter that he probably wouldn't be able to afford the wines on the wine list. Instead of a hard-hitting exposé of discrimination, the paper had to make do with publishing a collection of ordinary restaurant reviews.[30]

The only surprising thing about this is that everyone was so surprised. Businesses that insult their customers tend to go bust. South Africa's former white rulers always assumed that capitalists would be slow to discriminate if it hurt profits, which is why they passed so many laws to force them. The Mines and Works Amendment Act of 1926, for instance, which barred blacks from most well-paid positions, was passed because white labor unions appealed to the government to stop firms hiring blacks. Entrepreneurs – even racist ones – objected to "job reservation" because it affected their bottom line. Racist laws forced them to overpay their white employees, to forgo the benefit of black skills, and to suffer volcanic labor relations.

Apartheid, and the sanctions that it provoked, made the South African economy stagnate. As Themba Sono, professor of business studies at the University of Pretoria, put it:

> [V]ery few South Africans realise just how badly the [apartheid] government impoverished the entire nation. The per capita income of black Americans, for instance, is higher than that of white South Africans, and the descendants of the Dutch and French who settled in South Africa are much poorer on average than those who stayed behind in Europe. A measure of the damage [apartheid] did can be obtained from a comparison with Japan, which had approximately the same per capita GDP fifty years ago. Today, South Africa's per capita GDP is only 20 per cent of Japan's.[31]

As apartheid rules became progressively harder to enforce, black incomes began to catch up with white ones. Between 1975 and 1990, average real black earnings in manufacturing rose by almost 50 percent. For whites, the figure was only 1 percent. On the one hand, the government and white labor unions were struggling to preserve the gap between black and white wages. On the other hand, black labor unions and market forces were working to narrow them. White unions insisted that white workers should be paid much more than blacks, irrespective of how much they produced. But employers objected. When a job could be done equally well by a black employee, it made no sense to pay extra to have it done by a white one.

Winners and losers

Whites will probably cope in the new South Africa. They may be politically powerless, but they have money and skills. Those who are unsatisfied can emigrate, as many have, to Europe or Australia. For those who stay behind, legally mandated discrimination will provide an incentive to acquire marketable skills.

Under apartheid, many young whites studied politics or public administration at university and aspired to careers in government. In the new South Africa, they are more likely to study accounting or computing and to go into business or set themselves up as consultants. Unskilled whites will suffer. But most whites will succeed in making themselves commercially indispensable. In the long run, this will probably make them richer. Civil servants' salaries are generally lower than those paid by software firms.

Something similar happened in India, when the reservation of a large proportion of government jobs for the formerly "untouchable" caste prompted other castes to quit the civil service, go into business, and end up wealthier than before. In several countries commercially astute minorities have prospered despite laws that discriminated against them. Jews in medieval Europe were barred from many trades and often confined to ghettos but still ended up banking for kings. Countries such as Indonesia and Malaysia still maintain laws that discriminate against ethnic Chinese citizens, but the Chinese are richer than the locals. The future for white South Africans may be similar: politically impotent, often unpopular, but rich.

Affirmative action is portrayed as a means of helping the poor. But the beneficiaries are mainly middle class, which is to say, those who have already largely overcome the legacy of past discrimination. It is the best-educated blacks who are accelerated into managerial jobs. The poor lose, in two ways. First, they receive worse public services than they otherwise would. Second, affirmative action retards economic growth and so makes it harder for the jobless to find work. This is hugely important: in 2001, South African unemployment stood at 31 percent or 43 percent, depending on whether you count those who have given up looking for non-existent jobs.[32]

As in other countries where corrective discrimination is allowed, it is implemented much more aggressively in the civil service than in private companies. This is because government has no competitors, so political objectives often outweigh practical ones. If a private firm offers shoddier or more expensive goods than its rivals, customers will flee. The civil service, by contrast, is only indirectly accountable. The public can vote once every five years for a change of government, but that is about it. So bureaucrats find it easier to recruit by race than do firms that have to make a profit to survive.

In the new South Africa, most poor people, who are mainly black, receive much better public services than they did under apartheid. Whereas the old regime spent little money in black areas, the ANC has tried hard to bring piped water, roads, and electricity to the poor.[33] But the government could have provided more of these good things if it had been color-blind.

All firms bidding for public works contracts are required to have black partners or managers. Firms deemed "blacker" than their rivals are allowed to charge up to about 10 percent more and still win the contract. This is wonderful for blacks who own construction companies. But since the government is paying more than it needs to, the poor receive fewer houses, water pumps, and village roads than they should. In effect, "affirmative procurement" is a transfer of wealth from the poor to the well-off.

It can also provide a convenient cover for corruption. ANC officials can award contracts to their friends and justify it by pointing out that these friends are black. Many seem wholly unembarrassed at such apparent conflicts of interest. Several retired ANC politicians have made fortunes by exploiting their contacts. Because most of the poor are black, the government treats blackness as a proxy for poverty and argues that anyone black is in need of a leg-up. But the beneficiaries of this largesse are often millionaires.

In the private sector, affirmative action is less enthusiastically pursued. But because firms have to be seen to comply with the law, it is still a hefty burden. Time and effort devoted to meeting racial quotas cannot be spent improving products. Hiring on grounds other than merit is unlikely to foster excellence. The rest of the world will not buy an inferior South African product simply to assist in "transformation." Nor will many South Africans.

Economic growth in South Africa has been further hindered by delays in privatization. The ANC is torn. On the one hand, selling the state-owned power, telephone, and transport companies would bring much-needed foreign investment and skills. If more competition were allowed in these markets, power and bandwidth prices would fall, benefiting everyone and making South Africa an easier place to do business. This is why, in 1997, the government sold a 30 percent stake in Telkom, the telephone firm, to an American-Malaysian consortium and has promised gradual deregulation.[34]

But at the same time the ANC knows that if big companies remain publicly owned, they can more easily be used for political ends. State-owned firms take their orders from politicians and so work harder to promote blacks and to roll out services to poor and rural areas. The government hesitates to abandon such important levers of control.

Similar reasoning causes the government to give away licenses to use limited public resources. The supply of fish in South African waters, for example, is finite, so fishing boats are not allowed to catch more than their quota. These quotas could be auctioned, which would be easy to administer and raise large sums of money. But the government fears that black firms, which tend to have shallow pockets, would be outbid. So it apportions quotas to the firms it considers the most deserving. The process is slow, raises no money, and is open to corruption. It is applied to mobile telephone licenses, too. In 2001, after a long delay, the government gave away the country's third such license to a partly black-owned firm of questionable competence. The license could probably have been auctioned to a world-class firm for about $200 million: enough to build 100,000 houses for the poor.

South Africa's ethnic problems are nowhere near as grave as Rwanda's, and affirmative action has not crippled or corrupted its civil service to anything like the same degree as it has Nigeria's. The example of Malaysia shows that it is possible to combine laws that discriminate in favor of a racial majority (albeit less extreme laws than South Africa's) with rapid economic growth. But South Africa's neighbor, Zimbabwe, shows that such laws can become little more than a cloak for the award of contracts and licenses to cronies of the ruling party. And there is little evidence from anywhere that corrective discrimination improves the lives of more than a small minority. This improvement, moreover, usually comes at a heavy cost in lost growth and increased racial tension. It goes without saying that those who are discriminated against resent it.

I once asked President Mbeki how long he expected affirmative action laws to remain on the books. He predicted that they would eventually "fall into disuse" when they were no longer needed. Asked to name another country where this had occurred, he could not. This is not surprising. Affirmative action has been pushed back a pace or two in the United States but only after determined legal action by its opponents. In other countries with similar laws, such as India and Sri Lanka, these laws have tended to multiply and expand in scope.

Judge a man by the content of his character

Tribal passions are not, in themselves, a bad thing. Most people love not only their country but the town they grew up in and the people and the food and the songs they grew up with. Tribal loyalty is not so very different from family loyalty, from the admirable urges that impel so many Africans to feed and shelter orphaned nieces and cousins.

Governments, however, are supposed to represent the entire population of the country they rule. To favor one tribe over another instantly violates that ideal. Since governments are so powerful, groups seek their favors avidly and grow angry if rebuffed. Few people care that the owner of the Chinese restaurant on the corner employs only his cousins. (And nor should they: family businesses are often wonderfully efficient.) But members of virtually every African tribe seethe that their neighbors have grabbed a bigger plateful of the public pie. Tribal politics lead to ethnic tension, inefficient government, and slower wealth creation, as in South Africa, or worse, as in Rwanda.

The only sensible solution is a separation of tribe and state, much as faith and state are formally separated in America. Governments should not discriminate on grounds of ethnicity, period. Civil servants should be recruited on merit alone. State contracts should be awarded to the bidders who offer the best value for money. Aid to the poor should go to the poor, not to rich members of ethnic groups that are, on average, poor. As for private companies, it is none of the state's business whom they hire. Workers and employers enter into contracts if both parties think they will benefit. Such voluntary agreements tend to increase the sum of human happiness, and governments should not forbid them.

This may seem hopelessly idealistic. Many of the world's most powerful interest groups passionately oppose the idea of equality before the law. But all the alternatives are worse.

In Africa, the country that has come closest to separating tribe and state is Tanzania, which is home to 120 ethnic groups, each with distinct and sometimes mutually incomprehensible cultures. Yet in the decades since independence the country has suffered almost no communal bloodshed. This achievement is marred somewhat by occasional spats in Zanzibar, a semi-autonomous island off the Tanzanian coast. But only somewhat. The reason so many people like Nestor Nebigira, the Burundian refugee I mentioned at the beginning of this chapter, find sanctuary in Tanzania is that the place is more peaceful than any of its neighbors.

The first president, Julius Nyerere, despite his woeful economic policies, showed unusual wisdom in tribal matters. He recognized that ethnic politics could tear the country apart. While other African leaders stirred tribal rivalries to keep themselves in power, Nyerere sought to soothe them instead. He imposed a single official language, kiSwahili, and urged every Tanzanian to learn it so that they could talk to each other. He banned ethnically divisive talk from politics.

It was a great success, with one caveat. Nyerere had the power to ban tribalism at least partly because his regime was thoroughly undemocratic. With only one party allowed, there was no incentive for politicians to try to win votes by appealing to voters' tribal prejudices. Some argue that multiparty politics in Africa inevitably leads to ethnic politics. Yoweri Museveni, president of Uganda since 1986, has effectively banned political parties for precisely this reason, although he started to talk about lifting that ban in 2003.

Many African politicians find it hard to imagine a political contest based on class interests or ideas rather than tribal horse-trading. This is not always their fault. Often they behave this way because that is what their supporters demand.

Writing about Zambia, Patrick Chabal and Jean-Pascal Daloz, two European academics, argue that patron–client links, usually ethnically based, are the "fundamental" determinant of how people vote. "The populace expects to exchange political support for concrete help: that is the only way in which politics makes sense to them. . . . The understanding of the concept of citizenship and of the purpose of the individual vote remains indelibly linked to the anticipation of the direct communal (or even personal) benefit which elections offer. . . . This is also the view at the top. A Zambian minister was quoted as saying: 'If I don't appoint people from my own region, who else will?'"[35]

Such expectations can create a vicious circle. When voters assume that politics is a struggle between ethnic groups for the spoils of government, they tend to vote along ethnic lines and especially for candidates perceived to be good at grabbing and distributing those spoils. The more such candidates win power, the more tribal politics becomes, and the greater the incentive voters have to keep voting tribally. Breaking free of this cycle will be extremely hard.

That said, as African democracies mature it may grow easier for tribal disputes to be solved, if not amicably, at least according to laws that everyone respects. A recent worldwide study found that ethnic diversity reduced annual economic growth by a shocking 3 percent in undemocratic states but made no difference in democracies. One reason may be that people have fewer grievances in liberal democratic states than in tyrannous ones. If they do not feel oppressed, they are unlikely to blame the tribe next door for their oppression.[36] Power should also be decentralized rather than concentrated in the hands of an over-weening presidency, as is the case in most African countries today. If regions are self-governing and self-financing, they will have only themselves to blame if things do not go well.

There are no multi-ethnic African states where multiparty politics are wholly unsullied by tribalism. But there are reasons for hoping that ethnic hatred need not hold the continent back forever. Tanzania became a multiparty democracy in 1995, and inter-tribal relations remain largely cordial. So it can be done.

At his trial in 1964, Nelson Mandela gave a rousing speech from the dock. He declared: "During my lifetime, I have dedicated myself to [the] struggle of the African people. I have fought against white domination, and I have fought against black domination. I have cherished the ideal of a democratic and free society in which all persons live together in harmony and with equal opportunities. It is an ideal which I hope to live for and to achieve. But if needs be, it is an ideal for which I am prepared to die."[37]

Wise words, little heeded.

6. FAIR AID, FREE TRADE

Why aid fails, and how it could work

Somalia has no government, unless you count a "transitional" one that controls a few streets in the capital, Mogadishu, and a short stretch of coastline. The rest of the country is divided into warring fiefdoms. Warlords extract protection money from anyone who has money to extract. Clans, sub-clans, and sub-sub-clans pursue bloody vendettas against each other, often fighting over grudges that pre-date the colonial period. Few children learn to read, but practically all self-respecting young men carry submachine-guns.

I was at one of the country's countless road blocks, on a sandy road outside Baidoa, a southern town of shell-blasted stone walls and sandy streets. The local warlord's men were waving their Kalashnikovs at approaching trucks, forcing them to stop. Many of the trucks carried passengers perched atop the cargoes of logs or oil drums. The men with guns then ordered all the children under five to dismount and herded them into the shade of a nearby tree. There, they handed them over to strangers with clipboards, who squeezed open their mouths and fed each one a single drop of polio vaccine.

This was foreign aid at its most heroic. The World Health Organization (WHO) is trying to eradicate polio. It's a foul disease that paralyzes small children and sometimes kills them by causing their lungs to seize up, but it's vaccine-preventable. As recently as 1988, it afflicted an estimated 350,000 people, but since then, under the WHO's auspices, over 2 billion children have been vaccinated. In 2001, there were only 537 reported cases of polio, and the true total was thought to be no more than twice that.

Polio could be completely eliminated, like smallpox was in 1979. The wild polio virus cannot survive long outside its human host, so if enough people are vaccinated, it has nowhere left to hide. But it is holding out in places like Somalia: poor, often violent countries, where local health services are too dysfunctional to organize proper vaccination campaigns. This is where foreign aid workers come in.

Somalia has no public health service, so the WHO has to work with the only local authority that exists, which is to say, the warlords. It is a difficult and nerve-racking task, but somehow they manage it.

In each fiefdom, they make contact with the local thugocrat and ask, in language oozing feigned respect, his permission to carry out hut-to-hut vaccinations. They are careful to hire members of all the big local clans to help and to rent the cars they need – but no more – from whomever the local warlord nominates. The cars come with drivers and gun-toting guards but cannot be used to transport vaccines over long distances. If driven into a rival clan's territory, they are liable to be hijacked.

In Somalia, the men with guns make the rules, and aid workers have to adapt to this, just as locals do. Somali women make money by building stick-and-plastic shacks at road blocks and selling tea to all the travelers forced to stop and wait there. The WHO learned from their example and placed a vaccinator with a cooler at every possible road block to catch peripatetic children. As described above, the men with guns sometimes help, in their own bossy way.

The obstacles are numerous but not insuperable. Some Somali parents refuse to let their children be vaccinated. In an oral culture rumors proliferate, including the rather unhelpful ideas that vaccines are un-Islamic or that they give you AIDS. But the WHO persuades the reluctant by getting people from their own clans to talk to them and by driving trucks around broadcasting pro-vaccine messages over loudspeakers.

To reach more dangerous areas, the vaccinators wait for a pause in the fighting and then pounce. There is a polio officer in every district. Because anyone with a foreign employer is assumed to be rich, they are obvious targets for kidnappers so some sleep in a different house each night. Whenever it looks safe enough to fly in the coolers, they holler. When I visited, in April 2002, their task was nearly done. There had been no new polio infections reported since the beginning of the year, and they were hoping soon to declare Somalia polio-free.

It was a staggering achievement, of which the WHO can be proud, as can UNICEF and Rotary International, who also helped. Vaccination campaigns are universally and rightly applauded. But there is more to aid than jabbing babies, and many of the other ways in which rich countries have tried to improve the lives of the poor have been much less successful.

A deep hole

Running through the rocks beneath northern Zambia is one of the world's richest seams of copper, and there's plenty of cobalt down there, too. Large deposits were first discovered near Nchanga in the 1920s[1] and there could be another fifty years' supply still to dig up.[2] An opencast mine has been established there since 1955, a vast pit almost five kilometers long and 500 meters deep that makes the mechanical diggers scrabbling at the bottom look no bigger than the plastic sort that fall out of cereal boxes.[3]

Drop a coin into the pit at Nchanga, and it is gone forever. Drop in a million dollars, and you'll lose most of that, too. Some notes will be buried in the earth as it is churned beneath the shovels or blown off into the bush to be eaten by browsing antelopes. Some will disappear into the foreman's pockets.

Several lucky workers will grab an armful and perhaps then stop working. The people in the surrounding villages will maybe find a few dollars in their backyards, but not enough to make a real difference to their lives.

This is pretty much the story of foreign aid to Zambia. Perhaps because the country is, unlike Somalia, marvelously peaceful, or perhaps because Zambians are such nice people, donors have lavished more aid on Zambia, per head, than almost any other country in the world. The aid was supposed to make Zambians less poor. It failed. Between independence in 1964 and 2000, average incomes in Zambia actually fell, from $540 to $300.[4] The main difference between aid to Zambia and throwing a million dollars down a mine is the amount. By one estimate, between 1980 and 1996, counting only grants, not loans, 5,944 million-dollar bundles were thrown into Zambia.[5]

Six Marshall Plans

African leaders sometimes talk of the need for a "Marshall Plan" for Africa, a reference to the generous American aid program that helped Western Europe to recover after the Second World War. In fact, Africa has already received aid equivalent to six Marshall Plans.[6] But whereas the original Marshall Plan was a triumph, aid to Africa has failed to alleviate the continent's poverty.

This is also true of aid to poor countries in general. Few studies have found any robust link between aid and faster growth.[7] Countries that receive lots of aid do no better, on average, than those that receive practically none.

Why is this? One reason is that faster growth is not always donors' first priority. A hefty whack of Saudi Arabian aid, for example, is aimed at alleviating spiritual rather than material poverty by handing out free Korans. Much aid from some countries is a sly way of slipping money to domestic interest groups. Japanese donations, for example, have often been made on condition that the recipient buys chemicals or machine tools from Japanese firms.[8]

During the Cold War, the superpowers dished out much of their aid for strategic reasons. In the 1980s, for example, American aid kept the murderous (but anti-communist) Liberian President Samuel Doe in power, for which other Liberians are not particularly grateful. Soviet aid was less generous, but the possibility of pocketing a few million roubles led several African governments to nationalize industries, collectivize farms, and generally pursue policies that kept their citizens poor and hungry. (Greed was not the main reason for adopting statist policies – many African leaders believed in them – but aid doubtless encouraged a few waverers.)

Today, strategic considerations continue to guide much aid. Iraq swallows a huge chunk of American aid because America, having conquered the place, feels morally obliged to rebuild it and has a powerful interest in seeing it become a functioning democracy. Israel has long floated on American largesse, partly because it is the only (more or less) stable democracy in the Middle East and partly because a large domestic lobby demands that it be supported. Russia and Ukraine receive large sums for fear that they would otherwise sell their surplus nuclear warheads to terrorists. France hands out millions of euros to countries where French is spoken.

Even where aid has been intended to spur development, it often hasn't. Until recently, big donors liked to finance big, showy projects such as dams and sometimes failed to notice the multitudes whose homes were flooded. When individual Westerners empty their drawers and cupboards to find things to donate to Africa, the results are often laughably inappropriate: starving Somalis have received heartburn pills; barefoot Mozambicans have been sent high-heeled shoes.[9]

Shoddy research can render aid worthless. In Mali, donors once built a fish farm in canals that, had they asked the locals, they would have learned were dry for half the year. In Kenya, the government of Mwai Kibaki, which won office in December 2002, argues that although the country receives plenty of aid, it is hard to find time to govern when ministers have to receive half a dozen delegations of donors each day to explain what they plan to do with it.

Turmoil in recipient countries can prevent aid from bearing fruit. I once stood on a dock in Kinshasa and watched medical aid workers close to tears as they described how a power failure, caused by a rebel attack on a hydroelectric dam, had shut down their refrigerators, destroying the vaccines they contained.

Less spectacularly but more commonly, corruption, incompetence, and bad economic policies can often be relied on to squander any amount of donor cash. The Zambian example speaks for many.

A "Z" grade for Zambia

At independence in 1964, Zambia seemed poised for success. The second-wealthiest nation in Africa, after South Africa, it had a popularly elected government committed to helping the poor, some of the world's best copper mines, and a generous stream of aid. Most donors at the time believed that the main obstacle to development was lack of money and that giving poor governments cash to invest would spur rapid growth.

It was not so simple. Zambia's first president, Kenneth Kaunda, set up a one-party socialist state and nationalized everything from the copper mines to hair salons and dry cleaning shops. In order to promote "self-sufficiency," he erected tariff walls and currency controls, thereby shutting the Zambian economy off from the rest of the world. His officials told farmers what to grow, bought their crops, and then sold them at heavily subsidized prices. Generous loans were granted to farmers, and little attempt was made to make them repay.

Zambians came to see government loans as a perk of freedom from colonial rule.

In state hands, Zambian industry withered. Kaunda assumed that the copper mines would be an inexhaustible source of revenue. Thousands of unnecessary hands were hired. Contracts to supply the mines with anything from pencils to pickaxes were awarded to ruling party cronies, who gleefully padded their invoices. When mining tools broke down, they were only occasionally mended. Copper production peaked in 1969, just before nationalization, at 825,000 tons a year. By 1999, it had plunged to less than a third of this level.[10]

From 1974, the copper price fell, and suddenly the government could not pay its bills. But any shortfall was picked up by foreign donors. As Kaunda's economic policies grew more foolish, aid climbed steadily, reaching 11 percent of GDP by the early 1990s. IMF loans in the 1980s were tied to free-market reforms, but these were enacted without enthusiasm and frequently reversed. Aid kept the treasury full even as Kaunda destroyed most of the productive businesses in the country. A gentle and amiable man, and not a bad guitar-player besides, Kaunda is still widely respected in Zambia. But when he left office in 1991, after twenty-seven years in power, he left his countryfolk poorer. Zambians remember his rule as a time when the shops were so bare that even the well-off had trouble buying soap.

In the end, Kaunda's disastrous handling of the economy led to his downfall. In 1990, donor pressure forced him to allow opposition parties. The next year, donors pushed him into calling an election. To his surprise, he lost. Frederick Chiluba, a former union leader, won on a platform of allowing greater democracy and liberalizing the economy.

Donor funds rose anew. Buoyed with foreign cash and goodwill, Chiluba enjoyed some early successes. He brought inflation down from over 100 percent to only 20 percent in 1999. He cut tariffs, repealed exchange controls, and welcomed foreign investors. This filled the shops with fancy foreign goods: wine and lawn furniture from South Africa, Japanese televisions, and dozens of flavors of ice cream. But only the wealthy could afford these things, and most Zambians continued to grow poorer under Chiluba, despite receiving roughly $900 a head in aid and debt relief during the 1990s.[11]

The torrent of foreign aid allowed Chiluba to delay or avoid essential reforms. For instance, before coming to power, he promised voters that he would trim the bloated and inert civil service he inherited from Kaunda. Instead, he recruited yet more bureaucrats in the hope that they would be grateful and vote for him. Without aid the wage bill would have bankrupted the government, but with donor support Chiluba was able to pay thousands of the brightest Zambians to shun the kind of productive enterprise that might have made the country less poor.

Worse, Chiluba failed for almost a decade to privatize the copper mines. Even after years of decay, the mines were still Zambia's only significant exporter. Apart from foreign aid, they were the only way the country could get hold of hard currency, which they needed to buy things that could not be produced in Zambia. These included oil and practically everything more technologically advanced than a bowl of stew.

Under state control, copper output fell by the year, and the mines recorded huge losses. Without aid, the government would have had no choice but to sell them immediately. But donor support allowed Chiluba to dawdle. The idea of privatization was not popular with ordinary Zambians – many saw it as surrendering the country's most prized asset to foreigners. But probably a more important reason for the delay was that in state hands the mines were a tremendous source of patronage. If anything, they were looted more systematically in the 1990s than they had been under Kaunda.

Under pressure from donors the government put the mines on the auction block in 1997 but then rejected all offers. Exasperated donors starting cutting aid, which forced the government to try again in 1999. By this time, most foreign mining groups had lost interest. But in 2000 Anglo American, the firm from which the mines had originally been expropriated, bought most of them for $90 million. By one calculation, the delay cost Zambia $1.7 billion – about half a year's GDP.[12] No French or American president could have cost his country as much, in relative terms, without using nuclear weapons. To cap it all, two years later Anglo pulled out of Zambia, saying that the mines were in an even worse state than they had realized and could not be salvaged.

Meanwhile, Chiluba filled his government with an astonishing array of crooks, arms-traffickers, and drug-dealers.[13] One of his former cabinet ministers, who resigned in disgust in the mid-1990s, handed me a parliamentary report into the misappropriation of state assets which would have been enough to bring down any normal government but which Chiluba's regime simply suppressed. Another told me how even the money intended to buy corn for starving Zambians was stolen by Chiluba's cronies. According to William Easterly of the World Bank, if aid had had the predicted accelerating effect on growth between 1961 and 1994, Zambians' average income would have exceeded $20,000.[14] Today, it flounders at less than a sixth of that.

An "A" grade for Botswana

Aid failed in Zambia. But in neighboring Botswana it helped fuel a protracted economic boom. It is a remarkable story.

Botswana was, at independence in 1966, one of the poorest countries in the world. Cows grazed the few patches of ground that were not desert. Herdsmen herded them. That was pretty much the sum total of economic activity in Botswana.

To begin with, aid funded virtually all government investment and much of its recurrent expenditure, too. In 1971 aid was equivalent to 98 percent of state revenue.[15] But shortly after independence prospectors found diamonds under the Botswanan desert.

Unlike successive Zambian governments, Botswana's did not squander the windfall. Diamond dollars were ploughed into infrastructure, education, and health. Private business was allowed to grow unmolested, and foreign investment was welcomed. A group of South Africans came and set up safari lodges in the Okavango delta, where a river runs into the desert and stops, forming a 15,000-square-kilometer oasis for all the wildlife in the country. Tourists flocked to gawk at the elephants and wild dogs and to be punted around water-bird sanctuaries in hollowed-out logs.

Donors' suggestions were carefully evaluated; projects were only approved if the proposers could demonstrate that they were sustainable and did not duplicate work being carried out by others. Aid programs were transparent, too. Donors could come at any time and observe how their money was being spent.

In the last thirty-five years, Botswana's economy has grown faster than any other in the world. Yet cabinet ministers have not awarded themselves mansions and helicopters, and even the president has been seen doing his own shopping. Exchange controls were abolished in 1999, the budget has usually been in surplus (although this has slipped recently), and GDP per head tops $3,000. The country remains vulnerable to swings in the price of diamonds and has not diversified enough into other industries. But all in all its record is impressive. Their task completed, donors are packing their bags.[16] The country still has a horrific AIDS problem, but the government is now rich enough to offer drug therapy to people who need it.

Why the difference?

Aid helped lift Botswana out of poverty but was wasted in Zambia. Why the difference? Both countries had minerals. The two countries' cultures are quite similar. Educational levels were different at independence, but it was Botswana that had the less literate population. What really mattered, however, was that Botswana had good economic policies, soundly administered, whereas Zambia did not.

All around the developing world aid works or fails according to whether the recipient country competently implements sensible economic policies. We're talking about the basics here: spending approximately within your means, not cutting yourself off from the rest of the world, and not allowing civil servants to steal too much. A recent study by two economists at the World Bank sorted fifty-six aid-receiving countries by the quality of their economic management.[17] Those with good policies (low inflation, a budget surplus, and openness to trade) and good institutions (little corruption, strong rule of law, effective bureaucracy) benefited from donor funds. Those with poor policies and institutions did not. Badly run countries showed negligible or even negative growth, irrespective of how much aid they were given. Well-run countries that received little aid grew steadily, at 2.2 percent, per head, per year. Well-run countries that received a lot of aid grew much faster, at 3.7 percent, per head, per year.

This huge difference can be explained by a number of factors. In badly managed countries, aid is sometimes stolen. When it is not, it tends to displace, rather than complement, private investment, perhaps because there are fewer opportunities to choose from in such countries. In countries with good management, by contrast, aid tends to "crowd in" private investment. This is probably because if an economy is growing fast, the returns on, say, road-building or setting up a new airline are likely to be greater.[18]

For aid to be most effective in lifting people out of poverty, it should be directed toward well-managed countries with lots of poor citizens. But too often it isn't. Bilateral aid tends to favor allies and ex-colonies. A 1998 study by Alberto Alesina and David Dollar found that a former colony with a closed economy received about twice as much assistance as a non-colony with an open one.[19] Undemocratic ex-colonies also received twice as much as democratic non-colonies. After controlling for population and average income, badly run countries received just as much bilateral aid as well run ones. (Nordic aid was a notable exception to this dismal trend.)

Aid is supposed to help the poorest but often doesn't. The adage that foreign aid is a transfer of wealth from the poor in rich countries to the rich in poor countries is often true. A typical poor African country receives aid equivalent to about 10 percent of GDP, but the poorest fifth of the population disposes of only 4 percent of GDP.[20] In other words, a lot of the aid is paying for conferences at five-star hotels, study trips for MPs to Washington, and Toyota Landcruisers to ferry aid workers around.

For the foolish – advice

Can aid persuade bad governments to shape up? Probably not.

In the 1960s and 70s, many donors believed that statist policies, of the sort practiced in Zambia, were the quickest way to develop. So several African countries were actually paid to adopt policies that impoverished them. From the early 1980s, the failure of these policies was hard to ignore. So the IMF and World Bank started to make assistance conditional on more laissez-faire policies – "structural adjustment," in the jargon.

This has not been terribly successful either. African leaders, on the whole, distrust the IMF and the World Bank – understandably, given these institutions' policy flip-flops. More important, few African leaders like markets or the idea of spending within their means, and donors have discovered that it is virtually impossible to force governments to implement policies they do not like. They often agree to cut subsidies, tackle corruption, or whatever in return for loans. But as soon as they have cashed the aid check, they tend to backtrack.

The Kaunda government in Zambia, for example, had to beg the IMF to bail it out in 1985 and again in 1989. Both times, large amounts of cash were exchanged for promises to keep spending under control and to liberalize the economy.[21] Both times, the government broke its promises. This should not have come as a surprise. Neither Kaunda nor many of his officials wanted to reform. They passionately believed that the state should direct the economy and expected the copper price eventually to recover and plug the hole in the budget. It didn't.

In the 1990s, donors sent mixed messages to Zambia. Bilateral donors such as Britain and the Nordic countries made much of their aid conditional on the Chiluba government behaving democratically. The World Bank and the IMF emphasized instead the need to stick with free-market reforms. Bilateral donors cut aid when, for example, Chiluba had the constitution changed to bar his only serious opponent – Kaunda – from contesting the 1996 presidential election. The Bretton Woods institutions only protested when, for example, the privatization of the copper mines was delayed once too often.

Neither type of threat did much good. In economic matters, attaching conditions to loans made the Zambian government what one writer called a "receiver of policy, rather than an initiator."[22] Ministries devoted their efforts simply to meeting the letter of donor conditions rather than energetically pursuing the spirit of free-market reforms. They also fiddled the numbers to make it look as if they were keeping promises when they weren't.

Similar stories can be told of other countries. Daniel arap Moi, who ruled Kenya for nearly a quarter of a century, used to promise one thing to donors and the opposite to domestic interest groups. Even when recipients blatantly flout aid conditions, donors often hand over the money anyway, fearing that to refuse might spark an economic collapse.

According to the World Bank, "reforms rarely succeed unless the government is genuinely convinced that the reforms have to be implemented and considers the reform programme its own."[23] Richard Dowden, my former colleague at the *Economist*, expressed it more trenchantly: "If you give money to a recalcitrant junkie, he will waste it."[24]

As a rule, elected governments are more likely to implement reforms than unelected ones, as voters who keep on getting poorer will protest at the polls. And new regimes are more likely to reform than old ones: governments, like people, get set in their ways.[25]

For countries with foolish governments, large-scale monetary aid is wasted, so the best approach is to offer ideas instead. The architects of successful reforms in Indonesia in the 1970s, and in several Latin American countries in the 1980s and 90s, were largely educated abroad, often at donor expense. The crash course in market economics given to senior African National Congress members shortly before the ANC won power in South Africa in 1994 was crucial in helping the new government to understand the importance of financial stability.

In the meantime, perhaps the only valid reason for attaching detailed conditions to aid is to provide a scapegoat for governments that are trying to push through wise but unpopular reforms. If a minister who wants to privatize a loss-making airline can say that an IMF loan will not materialize unless he does so, it may be harder for unions to block the deal.

For the virtuous – cash

Donors usually like their money to be used for worthy things such as agriculture, education, and health. A high proportion of aid is disbursed for specific projects, such as irrigation or building schools. Since the schools are usually built and the ditches dug, donors are usually satisfied that their money has served the purpose for which it was intended. But often it has not.

Most of the available evidence suggests that aid money is

fungible – it goes into the pot of public funds and is spent on whatever the recipient government wants to spend it on. If donors earmark money for education, it may cause the government to spend more on education, or it may free up the money that the government would otherwise have spent on education to be spent on something else. If the government is benevolent, this may mean agriculture or tax cuts. If it is not, this could mean limousines for ministers and batons for cracking demonstrators' heads.

The important factor is not the donor's instructions but the recipient government's priorities. A study carried out a decade ago in Indonesia found that for every extra aid dollar earmarked for agriculture, public spending on agriculture increased by ninety-two cents.[26] By contrast, a fourteen-country study published in 1998 showed that each extra aid dollar aimed at agriculture actually *decreased* total agricultural spending by five cents.[27] So the uncomfortable answer to the question "What is all our aid money being spent on?" is "Who knows?"

Many donors, if they put money into a road-building program that shows a return on investment of 100 percent, imagine that the return on their aid is 100 percent. But it may be that the government would have paid for the roads anyway, and the actual effect of the aid is to free up funds for a marginal project that would otherwise not have been carried out. The return on this project could be much lower. It could even be zero.

This does not mean that donors should never finance specific projects. Sometimes the real value of a donor-funded dam or telephone network lies in the technology that is transferred and the advice given on how to operate and maintain the completed infrastructure.

But the fact of fungibility suggests that the aid-giving process could be greatly simplified if most donations took the form of untied, unconditional "balance of payments support." In other words, cash. Such support should go only to competent governments, and priority should be given to countries with lots of poor citizens.

There are not many such countries. India and Vietnam probably qualify, as do Mozambique, Tanzania, and Uganda, although corruption is a problem in all five.

Rich countries currently devote a miserable amount to aid. They may dig into their pockets to help tackle sudden, telegenic emergencies, such as floods in Mozambique or famines in Ethiopia (which is as it should be). But they have grown weary of funding the long slow struggle to help the bulk of the poor – the 2 billion or so who are not currently clinging to trees above raging floodwaters – grow a bit richer. Development aid to Africa withered in the 1990s, from $19 billion in 1990 to $14 billion in 1999, probably because rich-country taxpayers are fed up with bankrolling failure.[28] If aid could be made to work, however, people in rich countries would surely be more generous. The necessary sums are, by rich-country standards, not very big.

Donors should be both more generous and more selective. Countries that are genuinely trying to implement sensible policies should be given more money. Countries that are not should be offered advice but no money. Donors should be ready to help new governments if they seem earnest about reform.

At the same time, however, donors should probably devote a smaller proportion of their aid budgets to helping individual countries and more to fostering the kind of technology that benefits poor people everywhere, such as vaccines. This approach has recently become more popular. Large though not yet adequate sums have been pledged to the UN-backed Global Fund to Fight AIDS, Tuberculosis, and Malaria, and charitable individuals, most notably Bill Gates, have supported some hopeful research into vaccines for diseases that afflict the poor.

Most important, rich countries should open their markets to goods from poor countries. Trade has far more potential to reduce poverty than aid.

The right to trade

In the energy-sapping heat of Uganda, I watched women bent double to tend rows of flowers destined for export. They toiled and sweated long hours for a pittance so that pampered Westerners could buy roses all year round. Bono, the Irish rock star and conspicuous campaigner for worthy causes, was also watching. One might have expected him to protest at this scene of back-breaking drudgery. Instead, he said it represented "globalization at its best."[29]

He was right, of course. Growing flowers is hard work, but no more so than subsistence farming, which was the alternative; and it pays better. Everyone benefits: Europeans get roses in winter, and Ugandan rose-growers earn enough to put their children through school.

This is the sort of thing that advocates of heartless global capitalism, such as the *Economist*, have been banging on about since the 1840s, but it is rare to hear a rock star make the same point, which is why I was following Bono around Uganda. I don't normally chase celebrities, and my employer doesn't normally publish interviews with them, but in Bono's case we made an exception.[30] The shades-wrapped rock star had ventured onto our turf, and we were actually quite glad to see him.

It was in 2002, when a number of charities had started to notice that north–south trade is not always exploitative. Oxfam had just released a fat report on trade, which denounced rich countries' tariff barriers against imports from poor countries and their subsidies for farmers. Christian Aid had also condemned northern protectionism. Few charities were yet calling for poor countries to reduce their own tariffs and subsidies, but it struck me as a good start that some realized that, as Bono put it, Africans "don't want to spend the rest of their lives on the nipple of aid."

Bono was on a tour of Africa with, of all people, America's

treasury secretary, Paul O'Neill. It was an odd spectacle. O'Neill was a hard-boiled company-boss-turned-politician, who wore a dark suit and kept doing sums out loud and in public. Bono, by contrast, was a bit hazy with numbers and apt to say lyrical things in his soft Irish brogue that sounded beautiful but, on closer examination, meant nothing. "People say that politics is the art of the possible," he lilted, "but I think it should be the art of the impossible."

I'm not going to mock the rocker. He's a fabulously wealthy musical genius, and I'm not. More important, regardless of whether he understands the issues in much detail, he is uniquely able to publicize them. His ability to occupy magazine covers and television screens helped make the "Jubilee 2000" campaign for debt relief for poor countries such a success. And now he was fronting for a group of charities arguing that trade was at least as important as aid and that rich countries should tear down their trade barriers. That had to be a good thing.

Africa has lots of fertile land and cheap labor, so it is ideally placed to grow food and sell it to rich countries. Cheap labor should also make Africa a good place to make simple manufactured goods, such as textiles. Unfortunately, rich countries have erected towering trade barriers to keep precisely these products out.

Farmers in rich countries are especially well protected. In Western Europe, Japan, and (to a lesser extent) America, land and labor are expensive. Most things that French or Japanese farmers grow can be grown more cheaply in poor countries. Given the choice, thrifty Western consumers would probably buy a lot of groceries imported from the Third World. Western farmers know this and fear that it would put them out of business. So they lobby their governments for protection, which the governments seem happy to provide.

Rich countries impose hefty tariffs on imported crops; these tariffs are high enough to keep all but a few bags of foreign grain from being sold in supermarkets in Seoul or Tokyo. As if this were not favor enough, farmers in rich countries also receive all manner of subsidies. Sometimes they are paid to grow stuff. Other times they are paid to stop growing stuff that they have grown too much of because they were paid to grow it. Because prices fluctuate, governments sometimes guarantee a floor beneath which prices will not be allowed to fall. When prices fall below this floor, the government buys up all the surplus milk or wheat or whatever, which brings prices back up again.

Farm subsidies in rich countries are running at about a billion dollars a day. This is roughly equivalent to the entire GDP of sub-Saharan Africa. African farmers simply cannot compete. A huge potential source of profit is closed to them. What's more, subsidies make farmers in rich countries produce more than rich-country consumers can eat. This surplus is often dumped on African markets, which lowers the prices that African farmers can get at home.

When rich countries cut subsidies or tariffs, farmers in poor countries swiftly benefit. Those Ugandan flower-growers used to have to compete with heavily subsidized Dutch flower-growers whose prices they could only beat during the European winter. But as those subsidies were pruned, the Ugandans started to harvest all year round, and their country's flower exports blossomed from approximately nothing in the mid-1990s to $16 million in 2001.

Even so, compared with what Uganda could make selling peanuts to America if only they did not face tariffs of up to 164 percent, this is, well, peanuts. Ugandans who want to sell rice to Japan are hobbled because 93 percent of the market is reserved for Japanese growers. If they want to sell sugar to Europe, they must hack their way through a jungle of rules so thick that even experts cannot get through it. This is not an exaggeration. I called up Wyn Grant, an expert on European Union agricultural policy, and asked him to explain the sugar regime to me. He admitted that he couldn't, not without referring to some heavy reference books. God knows how African sugar farmers cope. Even if they were to master the rules, they still face tariffs of up to 140 percent.

In all, rich country protectionism costs poor countries $100 billion a year, or twice what they receive in aid. At any rate, that's the suspiciously round number that Oxfam's policy analysts calculate the damage to be, and I can't find a better one. What Oxfam, Bono, and other charitable types fail to notice, however, is that northern protectionism hurts the north, too.

Northern taxpayers lose out to the tune of those aforementioned billion dollars a day. Those northerners who eat food lose out, because they have to pay more for everything from bread to oranges. Among rich countries only New Zealand has taken the plunge and slashed agricultural tariffs and subsidies. As a result, New Zealanders pay half as much for the same basket of groceries as Western Europeans do. Bigger grocery bills particularly hurt the poor in rich countries because they spend a large chunk of their disposable incomes on food. Lawyers and lobbyists may not bother to read the price tags in the grocery store, but the jobless do.

The only people who win are the farmers who receive the subsidies. In Europe and America the biggest subsidies go to the biggest farmers, so a lot of the people being helped are rich. The average American farm reports a net worth of $564,000, twice the average household's. The needy recipients of farm subsidies include Ted Turner, the media baron, Scottie Pippen, the basketball star, and twelve of America's 500 largest companies.[31]

For smaller farmers, subsidies can make the difference between staying afloat and going bust. But is that as kind as it sounds? The torrent of handouts does not seem to have made them happy: British farmers are 50 percent more likely to kill themselves than other Brits. In effect, we're paying them to stay in a dying industry, instead of learning a new trade. I don't know about you, but if my son asked me for career advice, I probably wouldn't say, "Go work in a doomed industry, and here's ten grand if you stick at it."

Agricultural protectionism – a pig that can't be slaughtered

Given the harm that farm protection wreaks, it is strange that nearly every rich government does it. There are several reasons. First, people worry about "food security." They fear that if they cannot grow their own food they will starve if war breaks out and their imports are torpedoed. This is a fair point, with roots in the Second World War, when German submarines caused havoc with Allied ships. But it is greatly overstated. In the nuclear age, if France went to war with a country advanced enough to seize control of French shipping routes, the last thing anyone would be worrying about would be whether there was enough sugar to make almond croissants.

Another argument is that farmers are the guardians of the natural beauty of the countryside and should be paid for this public service. Perhaps so, but if that is the excuse for farm subsidies, it would be cheaper and more effective to pay someone actually to preserve unspoilt fields and woodlands rather than paying to have them ploughed up and slathered with pesticides.

The main reason that farm subsidies persist is the reason that all subsidies persist. The benefits are concentrated, but the costs are dispersed. The average rich-country citizen spends over $300 a year on farm subsidies but probably doesn't know it.[32] The price tag on a loaf of bread does not tell her how much cheaper it would be if foreign wheat could be imported without tariffs. No one ever asks her to press $300 into the palm of a California rice-grower. And even if she did realize where the money was going, it's less than a dollar a day, so she probably wouldn't organize a protest march about it. She's too busy earning a living. For the farmers who pocket them, however, farm subsidies are the single most important political issue. To defend them, they will certainly hire lobbyists, organize protests, and dump piles of fertilizer on their senators' front lawns.

Those who would restrict trade with poor countries often argue that the way poor countries compete – by paying workers less – is unfair. This argument is emotionally appealing. Many Westerners would choke on their cornflakes if they thought that the corn was grown with child labor. Even if the corn-planters were adults, many people in rich countries would not like to think of them being exploited, and a typical African farm-worker's wage of a couple of dollars a day sounds horribly exploitative to most Americans or Swedes.

This kind of thinking is behind moves by labor unions in rich countries to block imports from countries that do not adhere to rich-country labor standards. But it does the poor no favors. For most Africans, the alternative to long hours at low wages is long hours at no wages – unemployment. By preventing Africans from trading, well-meaning Westerners make them poorer.

Trade allows specialization. A plumber, for example, special-izes in fixing water pipes. He gets good at it, so he can fix lots of water pipes in a day. He trades his services for money, which he can then spend on everything he needs. If he had to grow all his own food, weave his own clothes, and build his own house, he would be unlikely to do any of these things well. He would probably end up as poor as Nashon Zimba, the Malawian sub-sistence farmer I mentioned earlier. Poorer, in fact – Zimba trades his surplus corn for soap and T-shirts.

On a larger scale, countries prosper through the specializa-tion that trade allows. British people are quite capable of growing wheat; they've been doing it for millennia. But South Africans can do it more cheaply, so it makes sense for Britain to sell South Africans insurance and buy their wheat.

Trade benefits both parties even when one party is better at more or less everything. This surprising observation was first made by David Ricardo, a British economist, who called it the law of "comparative advantage." Ricardo said that if you can make A better than B, and your neighbor can make B better than A, but he can make both A and B better than you can, it does not follow that your neighbor should do both jobs. Both of you would profit more if each concentrates on what he does best. So would society as a whole.

The most digestible illustration of this I've heard was concocted by P. J. O'Rourke, an American humorist who likes to grapple with serious subjects. Let us decide, he writes,

> that one legal thriller is equal to one pop song as a Benefit to Society. (One thriller or one song = 1 unit of BS.) John Grisham is a better writer than Courtney Love. John Grisham is also (assuming he plays the comb and wax paper or something) a better musician than Courtney Love. Say John Grisham is 100 times the writer Courtney Love is, and say he's 10 times the musician. Then say that John Grisham can either write 100 legal thrillers in a year (I'll bet he can) or compose 50 songs. This would mean that Courtney Love could write either 1 thriller or compose 5 songs in the same period.
>
> If John Grisham spends 50 percent of his time scribbling predictable plots and 50 percent of his time blowing into a kazoo, the result will be 50 thrillers and 25 songs for a total of 75 BS units. If Courtney Love spends 50 percent of her time annoying a word processor and 50 percent of her time making noise in a recording studio, the result will be 1 half-completed thriller and 2.5 songs for a total of 3 BS. The grand total benefit to society will be 78 units.
>
> If John Grisham spends 100 percent of his time inventing dumb adventures for two-dimensional characters and Courtney Love spends 100 percent of her time calling cats, the result will be 100 thrillers and 5 songs for a total of 105 BS.

Applying this principle to foreign trade, O'Rourke notes that "the Japanese make better CD players than [Americans] do, and they may be able to make better pop music, but we both profit by buying our CDs from Sony and letting Courtney Love tour Japan."[33]

JOHN GRISHAM AND COURTNEY LOVE EACH SPEND EQUAL TIME WRITING AND COMPOSING

	THRILLERS		SONGS		BS PRODUCTION
John Grisham	50.0	+	25.0	=	75
Courtney Love	.5	+	2.5	=	3
					78 Total BS

JOHN GRISHAM SPENDS ALL HIS TIME BASHING THE LAPTOP KEYBOARD AND COURTNEY SPENDS ALL HER TIME CATERWAULING AND PLINKING GUITAR STRINGS

	THRILLERS		SONGS		BS PRODUCTION
John Grisham	100	+	0	=	100
Courtney Love	0	+	5	=	5
					105 Total BS

Eat the Rich by P. J. O'Rourke

Joking aside, this works in practice, too. The Cato Institute, a libertarian think tank in Washington, has taken the trouble to rank ninety-one countries by their openness to trade between 1980 and 1998. The trade openness index (TOI) takes account of tariff rates; the severity of exchange controls, as measured by the difference between the black market exchange rate and the official one; restrictions on capital movements; and the actual volume of trade, compared to an expected volume calculated by looking at a country's size, population, proximity to big markets, and so on.[34]

Cato's researchers then tried to assess whether free trade made countries richer. The results were striking. The twelve most open economies had a GDP per head in 1998 of $23,387 – seven times the figure for the twelve least open. Average incomes in the most open countries grew by 2.5 percent annually over those nineteen years, leaving them on average 1.6 times richer at the end. In the twelve least open countries, average incomes grew by a pathetic 0.3 percent per year over the period, leaving them on average only 6 percent better off at the end. (The countries in the middle showed middling income and middling growth.) The bottom twelve contained five African countries; the top twelve none. Half of the countries in Africa were not ranked, mainly for lack of data.

The relationship between openness and growth remained similar when the study looked only at poor countries. If anything, poor countries appeared to benefit more from openness to trade. And when the researchers tried to allow for other factors that may be correlated with openness, such as country size, inflation, and security of property rights, they still found that trade openness boosts growth. Other economists agree. Using somewhat different measures, two Harvard economists found that developing countries with open economies grew by an average of 4.5 percent per year in the 1970s and 80s, while those with closed economies grew by only 0.7 percent.[35]

The good news for Africans is that their borders are opening. After several disastrous attempts at self-sufficiency in the 1960s and 70s, trade barriers started to fall in the 1980s and 90s. On the Cato scale of one to ten, seven out of twenty-two African countries improved by more than one point between 1980 and 1998, while only one African country (Sierra Leone) regressed.

The bad news is that Africa still has towering informal trade barriers: muddy roads, bad ports, crooked customs officials, and policemen who specialize in highway robbery – as I found out when I rode in the cab of a Cameroonian beer truck.

7. OF POTHOLES AND GRASPING GENDARMES

The risks and rewards of investing in Africa

Douala, Cameroon's muggy commercial capital, is one of the busiest ports in Africa, so the city's rotten infrastructure is a bit of a problem. The roads are resurfaced from time to time, but the soil is soft and the foundations often too shallow, so small cracks yawn quickly into great potholes. Street boys fill them with sand or rubble and hold out their palms for tips from the motorists who roll slowly by, but their amateur repair work rarely survives the first downpour.

In the middle of the day, the streets are horribly gridlocked, as I could see quite clearly from up in the cab of a sixty-ton beer truck. I was riding with Martin, a mild and amiable truck driver, and Hippolyte, his young, handsome, and green-hatted assistant. We were at the entrance of a Guinness factory, where Martin had just picked up 30,000 bottles of black velvety stout and other refreshing brews. We were trying to leave but couldn't. The road we wanted to join was narrow and packed with stationary cars, none of whose drivers wanted to let us pull out in front of them.

Martin, however, knew his stuff. He inched the eighteen-wheeled beast forward with skill and calculated aggression and gradually barged his way into the fast lane, where he immediately had to stop again. Far into the distance, motionless traffic blocked the way. With no cooling breeze coming through the windows, it was monstrously humid. After five minutes in the cab, I was sweating like a pig in a plastic jogging suit.

When we eventually got moving again, we had to dodge both the potholes and the wrecks of cars that had crashed. Under Cameroonian law these may not be moved until the police, who are in no hurry, have arrived. It took us half an hour to reach the first gas station and another half an hour to fill up, owing to arguments about paperwork. Another hour and two police road blocks later, we finally left the city. That was the end of the easy part of the journey.

Visitors from rich countries rarely experience the true ghastliness of Third-World infrastructure. They use the smooth roads between airports and hotels and fly any distance longer than a hike to the curio market. But the people who live or work in countries with lousy infrastructure have to cope with the consequences every day. These are as profound as they are malign.

I had hitched a ride in Martin's truck in the hope of following a bottle of Guinness from the brewery in Douala to a bar in the rainforest where some thirsty Cameroonian might drink it. The trip did not go entirely according to plan but it was educational. I saw, at first hand, just how difficult it is working in a country with wretched roads. I also saw how smart and persistent businesspeople can make good money in the most unpromising places.

Guinness Cameroon, the local arm of the global beverage giant, was very helpful. The managing director, Brian Johnson, asked one of the trucking companies that deliver his products to let me ride with them, and the head of logistics, a personable Scot named Ross Paterson, gave me a schedule that turned out to be as realistic as a James Bond movie.

At 2 p.m. on a Thursday in October 2002, I was to join 1,600 crates of stout on board a big truck bound for Bertoua, a small town in Cameroon's south-eastern jungle. As the crow flies, this is about 500 kilometers – as far as from London to Edinburgh, or New York to Pittsburgh. The journey was supposed to take eighteen hours, including an overnight rest stop. It took four days, and when the truck arrived it was carrying only two thirds of its original load.

Along the way, the scenery was staggering. Thickly forested hills stretched into the distance like a stormy green sea, punctuated with explosions of red and yellow blossoms. Beside the road were piles of cocoa beans laid out to dry in the sun, and hawkers selling engine oil, tangerines, and twelve-foot pythons for the pot. I was able to survey it all at leisure, not least because we were stopped at road blocks forty-seven times.

These usually consisted of a pile of tires or a couple of oil drums in the middle of the road, plus a plank with upturned nails sticking out which could be pulled aside when the policemen on duty were satisfied that the truck had broken no laws and should be allowed to pass. Sometimes they merely stared into the cab or glanced at Martin's papers for a few seconds before waving him on. But the more aggressive ones detained us somewhat longer.

Some asked for beer, which they couldn't have because it was in a locked cage on the back of the truck and Martin had no key. Some complained that they were hungry, often rubbing their huge stomachs for emphasis. One asked for pills, lamenting that he had indigestion. But most wanted money and figured that the best way to get it was to harass motorists until bribed to lay off.

At every other road block, they carried out "safety checks." Typically, Hippolyte had to climb down and show the truck's fire extinguisher to a gendarme relaxing in the shade of a palm tree, who would inspect it minutely and pore over the instructions on the side. Similar scrutiny was lavished on tail-lights, axles, side-view mirrors, and tires. Strangely, no one asked about seat belts, which Cameroonians wear about as often as fur coats.

At some road blocks, the police went through our papers word by word, in the hope of finding an error. Some found fault with me, although I tried to avoid confrontation by pretending not to speak French. One frowning thug declared that my

Cameroonian visa was on the wrong page of my passport; another insisted that I was obliged to carry my yellow fever vaccination certificate at all times, which was not true. Most of the demands for bribes, however, were directed at Martin. Because trucks have to abide by so many more regulations than passenger vehicles, truckers are easier to catch out breaking some trivial rule or another, and the Cameroonian police persecute them accordingly.

In the town of Mbandjok the police decided that Martin lacked a particular permit and offered to sell him a new one for twice the usual price. When he asked for a receipt, they kept us waiting for three and a half hours. A gaggle of policemen joined the argument. The total number of work-hours wasted (assuming an average of seven policemen involved, plus three people in the truck) was thirty-five – call it one French working week. And all for a requested bribe of 8,000 CFA francs (about $12).

The pithiest explanation of why Cameroonians have to put up with all this came from the policeman at road block no. 31, who had invented a new law about carrying passengers in trucks, found Martin guilty of breaking it, and confiscated his driving license. When it was put to him that the law he was citing did not, in fact, exist, he patted his holster and replied: "Do you have a gun? No. I have a gun, so I know the rules."

Cameroon's robber-cops are worse than the African norm. But even without their attentions, the journey would have been a slog. Most Cameroonian roads are unpaved: long stretches of rutty red laterite soil with sheer ditches on either side. Dirt roads are fine as long as it doesn't rain, but Cameroon is largely rainforest, where it rains often and hard. Our road was made impassable by rain three times, causing delays of up to four hours.

The Cameroonian government has tried to grapple with the problem of rain eroding roads by erecting a series of barriers with small gaps in the middle that allow light vehicles through but stop heavy trucks from passing while it is pouring. The barriers, which are locked to prevent truckers from lifting them when no one is looking, are supposed to be unlocked when the road has had a chance to dry. Unfortunately, the officials whose job it is to unlock them are not wholly reliable. Early on the second evening, not long after our stand-off with the police in Mbandjok, we met a rain barrier in the middle of the forest. It was dark, and the man with the key was not there. Asking around nearby villages yielded no clue as to his whereabouts. We curled up in the mosquito-filled cab and waited for him to return, which he did shortly before midnight.

The hold-up was irritating but in the end made no difference. Early the next morning a driver coming in the opposite direction told us that the bridge ahead had collapsed, so we had to turn back.

Six hours, eleven road blocks, and three toothsome sardine sandwiches later, we arrived in Yaoundé, the political capital, where Guinness has a depot. The alternative route to Bertoua meant passing a weighing station, where vehicles weighing more than fifty tons faced steep tolls. Since we were ten tons overweight, Martin needed permission to offload 600 crates. But it was a Saturday, the man in charge was reportedly at lunch, and we did not get permission until the next morning. It then took all morning to unload the extra crates, despite the fact that the depot was equipped with forklifts. Finally, after twenty-five hours without moving, we hit the road again and met no road blocks for a whole fifteen minutes.

For much of the rest of the journey, which took another seventeen hours, I was struck by how terrifying Cameroonian roads are. Piles of rusting wrecks clogged the grassy verges on the way out of Yaoundé. We saw several freshly crashed cars and a couple of lorries and buses languishing in ditches. None of the bridges we crossed seemed well maintained. And when we arrived in Bertoua we heard that two people had been crushed to death on a nearby road the previous day, when a logging truck lost its load onto their heads.

OF POTHOLES AND GRASPING GENDARMES

Coping with chaos

Cameroon's roads have wasted away. In 1980, there were 7.2 kilometers of roads per 1,000 people; by 1995, this had shrunk to only 2.6 kilometers per 1,000. By one estimate, less than a tenth are paved, and most of these are in poor condition. In recent years, however, aided by a splurge of World Bank money, things have improved a bit. The roads around Douala have been substantially rehabilitated. A more streamlined government helps: it used to take three years for officials to approve plans for new roads.

But there is much still to be done, and firms still have to find ways to cope with dire highways. Guinness used to buy second-hand army trucks, which was a false economy because they kept breaking down. Now, it buys its trucks new from Toyota, with which it has a long-term agreement to ensure that it will always be able to get hold of mechanics and genuine spare parts (as opposed to fake or stolen ones, which are popular in Cameroon, but of variable quality). The firm is also making more use of owner-drivers, who have a greater incentive to drive carefully.

"Just-in-time" delivery is, for obvious reasons, impossible. Whereas its factories in Europe can turn some raw materials into beer within hours of delivery, Guinness Cameroon has to keep forty days of inventory in the factory: crates and drums of malt, hops, and bottle tops. Wholesalers out in the bush have to carry as much as five months' stock during the rainy season, when roads are at their swampiest. Since they tend to have shallow pockets, Guinness has to offer them credit on exceptionally easy terms.

Out in the forest, the firm does whatever it takes to get beer into bars and liquor stores. It is an exercise in creative management. At the depot in Bertoua, crates are unloaded from big trucks and packed into pick-up trucks, which rush them to wholesalers in small towns. The wholesalers then sell to retailers and to small distributors, who carry crates to villages in hand-pushed carts, on heads, and even by canoe.

No matter how hard Guinness tries, however, the bars that sell its brew sometimes run dry. I spoke to Jean Mière, a tall young bar-owner with slightly bloodshot eyes, in a small village called Kuelle. "I'm not going to open the bar this evening," he said, "because I don't have any beer to sell to my customers." The local wholesaler's driver, apparently, was in jail.

I had arrived in an empty pick-up truck with the local Guinness depot chief, Yves Ngassa. We had been given directions by the wholesaler who normally supplied Mière, but the wholesaler had not mentioned that Mière had no beer nor asked if he could load some into Ngassa's empty pick-up. Ngassa was furious. "This is so stupid," he spat. "I'm losing sales here."

The famished road

The biggest losers from lousy infrastructure are ordinary Cameroonians. Many environmentalists argue that roads in rain-forests are a bad thing because they facilitate illegal logging and destroy indigenous cultures by bringing them into contact with aggressive, disease-carrying, rum-swilling outsiders. But the absence of roads probably harms Africans far more.

I tried to measure that harm, crudely, by jotting down the price of each Coca-Cola I bought and seeing how much more expensive it became as we moved away from Yaoundé, where it was bottled. I don't normally drink Coke when I'm in Europe; I prefer water. But in places like Cameroon even bottled water can be a bit iffy, whereas the Coke brand name conveys the reassuring message that "drinking this will not give you unpleasant bacterial diseases." So I drink gallons of the horrible stuff.

Anyway, I found that a 60 cl bottle of Coke cost 300 CFA in Yaoundé but 315 CFA in the small town of Ayos, a mere 125 kilometers down the road. At a smaller village 100 kilometers further on, it was 350 CFA. Once you leave the main road, prices rise even more sharply. A Guinness that cost 350 CFA in Douala would set you back 450 CFA in an eastern village that can only be reached on foot.

What is true of bottled drinks is also true of more or less any other manufactured good. Soap, axe-heads, and kerosene are all much more costly in jungle hamlets than in the big cities. Even lighter goods, which do not cost so much to transport, such as matches and malaria pills, are significantly more expensive.

At the same time, the things that poor people sell – yams, cassava, mangoes – fetch less in the villages than they do in the towns. Yet, thanks to bad roads, it is hard and costly to get such perishable, heavy items to market. So peasant farmers are doubly squeezed by bad roads. They pay more for what they buy and receive less for what they sell. Small wonder that the African Development Bank finds "a strong link between poverty and remoteness."

Where roads improve, incomes tend to rise in parallel. In Cameroon, where the soil is wondrously fertile, farmers start growing cash crops as soon as nearby roads are repaired. Big commercial farmers benefit too. Along the highway to Douala, I saw great plantations of sugar cane and banana trees whose fruit is wrapped in blue plastic bags to keep at bay the birds and bugs that might mar the visual perfection demanded by European consumers.

Better roads also ease the drudgery of rural life. According to the World Bank, a typical Ugandan woman carries the equivalent of a ten-liter jug of water for ten kilometers every day. (Her husband humps only a fifth as much.) With better roads, both men and women can, if nothing else, hitch rides on passing trucks, thereby sparing their feet and getting their goods more swiftly to market. And no country with good roads has ever suffered famine.

Africans often find ingenious ways around infrastructure

bottlenecks. Buses designed for European roads do not last long in Nigeria, so Nigerians import the chassis of heavy European trucks and mount locally manufactured bus bodies on top. This is much cheaper than importing a whole truck, and the vehicle is more durable than an imported bus.

But there is no substitute for building and maintaining better infrastructure. Guinness's Johnson told me that Cameroon's bad infrastructure added about 15 percent to his firm's costs. The reason Guinness can still make a profit in Cameroon is that its competitors all face the same problems. It also helps that labor costs are low and that Cameroonians drink a lot of beer. Johnson said that the firm's annual return on capital was around 16 percent, which is not spectacular but it is pretty good. If the Cameroonian government were to lift those road blocks and put the police to work mending potholes, Guinness would do even better, as would everyone else.

If there's one thing worse than being exploited, it's not being exploited

In letting me watch Martin and Hippolyte delivering their beer, Guinness took a risk. I could have been planning an exposé of the dire conditions under which African truckers work as the first step toward organizing a boycott of Guinness's products. Plenty of Western journalists are convinced that Western companies exploit their Third-World employees and feel a duty to protest. Naomi Klein, a siren of the anti-globalization movement, asserts rather dramatically: "Our corporations are stealing their lives."[1]

My report could have started like this:

Weary and wincing with malaria, Hippolyte siphons diesel from a spare drum and pours it, jerry can by jerry can, into the juggernaut's fuel tank. Eighteen hours a day, lashed by rainstorms or wiping the sweat from his brow, he toils to keep a Guinness delivery truck roadworthy. Lunch is a bag of peanuts; supper, a fatty slice of goat eaten in pitch darkness at a roadside food stall; his bed, a mat on the bumpy ground. He hasn't seen his family for a week, but he has to keep on working. And for what? While his multinational employer reaps billions, Hippolyte barely earns enough each day to buy a pint of Guinness in a Dublin pub.

All of which is true but misleading. Hippolyte was indeed suffering from a mild bout of malaria when I met him, and it is no fun working with a fever even if you can afford anti-malarial drugs, which Hippolyte can. If he had been working in the fields, which is how most Cameroonians survive, he would have fallen ill just as often, but he would have found it harder to buy pills. His lunch was indeed a bag of peanuts, but they were the freshest, juiciest peanuts I've ever tasted, and he snacked all afternoon on fresh tangerines and bananas. He ate supper in pitch darkness, but that is because none of the roadside food stalls in the village where we stopped had lights. The goat was the best dish on offer, and believe me I looked. I'm fond of my food and had a thick roll of notes in my pocket.

Hippolyte's wages would not go far in Dublin, but he does not live in Dublin. His job is nowhere near as cushy as that of, say, a Western journalist, but as far as he is concerned it is not bad. He dresses smartly, feeds his family, and aspires one day (he is in his early twenties) to be promoted to driver, which, he told me, is a really good job. Often, when we were delayed, Martin would let him stop, start, and park the truck, for practice.

Given Cameroon's lower productivity and poorer consumers, a company that paid Irish wages there would soon go bust. Guinness and other multinationals pay much less but are still popular employers because they pay better than local firms and much better than subsistence farming.

One study found that the average wages paid by affiliates of

American multinationals to their non-American employees in middle-income countries were three times GDP per head. In low-income countries, local employees of American multinationals had to get by on only eight and half times the average income in their country.[2] The average income (i.e., the total national income divided by the total population) is not the same as the average wage, particularly in countries where most people do not draw regular salaries. But still the comparison is suggestive.

Foreign firms also bring ideas and technology. Even a humble clothing factory probably contains sewing machines, computers loaded with accounting software, and an opportunity for workers to learn new skills. For poor countries, mastering low-tech manufacturing is a crucial first step up the ladder to prosperity. As one writer recently reminded us, "In the 1960s, Westerners used to bemoan the conditions in Japanese sweatshops."[3]

For most African countries, the problem is not that their people are being exploited by rapacious multinationals but that those rapacious multinationals shun them. Foreign direct investment (FDI) in sub-Saharan Africa – long-term projects such as building shopping centers and digging mines, rather than buying shares or bonds – was $11.8 billion in 2001. This was much better than the average of less than $3 billion between 1987 and 1995, but foreigners invested nine times more in Asia.[4]

Multinationals hesitate to do business in Africa because it seems too difficult and risky. After years of chatting with people who actually do business in Africa, I'm inclined to think their fears are overblown. Sure, there are hideous obstacles. The head of Cadbury Nigeria, Bunmi Oni, once told me that, because there was no reliable water supply in Lagos, his firm had had to drill 2,500 feet into the ground for the 70,000 gallons of water it needed each hour for its food-processing plant. The water spurted out at 80 degrees Celsius, so it had to be cooled before it could be used. And Nigeria's bureaucrats are as bad as

Cameroon's. It can take six months just to get permission to make a new type of boiled sweet.[5] In much of Africa reliable services are so hard to come by that firms barter contacts: we'll let you share the electricity from our generator if you can help us find spare parts for it.

What few outsiders realize, however, is that investing in Africa can be extremely profitable. Between 1991 and 1997, the average return on FDI in the continent was higher than in any other region, according to the UN Conference on Trade and Development.[6] This is partly because the perceived risk of doing business in Africa is so great that firms only usually put money into projects that promise a quick profit. But it also suggests that there are greater opportunities there than most businessfolk imagine.

Because Africa lacks so much, firms selling more or less anything of a reasonable quality at a reasonable price can do well. In countries where local banks often fail, many people feel safer putting their savings into big foreign banks such as Citibank or Barclays. Mobile telephones are wildly popular in countries so wild that landlines are stolen for scrap. In February 2000 I spoke to Microsoft's top man in Johannesburg, who told me that the firm's African business was growing by about 30 percent a year. Even poor countries have a laptop-tapping middle class, and Microsoft's only serious rivals are software pirates, who charge less but offer little after-sales service.[7]

The risks in Africa are changing. In the 1960s and 70s, investors feared nationalization. Nowadays this is rare, but several African countries still lack clear laws impartially upheld by an honest and independent judiciary. In such places contracts are hard to enforce.

Some firms deal with this problem by forging an alliance with a well-connected local partner. But if that partner defrauds them, there is often little recourse. Another trouble with relying too heavily on political connections is that governments change, sometimes suddenly. Many firms that won state contracts in the last months of military rule in Nigeria saw them canceled when a civilian government took over in 1999. Companies that prospered from links with Mobutu Sese Seko in the former Zaire, or the apartheid regime in South Africa, lost out when their patrons lost power.

In some parts of Africa keeping employees safe can be a problem. In Algeria, for instance, where Islamic terrorists trade atrocities with pro-government militias, oil firms typically spend about 8 or 9 percent of their budgets on security. Much of the money is spent on crude precautions: fences, guards, alarm systems. For a hefty fee, security firms staffed by ex-soldiers provide protection for offices, mines, or pipelines. Managers' houses in high-crime cities are often equipped with a bewildering array of defenses. My home in Johannesburg had high walls, razor wire, and panic buttons in every room to summon pistol-brandishing guards. (I never used the panic buttons, and they did nothing to protect my predecessor as the *Economist*'s correspondent in Jo'burg, who was robbed at gunpoint in the same house.) One tobacco executive I knew had steel blinds and electric portcullises to seal off rooms that burglars had broken into.

Softer precautions are at least as useful. Teaching employees how to drive defensively (check who is outside your front gate before stopping, beware at traffic lights) can reduce the risk of carjacking. Explaining what to do when faced with an armed robber or kidnapper (cooperate, don't make sudden moves or eye contact) can make the difference between a scary experience and a fatal one. Some foreign firms in South Africa even offer "pre-rape counseling" to female expatriates and their daughters.

Countries that are actually at war are beyond the pale for most Western firms. Mining multinationals may drool over the opportunities in Congo or Liberia, but they cannot send salaried employees to prospect for minerals in minefields. Small, freebooting entrepreneurs, however, may be prepared to take greater risks in the hope of becoming seriously rich. If they find buried treasure, they will usually need the help of a larger firm to extract it. What often happens is that the larger firm buys the "junior" that has gotten lucky. Since it is easier to defend a copper mine than it is to guarantee the safety of geologists wandering around a wide area, extraction is less hazardous than prospecting. Most mining majors subcontract the bulk of their exploration to juniors, thus reducing the chances that their own staff will be shot at.

In some places, businesses face the hostility of local communities. The people of the Niger delta, for example, were for decades brutalized by the Nigerian army and denied any benefit from the oil that gushed from their ancestral lands. Angrily, they turned on the firms that pumped the oil and provided the military regime with most of its taxes.

This made sense: protests directed at the government would have resulted in the protesters being beaten up, jailed, or worse. An oil firm is a softer adversary. That said, the policemen guarding Nigerian oil installations did sometimes arrest and beat up demonstrators. Since foreign oil firms were obliged, by law, to pay those policemen's salaries, the firms were often blamed for their actions.

Nigeria is a democracy now, but the delta's inhabitants continue to sabotage pipelines and kidnap oil executives. Shell, the biggest investor in the region, is belatedly spending tens of millions of dollars on mending ties with locals. But old grievances die slowly. And lawlessness, once provoked, is hard to dispel.[8]

Relations between big companies and impoverished locals are always tricky, but there are ways of reducing the risk that they will turn bloody. Managers at Anglo American, a South African mining firm with operations in several African countries, take pains to explain to local communities what they are doing from the outset, to learn about local taboos, and to hire as many locals as is practical. In poor countries, local means very local: AngloGold discourages traders from neighboring districts from setting up stalls outside its mines in Mali, favoring those from nearer by. So far, the firm has suffered little sabotage.

In some countries investors will be asked for bribes in return for the swift issue of necessary permits. Until recently such expenses were tax-deductible for firms from many European countries. These days bribery can lead to bad publicity and even prosecution at home, so firms increasingly refuse to grease the palms held out to them. Guinness, for example, has a policy of never paying bribes. This can be tedious if you are stuck at a road block, but it is the only way since paying up encourages more demands.

Locally hired managers sometimes find it harder to stay clean. Faced with American-style sales targets, the temptation to clinch deals through baksheesh may be irresistible. They are also more vulnerable to threats than expatriates; they cannot fly home to France or Canada. So firms should teach them how to refuse demands for bribes without getting hurt. Techniques include insisting that someone else is responsible for the decision in question and never going alone to meetings with people who may demand bribes.

He that filches from me my good name . . .

Companies care about their reputations. An accounting firm that acquires a name for dishonesty, for example, will probably lose its clients and fold, as happened to Arthur Andersen in the wake of the Enron scandal in 2002. Similarly, a firm widely believed to be unethical will have trouble recruiting good staff. Who wants to work for a company that pollutes the planet or drives Third-World peasants off their land?

In the 1990s, a number of pressure groups started demanding that companies should practice "corporate social responsibility." Campaigners argued that businesses should not focus solely on maximizing profits; they should also do their bit for the environment and for the communities in which they work.

In the age of the Internet, companies that fail to live up to these standards are sometimes swiftly punished. When Belgian king Leopold II turned Congo into a vast slave-tended rubber plantation in the nineteenth century, it was years before anyone in Europe noticed. Nowadays, if a Western firm transgresses abroad, a local NGO may email details to an NGO in the firm's home country, and within days there may be pickets outside the firm's headquarters, a boycott of its products, and vituperative editorials in the press.

Shell was pilloried for polluting the Niger delta and for failing to prevent the execution of Ken Saro-Wiwa in 1995. It is far from clear that the company could have saved him. The governments of most of the world's rich countries appealed to Sani Abacha, the Nigerian dictator, to show clemency. So did many of his African brothers. He ignored them all. Nonetheless, because Shell was the biggest company in Nigeria and because Saro-Wiwa had criticized the firm's environmental record, it was widely accused of complicity in his death.[9]

British Petroleum, another oil firm, was pummeled for working with Angola's odious regime. Nestlé, the Swiss food giant, was roasted for selling milk powder to African mothers and so allegedly discouraging them from breastfeeding. Charities such as Oxfam have launched campaigns to improve the working conditions of Africans who pick coffee and cocoa for sale in the West.

One cannot fault these aims. Other things being equal, dictators should not be propped up. Better working conditions are obviously a good thing. But there is a catch.

Virtually any firm doing business in the Third World is vulnerable to ethical criticism. Poor, unstable countries tend to have lax or non-existent environmental or safety standards. Guinness's trucks have seat belts, but no one wears them, and out in the middle of the rainforest it is hard to police this sort of thing.

Doing business in Africa sometimes requires firms to deal with, pay taxes to, and form join ventures with vicious regimes. If a dictator shoots dissidents, the firm has a choice. It can denounce him, thus putting its investment at risk. Or it can remain silent and risk being accused of complicity.

Damage to a reputation is hard to quantify. I asked Bobby Danchin, head of exploration and acquisitions at Anglo American, how seriously he took the threat. He said he spent 10–15 percent of his time worrying about environmental and human rights issues, up from about 1 percent a decade ago. He estimated that such concerns added about 5 percent to operating costs.[10] This means that Anglo mines fewer marginal seams than it otherwise would and employs fewer people.

De Beers, the South African diamond cartel, has worked especially hard to distance itself from odious regimes and rebel groups. During the 1990s, the firm was flogged by NGOs such as Global Witness for buying gems from countries where civil wars were being fought, thus allegedly providing rebels with the cash to buy arms and carry on fighting. De Beers responded by shutting down its business in Angola, withdrawing its buyers from Congo and Guinea, promising to shun "conflict diamonds," and helping to set up a certification process to keep such stones out of Western jewelry shops.

The situation for De Beers is tricky. The firm has prospered over the last century by controlling most of the world's supply of diamonds and persuading consumers that glittering lumps of carbon are glamorous. A diamond has little intrinsic value, so to keep prices high De Beers restricts the supply and constantly polishes the stones' image. The latter could prove hard if diamonds become associated in the public mind with deadly wars instead of undying romance.

De Beers claims that only 2 percent of the world's diamonds come from war zones and points out that the diamond industry feeds hundreds of thousands of miners and gem-cutters in peaceful poor nations such as Botswana, Namibia, and India.

Will such arguments convince consumers? Perhaps, but fashion is fickle, and passionate campaigners can shift it. Remember how quickly animal rights activists turned fur coats from objects of envy to objects of scorn? Because poor countries rarely measure up to rich countries' standards in anything much, companies doing business there do so at their peril. There is practically no limit to what they could be condemned for allegedly condoning. What if gay rights activists or feminists decided to boycott firms that invest in countries where gays or women are mistreated? (Of which there are, sadly, a lot.)

Reputational risk is almost impossible to insure against. It is hard to put a value on a firm's good name.[11] The best way for any firm to avoid harmful publicity is to make sure that its environmental and human rights records are beyond reproach. Sometimes this is expensive, for instance when drug firms donate money to worthy causes in the hope of deflecting the criticism that they do too little to cure the poor. Sometimes, however, all it takes is common decency. Palabora, a South African subsidiary of mining giant Rio Tinto, managed to do business during apartheid without bad publicity simply by being nice to its workers. When an employee was arrested (as happened to many unionists), his manager would telephone the police and politely ask where and why he was being held. This was usually enough to prevent the detainee from being "disappeared." The firm also continued to pay salaries to the families of miners who were not working because they were in police cells – not standard practice in those days. As a result, Palabora has unusually good labor relations to this day.

But this did not protect its parent firm, Rio Tinto, from being sued for having allegedly propped up apartheid. In 2002, an American lawyer assembled a class action suit on behalf of some of apartheid's victims. Their targets were not the security policemen who beat them up (who don't have much money) but the big foreign firms that did business in the old South Africa. The new, black South African government pleaded with the plaintiffs to drop the suit because it was likely to deter foreigners from bringing their money and expertise to South Africa. The plaintiffs carried on regardless.

Miners and oil firms will not abandon Africa, of course. They have to dig where the treasure is buried. But for most firms the possibility of attracting negative publicity is a grave deterrent to investing in poor countries. The fear of association with sweatshop labor has almost certainly led some multinationals to close factories in the developing world, thereby destroying jobs. For example, in 2002, Reebok, the sportswear firm, stopped doing business with a subcontractor in Thailand because of press reports that its staff were working more than seventy-two hours a week.[12] These workers are now worse off.

Even before the anti-globalizers started demonizing multinationals, Africa found it hard to attract investors. Companies are attracted to large markets (such as China) or rich ones (such as Ireland). Africa is divided into dozens of small, poor countries. Cracking these tiny markets can seem like a lot of effort for a modest reward. When a manager adds to this the likelihood that his teenage children will accuse him of running a sweatshop, he may decide that it is not worth the trouble.

There is more than a whiff of racism in the assumption that workers in poor countries need to be prevented from working for Western firms. If working for a Reebok subcontractor were not better than the alternatives, Thais would not work there. Africans have even fewer choices, which is why every African government actively woos foreign investors. Even Zimbabwe offers incentives to platinum miners.

I have been a couple of times to the Niger delta, where the big bad Shell pumps oil. What struck me most, after interviewing local politicians, journalists, community activists, and people in the street, was that I did not meet a single person who wanted the firm to leave. One time, not long after I left, a group of armed youths broke into a Shell office, took hostages, and issued a list of demands. What did they want? Jobs.

Enterprise and trust

They cannot all have jobs, of course. Nigeria's oil industry only employs about 100,000 people out of a population of over 100 million. Most Africans will never be paid a regular salary of any kind, let alone taste the superior wages offered by multinationals. To live more comfortably than peasants, they must usually start their own businesses.

This is getting easier. Until the 1980s, small traders were aggressively persecuted in many African countries. The smallest of all, peasants with a few extra bags of millet to sell, were crushed with price controls that allowed governments effectively to confiscate most of their produce. Those who dodged such controls were harshly punished. In a typical case in 1980, a Ghanaian peasant woman was sentenced to five years' imprisonment with hard labor for trying to smuggle $4.36 worth of cocoa into neighboring Togo to buy some soap. In Zambia in 1988, when market traders refused to sell goods at government-dictated prices, the authorities arrested hundreds of them, pocketed their money, seized their stock, and smashed their stalls.[13]

These days, the main problems facing entrepreneurs are the ones I have described in this chapter: poor infrastructure, poor customers, and obstructive officials. In most African countries there seems to be a healthy entrepreneurial spirit. Some ethnic groups have a stronger commercial tradition than others, but few have none. I recall talking to Pakmogda Zarata, an energetic restaurateur from Burkina Faso. Her restaurant, in a marketplace outside Ouagadougou, was unpretentious. Rough-hewn logs propped up a ceiling of thatch and old trash bags; there were no walls to speak of. The menu matched the decor. "We only serve rice," Zarata told me, "but we do cook it."

Her business plan was simple. She borrowed a small sum from a microlender, which enabled her to buy rice

191

wholesale rather than retail. Her profits rose. She now employed seven people and swanked around town on a second-hand motorcycle.

Entrepreneurial flair can only take you so far, however. Many individual African businessmen have built empires, typically in fields such as trading, trucking, or retailing, but too often these firms rely on the founder's drive and vision and fall apart when he dies.

I asked a couple of Cameroonians why this was. Paul Fokam, who founded a private bank in Cameroon in 1987, when private banks were illegal, thought it had something to do with African traditions of inheritance. "A rich man will have three or four wives, and perhaps a hundred children, if you include the ones with his mistresses. Often, there's no clear succession, so when the old man who held it all together dies, his business unravels."

His colleague, an economist called Alamine Ousmane Mey, agreed and added: "The first generation of entrepreneurs learned by doing. They are often illiterate. When they make money, they send their children to school, but they don't necessarily get them involved in the business, so the kids end up not even knowing what assets their father has, let alone how to run the firm."

If Africa is ever to succeed in more technologically advanced industries, the continent will need more than a few gung-ho entrepreneurs. A man can make a fortune buying and selling real estate with little more than an eye for location and the back of an envelope to scribble numbers on. But the real estate will probably only be worth a fortune if other, more complex businesses want to operate in the same city. And lone entrepreneurs cannot easily manufacture cars or run large insurance firms. Such businesses need legions of skilled employees: engineers, accountants, designers, salespeople, and so on. In the rich world, these people tend to work together in impersonal, professionally managed companies, often with widely dispersed ownership, in the form of shares.

Africa does not yet boast many indigenous institutions like this. One reason is that so many African professionals have emigrated. Another is that complex institutions cannot operate without a measure of trust, a belief that most people will perform their jobs honestly and as well as they can. And Africans often do not trust each other. Two European academics claim that "outside [an African's] own community . . . where rules of civic behaviour apply, there is an assumption that graft presides over all forms of exchange."[14]

This is probably an exaggeration, but I have seen plenty of evidence that a lack of trust makes it harder to get things done in Africa. In Nigeria, guests at five-star hotels must pay cash, in advance, not only for their rooms but also for the meals the manager thinks they might eat and the telephone calls he thinks they might make. When paying in dollars at the Hilton in Abuja I have had to wait while the cashier scanned each bill to make sure it was not a forgery and recorded each individual serial number in triplicate to make sure that none of his colleagues could steal any.

Nigerians, being entrepreneurial types, find ways to profit from this sorry state of affairs. I once visited a firm in Lagos called Smartcard, whose business depended on the fact that no one accepts checks in Nigeria and banks do not generally entrust customers with credit cards. This means that Nigerians have to carry around uncomfortably large wads of banknotes, which attract thieves and are not terribly hygienic: according to researchers at the University of Lagos, 86 percent of the country's notes are infested with the sorts of microbes that cause diarrhea.[15] The solution? An "electronic purse": a card that can be loaded with "e-cash" and used at hundreds of stores. It's clean, it fits in your shirt pocket, and if it's stolen, you can cancel it.

8. WIRING THE WILDERNESS

How Africa can embrace technology

Genetically modified (GM) food is "poison." That was the reason Zambia's president, Levy Mwanawasa, gave for rejecting American food aid during a famine. It was in 2002, when all the badly governed countries of southern Africa were seriously short of food.

People were dying. It was hard to say how many, because most of the victims did not actually starve to death; rather, lack of food left them weak and unable to fight off infections that might not otherwise have killed them. AIDS, of course, aggravated matters.

According to the UN World Food Programme (WFP), 2.3 million Zambians – a quarter of the population – were dangerously hungry and in urgent need of aid. America, the largest donor, had sent a big shipment of corn and soybeans, some of which had been genetically modified. Two hundred fifty million Americans had been munching this sort of stuff for seven years without detectable harm, but President Mwanawasa decided it was too risky for his starving people.

All new technology carries potential risks, as well as rewards. Some fears are fanciful. When coffee first arrived in Europe, doctors warned that it would cause sterility, stillbirths, and paralysis. When electric light bulbs were introduced, the *New York Times* warned that they might blind people. Occasionally, new inventions really are dangerous: thalidomide causes birth defects, and cars crash, especially when the driver has a mobile phone pressed to his ear. One can never prove with absolute certainty that anything is safe. But in the case of genetically modified foods, seven years of trouble-free consumption in the world's largest rich country, a nation known for its health-consciousness, food fads, and tendency to sue at the first whiff of harm, comes pretty close.

Farmers have been manipulating genomes since before they knew about genes. For thousands of years, they sought to transfer desirable traits from one plant to another by cross-breeding: this is how wild grasses were turned into wheat. They also selectively bred animals to make them fatter and tastier: this was how wild boars became pigs.

GM technology aims to achieve similar, but faster, results. It typically takes eight to twelve years to produce a better plant by cross-breeding. But if scientists can isolate a gene in one species that is associated with, say, drought resistance, they can sometimes transfer it directly into the genetic code of another species without wasting years crossing and back-crossing successive generations.

Genetic modification is more precise than cross-breeding, too. As any parent knows, sexual reproduction is unpredictable. The union of a brilliant woman and an athletic man does not always produce a brilliant and athletic child. In plants as in people, some traits are inherited, others are not. In theory, genetic modification solves this problem by transferring only the gene associated with the trait that the farmer wants.

The final advantage of genetic modification is that it makes it possible to transfer traits between unrelated species. You cannot cross-breed cacti with corn, but you can take a cactus gene that promotes drought resistance and put it in a corn plant.

So far, scientists have produced GM crops that are more resistant to viruses or insects and more tolerant of herbicides. In the future, genetic modification could fill the world's larders with high-protein cereals, vegetables with extra vitamins, and all manner of cheaper, tastier, and more nutritious foods than we currently enjoy. Researchers at Cornell University have even created bananas that contain a vaccine for hepatitis B. A single banana chip inoculates a child for one fifteenth of the price of an injection, and with fewer tears.

Against these actual and potential benefits must be set the potential dangers. Shifting genes between different species could create health risks. For example, soybeans given brazil nut genes have been found to express brazil nut proteins of the sort that might trigger allergic reactions. Soybeans are used in thousands of food products, so this could make life hazardous for people with nut allergies.

Genetically modified crops may also cause environmental problems. Pollen from GM crops can blow into fields of ordinary crops and fertilize them, which might affect ecosystems in some unpredictable way. Also, crops genetically modified to repel pests might spur the evolution of super-pests or poison other species. Laboratory tests have found that butterfly larvae are harmed when fed the pollen of plants genetically modified to express a toxin called *Bacillus thuringiensis* (Bt), which protects corn and cotton from boll worms. There is no evidence, however, that this has happened in the wild.

All these dangers are rather speculative. It is essential to test genetically modified products carefully before releasing them and to keep monitoring them afterwards. But so far there is little or no evidence that GM crops hurt either humans or the environment. The available evidence suggests that GM crops actually help to protect the environment by reducing the need for chemical pesticides.

China has embraced GM crops with gusto. The Chinese government sees the technology as one of the most powerful tools available for making farms more productive. This is a matter of immense importance: if millions of Chinese peasants can grow more rice and cotton, they will become more prosperous. Africa has been much more wary of the new technology partly, perhaps, because of the continent's strong links to Europe.

In Europe, although regulators have concluded that GM products are safe, an energetic campaign by NGOs such as Greenpeace has convinced consumers that they are not and prompted supermarkets to refuse to stock them.

Africans heed these doubts. President Mwanawasa appears to accept the Greenpeace line in its entirety, although a Greenpeace spokesman told me he did not think him wise to reject food aid during a famine. Other Africans might like to experiment with planting GM crops but hesitate to do so for fear of wrecking their exports to Europe. This is not an unreasonable fear. If an African country were to plant GM crops which then fertilized (or "contaminated," as the NGOs say) neighboring fields, European supermarkets might start refusing to buy any farm products from that country, as they could not with confidence label them "GM-free."

In Zimbabwe, Malawi, and other countries stricken with food shortages, the problem was solved by milling American grain before distributing it. Milled corn cannot be replanted, so it cannot pollinate non-GM crops.

Of course all this milling took time and money. In November 2002, I asked Judith Lewis, the World Food Programme's personable director for eastern and southern Africa, about it. "This issue totally came out of left field for us," she said. "I mean, we've been handing out GM food aid for seven years, all over the world. There were no problems until now. But now, in Zambia, we're seeing just a drip of food aid going in. We have 100,000 tons of American maize [corn] sitting in nearby ports like Durban, Maputo, and Beira, just waiting to go. But we have to send samples to South Africa to test them. This takes ten days. Then we have to get the GM maize to a mill, mill it, and put it back on the road to wherever it was supposed to be going. That can take up to two or three weeks."

All the while, people were dying. The most spare milling

capacity, Lewis told me, was in Zimbabwe, where many mills had been mothballed. But the Zimbabwean government refused to let the WFP either grind GM corn on its territory or even transport it along Zimbabwean roads. The reason cited was "biosafety," but this may have been a pretext. Robert Mugabe's regime used its monopoly of grain distribution to reward its supporters and punish dissidents. It did not want Western charities to start handing out food to members of the opposition party.

Technology cannot solve all problems. Famines are usually caused by the interplay of bad weather and bad government, with war and pestilence often lending a helping claw. Biotechnology offers no cure for the likes of Robert Mugabe. But it does offer the prospect of more and better food, and in the long term there are few more important goals than that. The world's population is swelling while the area of cultivable land is not. Somehow, farmers will have to continue squeezing more calories out of each hectare.

Past predictions that overpopulation would cause mass starvation have always proven wrong, because people have found ingenious ways to raise agricultural productivity. The techniques of the "green revolution" of the 1960s and 70s – high-yielding hybrid seeds, chemical fertilizers, pesticides, and weedkillers – worked wonders in India and China and saved, by one estimate, a billion people from starving.[1]

Africa was slow to embrace the green revolution. In Asia by 1998 an impressive 86 percent of wheat fields were sown with modern hybrid seeds, as were 65 percent of rice paddies, 70 percent of corn fields, and 78 percent of millet fields. For Africa the figures were 52 percent, 40 percent, 17 percent, and 14 percent.[2] Partly, this reflects the fact that some of these seeds were not suitable for African soil. But it also reflects a reluctance or inability on the part of African governments to promote new technologies and a reluctance among many Africans to embrace them.

Among the very poor, such reluctance is rational. All change carries risks, and when you live perpetually on the brink of starvation, all unquantifiable risks are terrifying. If a peasant with no safety net tries a new hybrid seed and his crop fails, his family may starve. But governments have no such excuse. Official technophobia seems especially perverse when you consider the benefits that technology has brought to people's lives in the past century.

Getting better all the time

I once spent a piteous morning interviewing Angolans who had trodden on landmines. It was easy to imagine, as I glanced uncomfortably at their stumps, that twentieth-century technology has done more harm than good in Africa. Cluster bombs shred limbs. Helicopter-gunships keep evil men in power.

But even in Angola, the country UNICEF rated in 1999 to be the worst place on earth, people are living nearly twice as long as their great-grandparents. A life expectancy of forty-five sounds awful by Western standards. But a century ago, Angolans, like most people throughout human history, survived for an average of only twenty-five years.[3]

The main reason for this improvement is modern medicine. Even the sad souls in Luanda's refugee camps have access to drugs. Antibiotics clear up infections that would previously have been fatal. Vaccines prevent countless children from dying before they can walk. In Angola as a whole, two thirds of one-year-olds are immunized against tuberculosis. This is one of the lowest rates on earth, but it is a vast improvement on nobody 100 years ago.

The conventional wisdom is that as rich countries innovate with ever-increasing speed, the poor are left behind. This is not true. Technology certainly makes the rich richer, but it also makes the poor less poor, not to mention healthier, better-fed, longer-lived, and supplied with a wider variety of entertainment.

Consider the most basic (and least falsifiable) indicator of well-being: staying alive. Angus Maddison, an economic historian, estimates that life expectancy in 1900 in what we now call the developing world – roughly speaking, everywhere apart from Western Europe, North America, Australasia, and Japan – was twenty-six. In the West it was forty-six, about the same as in Angola today.

Westerners now live 70 percent longer than they did a century ago, to an average of seventy-eight. People from developing countries have done better: they can expect to live two and a half times longer than in 1900, to sixty-four. These figures are astonishing. In the millennium before 1900, lifespans in Asia, Africa, and Latin America barely budged. But then again, medicine has improved more in the past 100 years than in the previous million.

Brains v. bugs

Imagine a hospital where the water is dirty, where tuberculosis is rife, and where the doctors are so ignorant that a patient has only a fifty-fifty chance of benefiting from a consultation. Imagine, too, that most of the drugs are useless, and some are poisonous. This is a fair description of what health care was like in America a century ago. One in four children died before the age of fourteen, mostly from infectious diseases. In the early twentieth century, Oliver Wendell Holmes, an American wit, declared that if all the medicines of his day were tossed into the ocean, it would be better for mankind and worse for the fish.[4]

Health care in poor countries today is rather better than that. Poor people are living longer, not because the natural human lifespan has increased, but because many of the horrors that prevent people from reaching old age are being tamed. A child born in the developing world today can expect to live eight years longer than one born thirty years ago. Even in the forty poorest countries, infant mortality fell by a third between 1970 and 1999. A recent World Bank study concluded that technical progress was the biggest single cause of reductions in mortality, accounting for 40–50 percent of the improvement between 1960 and 1990.

Vaccines, for example, have had a startling effect. Influenza, which killed between 20 and 100 million people in 1918–19, is now largely under control. Smallpox has been eradicated and measles, whooping cough, rubella, diptheria, tetanus, and tuberculosis have been curbed by vaccination. In recent decades, technology has made vaccines easier to deliver in poor countries. A droplet of polio vaccine can be swallowed – no need for needles. More heat-stable vaccines have been created which do not need refrigeration. Combination vaccines can be delivered in a single shot.

Antibiotics have been a great blessing, too. Penicillin was discovered in 1928, but it was only during the Second World War that a way to mass-produce it was invented. Infections that used to be fatal can now be quickly cured.

One of the simplest and most effective medicines ever is oral rehydration therapy (ORT), which was developed in Bangladesh and has saved millions of babies from dying of diarrhea. Take a mixture of sugar and salt, dissolve it in water, and give it to the ailing child. It prevents dehydration and so keeps her alive. Before ORT, the standard treatment was an intravenous drip, at a cost of $50 per baby. Packets of oral rehydration salts were mass-produced in the 1980s: they cost less than 10 cents each.

Despite all these advances, people in poor countries, and Africans in particular, are much sicker than they need be. Technology has conspicuously failed to conquer AIDS, which, by scuppering people's immune systems, has allowed diseases that were retreating, such as tuberculosis, to rally and attack once more. In much of eastern and southern Africa, life expectancies have actually fallen in the last decade, often quite dramatically, because of AIDS.

How can Africans fight back? Better logistics would help. Existing medical technology is not nearly as widely used as it should be. In Ethiopia and Burkina Faso, for example, under 20 percent of those who need ORT receive it.

One problem that Africans are almost powerless to solve, at least in the short term, is that most medical research is done in rich countries for the benefit of rich people. The fattest profits are to be made tackling chronic conditions that affect lots of Westerners, such as heart disease and cancer. The ills of the poor are neglected: of the 1,223 drugs introduced between 1975 and 1996, only thirteen were aimed at tropical diseases. In 1998, the world spent $70 billion on health research, but only $300 million of this was directed at developing an AIDS vaccine, and a mere $100 million was devoted to fighting malaria.

When drug firms do produce pills that might help the poor, their patents allow them to charge monopoly prices which the poor cannot pay. The patented drugs that have curbed AIDS in rich countries used to cost $10,000 a year. For most Africans this is an outlandish sum. AIDS activists have gone so far as to claim that "patents kill."

This is unfair. Without patents, there would be no incentive for private companies to invent new medicines. Drugs firms spend $300–$500 million creating a single pill. They could never recoup this investment if others were allowed to copy their drugs and sell them at a thin margin over what they cost to manufacture.

Patent protection is temporary and conditional. To win it, an invention must be original, useful, and non-obvious. The inventor must reveal how his invention works, and this information is made public. The inventor is then typically granted the sole right to sell it for seventeen to twenty years from the time the patent application was filed. For drugs, the effective monopoly period is shorter. It can take a decade for a drug firm to develop, test, and bring to market a patented molecule. This leaves only seven to ten years for the firm to cover its research costs and turn a profit.

Abolishing patents would more or less halt progress in pharmacology. But there is a strong argument for pricing drugs differently in poor countries. A treaty that most countries signed in 1994 allows governments to override patent protection during a national emergency. AIDS in Africa obviously qualifies as such an emergency.

Several drug firms, partly because of international pressure and partly because they noticed that they were not generating significant profits in Africa anyway, have started to offer AIDS drugs to Africans for less than a tenth of their normal price. This gesture has certainly prolonged some lives, but the drugs are still too expensive for most Africans, and some have been bought up by corrupt officials, shipped back to Europe, and sold, illegally, at a huge profit.

Differential pricing will not, in any case, address the other problem, that drug firms' research concentrates on problems that affect rich people. Only public money can fill the gap. As I mentioned earlier, foreign aid would lift more people out of poverty if it bankrolled vaccine research instead of dodgy governments.

Some donors see this. In 2001, the UN announced the creation of the Global Fund to Fight AIDS, Tuberculosis and Malaria, asking rich countries to chip in $7–$10 billion. In the first year, it raised $2.1 billion, which is a start. Another organization, the International AIDS Vaccine Initiative, launched by the Rockefeller Foundation, which brings together states, academics, and drug firms, started clinical trials of its first vaccine candidate in Kenya in January 2001.

The more that developing countries themselves contribute to these efforts, the more likely they are to succeed. No African country, except South Africa, can plausibly handle the whole process of drug discovery, development, testing, and marketing. But several have pockets of unique expertise or a wide variety of potentially medicinal plants.

Turning biodiversity into medicine is not easy, however. Vietnamese scientists extracted an effective malaria drug from a tree long used in traditional medicine, but there are only a handful of other recent triumphs. Congo's jungles may well hide a cure for heart disease, but no one has found it yet. The trouble is that countries with rainforests tend to lack pharmacological expertise, while the big drug firms that have the know-how are all based in countries without rainforests.

Unscrupulous Western researchers sometimes solve the problem by stealing plants from poor countries. Some firms have learned about the healing properties of plants from locals, taken this information, and patented the plant's active ingredient without acknowledging the locals' contribution or rewarding them for it. Two cancer drugs, for example, were developed using a rose periwinkle plant found in Madagascar, but Madagascar received no benefit. Stopping "biopiracy" is tricky; bacteria are easy to smuggle. But multinationals hate bad publicity, so many are striking fairer deals. The Brazilian government, for example, receives royalties from Novartis, a Swiss drug firm, for providing it with micro-organisms. Monsanto, another multinational biotech firm, is working with the Kenyan Agricultural Research Institute to create virus-resistant sweet potatoes.

Some day, biotechnology may allow scientists to modify the insects that spread disease: perhaps to create a mosquito that cannot carry malaria. Using a more basic technology, irradiation, health workers managed to eradicate sleeping sickness, a horribly debilitating disease that hits both people and their cows, from the island of Zanzibar, off the coast of Tanzania. Tsetse flies, which carry the disease, were sterilized with radiation and then released. The sterile flies mated with fertile ones, producing no offspring but convincing the fertile flies that they did not need to mate again. Eventually, the island's tsetses died out. I spoke to John Kabayo, a doctor who was trying to organize a similar feat in Ethiopia. This was clearly going to be harder as Ethiopia is not surrounded by water. But Dr. Kabayo seemed confident.

"Sleeping sickness is a poor man's disease; no one is going to develop a vaccine for it," he told me, "So we're just going to have to wipe out the tsetse flies that carry it."[5]

Fishermen on the Net

Working as a journalist in Africa, I find myself using Internet cafes a lot. Television crews need their own satellite link-ups to whizz pictures home in time for the six o'clock news, but a scribe on a weekly paper can get by with much less fancy equipment. A humble laptop with a floppy drive is all I usually carry. When I have to send a story home, I save it onto a disk, walk into a cyber-cafe, order a strong black coffee, log on, and buzz the piece to London. It's cheap and more reliable than you might think. These days, even small African towns have Web access. Sitting at a terminal in Antananarivo, the capital of Madagascar, I've looked up facts about the history of an island that has not yet been properly mapped.

The Internet has been so loudly hyped that I hesitate to add to the noise. Africans need food and medicine before they need Google. But information and communication technology (ICT) could help them lay hands on both of these more easily.

While surfing in Tanzania, I've overheard locals using Internet telephony to bypass the price-gouging state phone company, call Hong Kong, and sell hand-carved elephants for hard currency. In Niger, weather forecasts are downloaded from the Internet, relayed to local radio stations, and broadcast to cattle-herders with wind-up radios. This tells the herders where to herd their cows for the best grazing, crucial information in a country that is mostly desert.[6]

Communication, as you may have heard, is getting cheaper. Any task that can be digitized can now be done at a distance. Dial a helpline for a British bank, and you may find yourself talking to someone in South Africa. It's in roughly the same time zone and has adequate telephone lines and a lot of English-speakers who will work for a quarter of the going rate in England. The operators are glad to have jobs (staff turnover is much lower at South African call centers than at British ones), British banks save money, and their customers enjoy slightly lower bank charges as a result. In Ghana, a firm called ACS employs 1,000 locals to process American health insurance claims and bounce them back to Kentucky via satellite. None of this remotely compares with what is going on India, where the software industry employs 400,000 people. But you have to start somewhere.

Accurate, timely information is useful in almost every field. Take health care. The Internet is the quickest and cheapest way yet devised of disseminating medical research. African doctors with Web access can read journals online that they could not afford to have mailed to them. In Gambia, nurses in remote villages use digital cameras to download images of symptoms on to a PC and email them to doctors in the capital for diagnosis. Throughout Africa, outbreaks of meningitis are tracked over the Internet so that epidemics can be stopped early.

Information and communication technology could make government more efficient and accountable. Email creates an un-shreddable paper trail for decisions. In Madhya Pradesh, in India, an experimental government intranet service allowed ordinary people to get hold of official documents (farmers, for example, might want land title deeds) for as little as 10 cents. Previously, such documents were only available if the farmers bribed corrupt officials to dig them up, which could cost as much as $100. And academics find the Internet invaluable. A decade ago if a researcher in Nairobi wanted to bounce ideas off lots of other experts each day, he probably had to move to Boston. Now, he simply logs on. Cheaper communications mean more North–South collaboration and indeed more South–South collaboration. Between 1995 and 1997, Kenyan scientists co-authored papers with colleagues from eighty-one other nations.

As I write, most Africans have still never made a telephone call. But by the time you read this book, that may no longer be true. Landlines are still expensive and unreliable, but mobile telephones are spreading throughout the continent with the pace and annoying chirrups of a swarm of locusts. In 1998, only 2 million Africans had cellphones. Four years later, 30 million did.[7]

Most African cellphone firms are privately owned, and many operate in competitive markets. It shows. Walk into a mobile phone shop in Lagos or Nairobi, and your handset will be up and ringing in five minutes. The old state-owned fixed-line monopolies used to take several years to connect your house to the network and then charged exorbitant rates for woeful service. A friend of mine in Nairobi whose telephone regularly broke down paid several bribes to engineers from the state phone company to fix it until he discovered that the engineers were deliberately cutting him off again after they fixed it to earn more bribes. Another friend, who lived in Nigeria, received a colossal bill one month because someone at the state phone company had hired his office line out at night to people who wanted to call relatives in Europe.

Most Africans cannot open accounts with traditional telephone firms because they have no credit history. Private mobile firms, however, sell them pre-paid cards. When they use up all their minutes, they buy another. There is no chance – and this is tremendously important for poor people – that they will receive an unpayable bill at the end of the month.

The mobile phone companies, because they receive payment in advance, waste none of the time and money that fixed-line firms do chasing bad debtors. So their cash flow is better, and they are able to expand their networks faster. In several African countries, the number of mobile users has overtaken the number of landline users in less time than it can take to get a landline installed.

How countries go high-tech

Visitors to the Ajaokuta steel plant in Nigeria are surprised to see goats grazing among the gantries and children playing by the silent rolling mills. The Nigerian government flushed away $8 billion trying to build a steel industry at Ajaokuta and elsewhere. The idea was first proposed in the 1970s, after the oil boom began. Nigeria's military rulers saw steel as the first goose-step down a forced march to industrialization. Steel mills would turn local coke and iron ore into shiny metal, which would then be used to build railways.

Contractors from the Soviet Union, bidding to build Ajaokuta, produced a twenty-one-volume feasibility study, but it was never translated from Russian and probably never read by any Nigerian decision-makers. They wanted a steel industry whatever the cost, partly as a matter of national pride and partly because big projects brought big kickbacks. Ajaokuta has yet to produce a single bar of steel and will probably never be able to do so at a profit. Other steel mills in Nigeria operate fitfully, at a loss, and usually at a small fraction of capacity.[8]

As this story illustrates, it is hard for governments to micromanage technological change. Most African politicians want their countries to become more technologically competent. But it is not easy. To make the best use of foreign technology you need some locals who understand it. Airplanes and telephone networks need to be maintained. Foreign products sometimes need to be adapted to local conditions. And if a country is to start coming up with inventions of its own, it needs the kind of political, social, and economic arrangements that foster innovation.

The example that everyone looks to is, unsurprisingly, America. How, ask politicians from Abuja to Cape Town, can we build a Silicon Valley in our own country? The short answer is, they can't. America's thriving high-tech industries were not planned. Silicon Valley is what happens when thousands of scientists and entrepreneurs migrate to a sunny rich state with tough patent laws, a sophisticated financial system, and a culture of inventing things and then making money out of them.

All these things take time to evolve. Governments can remove obstacles and prod things in the right direction. But when they start making detailed plans they tend to come unstuck. Public investment in basic science is useful, for those who can afford it. But public investment in developing high-tech products is usually wasteful. Politicians are slow to admit mistakes; hence Nigeria's steel folly.

The head of South Africa's Medical Research Council, Malegapuru Makgoba, argues that politicians find it hard to understand scientific method because it is more or less the opposite of politics. "Politicians are trained for loyalty, whilst scientists are trained for independence. Politicians get promoted for being economical with the truth, whilst scientists get fired for bending the truth."[9]

After making these observations, Dr. Makgoba and his colleagues produced a report, based on five years of research (it was leaked in 2001), concluding that AIDS was the leading cause of death in South Africa. This contradicted President Thabo Mbeki's odd beliefs, so the government was furious. Dr. Makgoba says that the minister in the presidency, Essop Pahad, Mbeki's hatchet man, called him and threatened that he would be fired and "forgotten by history." "Part of his portfolio is to phone and threaten scientists," said Dr. Makgoba. "He is trying to overrule science with politics. It is very frightening." Pahad denies it all.[10]

But Dr. Makgoba is not the only South African scientist to complain about the president's alleged meddling. Sipho Seepe, a physicist and newspaper columnist, argues that "Mbeki conflates and confuses his political authority with intellectual authority." Hence the difficulty of persuading the president that the global medical establishment knows more than he does about AIDS. "Of course scientists can be wrong," says Dr. Seepe, "but they are usually corrected by other scientists, not by a politician with no training in science."[11]

Many of the things that governments can do to promote technology are worth doing anyway. Establishing peace and stability, for example. Clever people are mobile and prefer not to live in war zones. Another crucial factor is openness to trade and investment. Isolating yourself from the rest of the world is a good way to stay technologically backward.

I once sneaked into North Korea, pretending to be a tourist, to take a look at the world's last totalitarian state. It was a useful reminder of how fortunate we all are that the Cold War didn't go the other way. I was followed everywhere by two official guides who, if I commented on how nice a building was, would reply: "Yes, thanks to the benevolent leadership of the Dear Leader Kim Jong Il, there are many great buildings in Pyongyang."

Everywhere I looked I saw the stultifying effect of the government's policy of "self-sufficiency." Nothing invented since the 1950s appeared to have entered the country. The government tried to hide this, naturally. At an exhibition I was shown a computer with a "North Korean" operating system. It didn't do much. I asked the party functionary in charge why, and he said it was "in display mode." I re-booted it and saw the logo "Texas Instruments" flash up on the screen. The functionary was so embarrassed I felt sorry for him.

"Self-reliance" used to be a popular mantra among poor countries. In Africa, as well as Latin America and India, many governments made a virtue of shutting out foreign goods and investment. Inevitably, they shut out ideas, too. With no foreign competition, local firms had no one to learn from and little incentive to make their own products better. In Tanzania, a ban on importing computers was not wholly lifted until 1994.[12]

In the last decade or two, most developing countries have opened up a bit. Freer trade has brought new products, which can be taken apart and copied. Foreign direct investment has spread skills and technology. When BMW and Daimler Chrysler build cars in South Africa, they train African engineers and transfer know-how to their local suppliers.

High-tech trade has made a big chunk of the developing world much richer. Between 1985 and 1998, developing countries' exports of high-tech products grew twelvefold. Exports of things dug out of the ground or grown in it rose by a paltry 14 percent over the same period. By 1999, high-tech goods were actually a larger slice of developing-country exports than they were of the exports of advanced industrialized nations.

Africa, sadly, missed out. Between 1970 and 1997 African exports per head fell, from $175 to $163 (in constant 1987 dollars). If we leave out South Africa and oil-producers, Africa's cumulative terms of trade losses between 1970 and 1997 were equivalent to 120 percent of GDP.[13] That is, the prices of the sorts of things that Africa traditionally produces have fallen. Most of Africa's exports are of primary products, that is, unprocessed raw materials: copper, cocoa, and all sorts of other crops and minerals. Apart from oil, the prices of such commodities have been sliding in real terms ever since the industrial revolution. As the world grows ever more technologically advanced, the proportion of its wealth that it needs to spend on raw materials falls.

Think of a computer. The cost of the metal and plastic that go into its wiring and casing is a minute fraction of the final price tag. The expensive parts are the skills that went into making it, the software that runs it, the promise of technical support that comes with it, and the advertising and marketing that persuades customers that the whole package is worth buying. Africa produces the copper from which some of its wires are made.

But the continent is not doomed to do so for ever. Countries that start at the bottom of the technology ladder can leapfrog. In building a railway network, they don't have to bother with the steam age. When setting up a telephone system, they can skip copper wiring and go straight to fiber optics and mobile telephones. And they don't necessarily have to pay for these things themselves.

The firms that know how to wire countries are usually willing to do so at no cost to the public purse so long as they are then allowed to charge people to make calls. In fact, they will pay good money for the privilege. In 2001 Nigeria raised $570 million auctioning licenses to set up mobile networks.

Intellectual property rights, and wrongs

I was once standing in a Zambian market, browsing through a fine selection of tapes. There was a lot of Congolese dance music and a good sprinkling of Western pop: Madonna, Kenny G, Dr. Dre, and so on. Both types of music are popular in Zambia, and both types of tape had fairly obviously been pirated. (The misspellings on the packaging were a bit of a giveaway.)

Suddenly, a furious crowd surged around the corner, pursuing a man I guessed was suspected of stealing something, because he was covered in blood. They caught him and started kicking and punching him. A man on the mob's periphery, noticing the shocked look on my face, shouted at me: "This is what we do with thieves!" The robber was dragged to the police station on the other side of the marketplace. I think he survived, but I am not sure. I put down the bootleg Papa Wemba tape I was holding and bought nothing.

In Africa, few people think that piracy is immoral. Unlike those who steal sheep or loaves of bread, thieves of intellectual property are never lynched. One can understand the Africans' point of view: most patents and copyrights are held by rich Westerners who will not go hungry if a few enterprising Zambians filch their ideas. Poor countries, runs the argument, need to steal ideas, for they will never scale the technology ladder if Merck and Microsoft extract royalties at every rung.

This is a reasonable argument but only in the short term. Piracy is a cheap way to climb the lower rungs, but failure to respect intellectual property rights deters high-tech investment.

Firms will not bring new technology to countries where it can be stolen with impunity. Furthermore, if poor countries do not reward innovation, their people will have no incentive to innovate. The most inventive African country by far is the one that takes intellectual property rights most seriously: South Africa. Scientists in South Africa are actually rewarded for their efforts. So are South African musicians, up to a point. Half a dozen bootleg CDs are sold in South Africa for every genuine one, but that still leaves *kwaito* stars from Soweto much better off than Congolese *rumba* bands, who sell almost no records at home (which is a pity; the Congolese musicians sound much better).

The one area where Africa can free-ride with impunity is in regulation. It takes time, money, and expertise to determine whether a drug or foodstuff is safe. Agencies such as America's Food and Drug Administration have huge budgets and make few mistakes. Poor countries could save millions, and get valuable medicines on the shelves more quickly, if they simply decided that a product safe enough for Americans is safe enough for them, unless there is good reason to assume that, for example, it might work differently in a tropical climate.

Getting the basics right first

Most important, to take advantage of technology, Africa needs better scientific and mathematical skills. The good news is that education is improving in Africa. A hundred years ago, almost no Africans could read. Now, 60 percent of adults can. Since 1985, literacy has improved or stayed the same in every African country for which the UN Development Programme could find data. The bad news is that the data are incomplete, and the dataless countries tend to be battlefields such as Angola and Sierra Leone, so the true picture is less rosy.

One problem is that many African countries' education budgets have been captured by the elite, who want free university education for their children but are less worried about the masses who cannot even attend primary school. Zambia, for example, spends 135 times more public money on each university student than on each primary school pupil despite the fact that university students typically come from affluent families. Each year in Niger, 4,700 students receive university scholarships worth ten times the national average income while 900,000 rural children receive no education at all.[14]

This makes no sense. You cannot build an education system from the top down. There is no point having lots of universities before there are enough adequately prepared children to fill them. Besides, the benefits of primary education accrue to society at large, whereas those of higher education are more concentrated on the individual who receives it. So primary schools should have first claim on scarce public funds.

East Asian countries have tended to put first things first. Japan introduced universal and compulsory primary education in 1872, when its citizens were on average no richer than the people of Djibouti are today. Other East Asian countries achieved universal primary enrollment in the 1970s. Secondary enrollments initially lagged but surged ahead in the 1980s as the "tiger" economies boomed and demand for skilled workers soared. Tertiary enrollments rose last: in South Korea from 16 percent in 1980 to 68 percent in 1996.

The tigers have also, with the notable exception of Singapore, tended to make advanced students pay for their own tuition. In South Korea in 1993, 61 percent of upper secondary students attended private institutions, and 81 percent of university students. Poor but bright students can win scholarships. But for most university is a costly venture, which perhaps helps explain why so many Koreans opt for the kind of technical subjects that lead to well-paid careers. Koreans are 116 times more likely to study science at the tertiary level than youngsters from Burkina Faso.

Another lesson from East Asia is that how much you spend

on education is less important than how you spend it. Public education spending in East Asia was only about 2.5 percent of GNP in 1960, inching up to 2.9 percent by 1997. Other developing countries spent far more – 3.9 percent on average – while African governments spent a whopping 5.1 percent. As East Asia grew richer, the absolute level of spending rose, but not nearly to the levels common in Western Europe or North America. And yet East Asian students consistently thrashed everyone else in internationally comparable tests. How did they do it?

What went on outside the school walls was crucial: mothers nagged children to do their homework; the job market rewarded educational attainment. But what went on in the classroom was important, too. The state saw its role as making sure that every child learned to read, write, and manipulate numbers. Calculators were forbidden until students could do sums in their heads. Laggards were coached until they reached the required standard.

Teachers addressed the whole class at once, quizzing individual students from time to time to make sure everyone was following. Classes were large. In Korean primary schools in 1975 the pupil–teacher ratio was more than fifty-five to one; in secondary schools it was thirty-five to one. Big classes are thought to deprive students of individual attention. In other developing countries ratios were kept down to an average of thirty-six in primary schools and twenty-two in secondary schools, for this reason. But, given a limited budget, there is a trade-off between class size and teachers' pay. With fewer teachers, Korea was able to pay them more, relative to average income, than any other comparable country. This made it easier to recruit good teachers.

Recently, some African countries have begun to charge college students so that primary school can be free. During the 1990s both Uganda and Malawi went from spending less than half of their education budgets on primary schools to two thirds. The results have been excellent, especially in Uganda, despite protests from the elite.

Unfortunately, even in countries where primary schools are supposed to be free, parents are often hit with extra charges for books and uniforms or to supplement the teachers' salaries. Some of these charges are illegal: teachers are not supposed to demand bribes to do their jobs, and schools often keep no records of what happens to the extra cash they squeeze out of parents. Some charges are pointless: Uganda greatly increased enrollments by scrapping uniforms, which many poor families cannot afford.

There are many other things that African governments can do to foster a more educated population. Since money is always a problem, they could spend less on defense, which absorbs on average half as much as health and education combined (and four times as much in Sudan). They could stop expelling girls who become pregnant, a common practice. And they could copy South Africa's program of handing out free peanut-butter sandwiches to primary school pupils. Malnutrition stunts a child's ability to learn.

Once people have valuable expertise, however, keeping them is a problem. Africa loses 23,000 professionals each year,[15] which helps explain why Chad has only one doctor for every 30,000 people.[16] It is the brightest and best-educated who leave: émigré Africans in America are among the most highly educated of all ethnic groups in that country. The more demand there is for a particular skill, the easier it is for those who have it to find work in a rich country, so software specialists are especially flighty.

One recent emigrant was Mark Shuttleworth, by far the most successful South African Internet entrepreneur. Shuttleworth is best known among his compatriots as the first African in space: he paid the Russian space program several million dollars to let him join one of their crews in orbit. He could afford such an expensive holiday because, while still in his twenties, he created software that let people do business online without fear of having their credit card details stolen. In 1999, he signed a deal to sell his company for $575 million. At the time he said he would never leave Africa, but less than two years later he packed his bags for London, griping that South African capital controls prevented him from making the most constructive use of his money. "If I see some crazy project in Norway I want to invest in," he said, "I should be able to get the money from South Africa now, not in six months. That is what entrepreneurs do."[17] His case is not typical, of course, but if African countries want to keep their home-grown talent, they will have to allow them a bit more freedom. Still, Shuttleworth says he'll return one day.

9. BEYOND THE RAINBOW NATION

South Africa's prospects

Apartheid was beyond parody. Black and white South Africans were ordered by law to live separately, but whites employed several million blacks to clean their houses, cut their lawns, nurse their children, lay their bricks, and pick their grapes. Inequality before the law produced cruel absurdities. On one occasion a black woman was convicted of sleeping with a white man on the basis of her own confession and jailed. The white man was found innocent, however, because the only evidence against him was the testimony of his black lover.[1]

No one could come up with a foolproof definition of "black" and "white" (unsurprisingly, as it is not possible) but the authorities devised tests for borderline cases. If a pencil, placed in the subject's hair, stayed there, he was deemed curly-haired and therefore "Native." If he played rugby rather than soccer, he was possibly "colored" (mixed race) rather than black. Each year, hundreds of South Africans were racially re-classified.

No satirist could create fiction more grotesque than the reality of white supremacist rule. But some tried.

Tom Sharpe, a British writer who was deported from South Africa in 1961, wrote *Indecent Exposure,* a blood-flecked farce set in what is now KwaZulu-Natal. What would happen, Sharpe asked himself, if one took the thinking behind apartheid to a preposterous extreme? Take the apartheid leaders' horror of inter-racial sex, combine it with the brutality of the old South

African police force, and you have Luitenant Verkramp, the policeman anti-hero of Sharpe's novel. Verkramp tries to cure his constables of their habit of raping black women – not because he feels sorry for the women but because he believes it immoral for black and white to breed together. His solution is gruesome. He has his men strapped into chairs, shown pictures of naked black women, and given electric shocks to make them associate black womanhood with pain.[2]

It was an outrageous parody. But what Sharpe could not have known was that it was not far from the truth. The South African army really did use electric shock treatment – to try to make gay soldiers straight. They used pictures of naked men rather than black women, but the principle is the same.[3]

A paradise, for some

I arrived in South Africa in 1998, as Nelson Mandela's presidency was entering its final year, and was struck by all the things that usually strike new arrivals. Perhaps more so. My previous jobs were in London, Tokyo, and Seoul: three cramped, crowded, costly, safe, efficient cities with iffy weather. Johannesburg is rather different.

The weather is perfect, for a start: warm and sunny, but never humid. South Africa is huge and sparsely populated, so space is cheap. My wife and I rented probably the largest house we'll ever live in, eight minutes from the *Economist*'s office, with a kitchen bigger than my whole apartment had been in Tokyo and a swimming pool and a lemon tree in the garden. The food is great, too. In season, hawkers at traffic lights sell boxes of avocados, softer and more flavorsome than the little cannon-balls sold in British supermarkets and one twentieth of the price. Shop shelves groan with fresh asparagus, Knysna oysters, and unfeasibly large ribs. A bottle of good Cape chardonnay in a Jo'burg restaurant costs slightly more than a large can of beer from a Japanese vending machine. All in all, life in South Africa's commercial capital is pretty comfortable.

Except that I'm only describing the northern suburbs, an island of middle-class indulgence surrounded by grim workers' townships and plastic-shack squatters' camps. It is one of the worst travel-writing clichés to describe a country as a "land of contrasts," but the phrase is hard to avoid when describing South Africa. It is like a European archipelago dropped into an African ocean. The Third World lives in a shed at the bottom of the First World's garden, which he weeds on Wednesdays.

South Africa is Africa's best hope. It has by far the continent's largest and most sophisticated economy. If South Africa prospers, it could pull the rest of the continent in its wake, as Japan did in Asia. If it were to stagnate, or revert to tyranny, it would be as if someone had poured sugar into the continent's gas tank. So what are South Africa's prospects?

A gentler kind of government

In many ways, the leaders of the African National Congress, the party that has governed South Africa since 1994, have behaved well. Many senior ANC members were imprisoned and tortured by the old regime, but they have not sought revenge. South Africa is no longer a country where ordinary citizens are terrified of their government, although the police can still be rough. The death penalty has been abolished, as has corporal punishment in schools.

South Africa has become a freer, more tolerant place. Black South Africans are no longer barred from traveling where they please. Young white men are no longer conscripted to go and strafe neighboring countries. Anti-apartheid guerrillas have found jobs in government and started eating at smart restaurants instead of bombing them.

Abortion and gay sex are now legal. The constitution of 1996 promises freedom of expression, information, movement, and association, not to mention the rights to privacy, access to adequate housing, and a clean environment. For a country that until recently deprived nine tenths of its population of full citizenship, this has been a dramatic change.

Some of South Africa's new constitutional rights are harder to guarantee than others. The "right" to adequate housing implies that someone has a duty to build adequate houses for people who don't have them. In practice, this has been interpreted to mean that the government has to make reasonable efforts to provide the roofless with shelter. This it has tried to do: between 1994 and 2002, 1.4 million neat new brick houses were built with government subsidies of about $2,000 each. One study found that only a third of these houses were of a "suitable standard"; but they were still much better than the hovels they replaced.[4]

The government has done several other things that have greatly improved the lives of poor South Africans. By 2003, it was supplying free piped water, up to a modest limit, to 26 million of South Africa's 45 million people. The state has also brought electricity to many who previously relied on paraffin to light their homes and cook their food. Between 1996 and 2000, the proportion of homes with electric power rose from 55 percent to 70 percent.[5] This has meant fewer lethal fires in crowded slums.

Not only has the government brought services to the poor, but it has given them money too. Pensions, mostly. Having converged in the last years of apartheid, state pensions for black and white South Africans were equalized. In many townships and rural villages, old women have become the most reliable breadwinners for large extended families. The monthly pension was only about $80 in 2001, but for many households this meant the difference between eating and not eating.

A safer place to do business

All this was achieved without printing money. A glance over the border at Zimbabwe shows how important this is. South Africa's public finances under the ANC have been more carefully managed than they were under the old regime. Macroeconomic policy has been better than in living memory.

The government still spends a bit more than it receives in tax revenues, but the budget deficit shrank steadily from a worrying 9.1 percent of GDP in 1993 to an estimated 2.4 percent in 2003.[6] Inflation fell too, from a peak of 18 percent in 1986 to 5 percent by late 2003, although it crept back up to 12 percent by late 2002. Trades unions and left-wingers within the ANC put tremendous pressure on the government to spend more and let inflation rise, but the party leaders understand that the gains from fiscal irresponsibility would probably be fleeting.

With sanctions ended, South Africa has become, in many ways, an easier place to do business. Fiscal and monetary policies have been consistent and conservative. Trade barriers, once towering, have been lowered several notches. Currency controls have been relaxed and may yet be abolished. Corporate governance has improved: companies have been obliged to publish more transparent accounts, and insider trading has been curbed.

As I write, however, all these reforms have yet to spur much growth. Average incomes have not fallen under the new regime, but they have not risen much either. Between 1994 and 2002, economic growth averaged 2.8 percent a year, outstripping population growth of 1.8 percent. This was much better than the previous twelve years, during which growth was a wretched 0.6 percent a year. But many black South Africans actually grew poorer under black rule, mainly by losing their jobs.

Can't fire? Won't hire

Although the black middle class expanded swiftly in the early years of ANC rule, so did the number of poor South Africans, almost all of them black. Joblessness exploded. Using a strict definition (counting only those who actively sought work in the last month), the number of unemployed black South Africans rose from 1.6 million in 1994 to 3.6 million in 2001. Using an expanded definition, including those who want to work but have given up looking, the number rose from 3.2 million to 6 million over the same period. Put differently, between 31 percent and 43 percent of black South Africans were jobless in 2001.[7] Among unskilled rural black women, the figure was more like two thirds.

The rise in joblessness has largely been a consequence of the government's efforts to protect workers. Besides all their racial laws, the ANC, urged on by its union allies, has passed a series of laws obliging firms to treat their employees more generously.

Firms must grant maternity leave, increase overtime rates, and pay a "skills levy" that is reimbursed only if the firm spends money on the kind of training that the government thinks its workers need. How a bureaucrat might know the answer to this question is not explained. Minimum wages are negotiated between unions and the larger firms in an industry and then extended to smaller firms in the same industry, whether they were party to the agreement or not. Since larger firms can usually afford to pay more, this makes it harder for small businesses to get started. Jobless South Africans tell pollsters that they would be willing to accept pay packets roughly half the typical minimum wage, but union leaders insist that they should not be allowed to.

To a European, some of these rules might sound unremarkable. But South Africa is not Europe. The ANC has tried to grant First-World legal privileges to a workforce with largely

Third-World skills. The trouble is, workers with few skills do not produce enough to enable their employers to pay them generously – which is why the South African government has found its own laws impossible to obey. In 2000, the minister in charge of the civil service sought an exemption from some of the rules, as did the state-owned airline.

Some labor laws only apply to firms with more than fifty employees, so firms try hard to keep their headcount below this figure, by sub-contracting, for example. Thabo Mbeki, the president, sees this as quite a big problem. He once recounted how he had visited a factory and asked the boss how many employees he had. "About fifty," was the answer. But Mbeki could see 300. Most of them were contract workers, explained the boss, employed by labor brokers, and therefore not his responsibility.[8] The government later passed new rules restricting the use of sub-contractors.

When sacking staff or retrenching, bosses must follow long and complex procedures to the letter. A small technical violation of these procedures can lead to awards of up to a year's salary to each employee involved. Most businessmen I talked to in South Africa felt that the labor courts were biased against them. For small employers, sacking unwanted staff can be an excruciating hassle, as a friend of mine, Michael, found out. He was the Johannesburg bureau chief for a British newspaper, which is to say, he was in charge of a two-man office, consisting of himself and an assistant who was supposed to run errands and generally make life easier for him while he struggled to meet deadlines.

Michael told me that, shortly after he arrived in South Africa, he discovered that his assistant had borrowed the company car without permission or a driving license, crashed it, and tried to cover up his tracks. When Michael was out, he ran up a bill on the office phone that exceeded his salary, including 258 calls in four months to friends and relatives in Zimbabwe. Michael said he gave him five written warnings to stop and countless spoken ones, but to no avail. Eventually, he decided to fire him but found that he could not. After a year of preparing for hearings, attending hearings, and paying legal fees, he was ordered by a labor arbitrator to give the man another chance.

If you fire him, the arbitrator said, he won't find work again – which was doubtless true. But if workers are this hard to fire, employers have a strong incentive not to hire them in the first place. South Africa's labor laws are supposed to be pro-poor, but their effect is anything but. They may benefit those who already have jobs, but they also make it harder for the jobless, who are mostly much poorer, to find work.

A rough nation

Those with no other means of earning a living sometimes turn to crime. Joblessness can lead to alienation, and poverty gives people an incentive to steal. With guns easily available, plenty of rich people worth robbing, and a tradition of revolutionary violence that dates back to the days when the ANC called for the townships to be made "ungovernable," you would expect South Africa to be a dangerous place. It is.

According to one survey, an incredible 11 percent of fifteen-year-old boys think that "jack-rolling" (recreational gang-rape) is "cool," and one South African man in four admits to having raped someone.[9] The average South African is five times more likely to be murdered than the average American. (This rate is slightly better than it was in the early 1990s, largely because political violence has almost stopped.)

The popular mood seems to be that brutality should be met with brutality. Most South Africans want to bring back hanging. In 1999, a front page of the *Sunday World*, a black newspaper, showed a photograph of a dead man sitting in a lavatory cubicle, his brains smeared on the wall. The caption explained that he had stolen a mobile telephone and then shot himself rather than face the lynch mob outside.

The same year, the BBC aired footage of South African police officers, *who knew they were being filmed*, kicking, stubbing out cigarettes on, and goading their dogs to bite some carjacking suspects. The item attracted a volley of complaints from South African viewers, several of whom fumed that the BBC's reporter should have left the officers alone, as they were only doing their job.

Both crime and the response to it seem to be fired by a palpable anger in South African society. This anger may have political roots. Many whites are furious that they no longer run the country, while many blacks are frustrated that they are not yet rich. The least intelligent whites, for whom apartheid job reservation was most beneficial, are probably the angriest now that it has gone. A couple of white security guards used to patrol the street where I lived in Johannesburg in a state of permanent rage that they no longer had nice jobs working for the state railway firm. One used to cradle his pistol and say things like: "I hate the fucking *kaffirs*. I fucking hate them. I want to fucking shoot them all." He was soon fired and replaced with a more personable black guy.

In most parts of South Africa, but especially in rural areas, people assume that the police are powerless to catch criminals. So vigilante groups, including a couple of large, well-organized ones, are uncomfortably popular. I once arrived at a little hotel near Kruger National Park with a British friend, who saw a snarling leopard logo on the wall and asked me what it was. I explained that it meant that the place paid protection money to the local vigilante group, Mapogo a Mathamaga, which was notorious for dangling suspected thieves over crocodile-infested rivers until they confessed.

"No, really," he said, "what is it?" I assured him that I wasn't joking. Our guide, a kindly middle-aged lady, chipped in, recounting with approval how vigilantes "catch criminals, give them a bloody good hiding, and sometimes they don't get up again."

Under apartheid, the police's job was to crush subversion, and their main obstacle was that everyone hated them. Black policemen were deemed traitors and liable to be "necklaced," which meant having a burning tire filled with gasoline placed around their necks. At a police station in Soweto, officers told me how, in the 1980s, they sometimes awoke to the sound of hand grenades being lobbed through the window.

In the new South Africa, the same policemen are supposed to catch common criminals, and their main hurdle is their lack of detective skills. The ANC government, many of whose leaders have vivid memories of bleeding in police cells, have made it clear that police are no longer allowed to kick confessions out of suspects. The trouble is, many police are unfamiliar with more modern ways of securing convictions.

Some are barely literate and have trouble processing the paperwork on which they spend roughly two-thirds of their time. Even when charge sheets are properly filled in, they can vanish if the right person is slipped a few hundred rand. Courts are gridlocked. Prosecutors and police have not figured out how to cooperate smoothly. My reason for visiting that police station in Soweto was to see a new computer system, paid for by local businesses, which was supposed to help the police share and analyze data. But when I got there no one knew how to work it. The result of all this muddle is that for every fifty carjackings, only one hijacker is jailed.[10] The knowledge that they probably won't be caught emboldens criminals.

In 1999, the government launched an FBI-style elite detective corps called the Scorpions. The unit has enjoyed a few high-profile successes. But South Africans will not start laying off their security guards or disbanding their vigilante bands until ordinary policemen become effective.

The mind of the ANC

One of the less sensible tricks the government tried to ease citizens' fear of crime was to stop publishing crime statistics for a while, on the grounds that they were inaccurate. It's a minor, but revealing, example. Many within the ANC are comfortable with the constraints of an open, liberal democracy, but many are not. Officially, the party subscribes to all the ideals of the constitution, for example that "anyone has the right of access to any information held by the state."[11] But when such information makes those in power look bad, they are sometimes tempted to suppress it.

When a report by the respected Truth Commission mentioned that, while the ANC was a rebel movement, it had tortured and killed some of its own members who were suspected of treachery, the party tried to block its publication.[12] This was foolish. Had the party not drawn attention to this (well-documented) allegation, few people would have noticed it. The bulk of the report dealt with atrocities committed by the apartheid regime. The passages criticizing the ANC were shorter and less grisly. But because the then-deputy president, Thabo Mbeki, did not want his party to be criticized at all, he made it look less tolerant and democratic than it was. Fortunately, he was overruled by his boss, Nelson Mandela, and by the High Court.

How significant this incident was will become clear only with hindsight. Optimists dismiss it as an unthinking error by a party with less than five years experience in government. Pessimists fear that it could be an indication of how the ANC might behave if its grip on power were ever threatened, which currently it is not.

There are several reasons for optimism. The constitution, for one. South Africa also has a vibrant press that does not fear to lampoon the mighty (although the public broadcaster, which dominates radio and television, is tame and turgid). The judiciary shows no sign of kowtowing to the executive. Opposition parties in parliament energetically savage policies they think unwise and loudly complain about corruption.

But there are reasons for pessimism, too. One is the government's choice of friends. ANC leaders tend to be blind to the faults of anyone who chipped in to assist their fight against white rule. ANC MPs gave Fidel Castro a standing ovation when he made a speech in the South African parliament in 1998. On a state visit to Havana in 2001, President Mbeki praised Cuba's "passionate humanism." His foreign minister, Nkosazana Dlamini-Zuma, who had spent her life struggling for universal suffrage in South Africa, dismissed the idea that Cubans might also want it. "Would you rather be . . . lying in the gutter with a vote, or a poor person in Cuba?" she asked.[13]

The ANC's apparent support for Robert Mugabe is even more worrying. It is not universal, by any means. Nelson Mandela has made it clear he thinks that Mugabe is a despot and even made a veiled call for Zimbabweans to overthrow him by force.[14] Tito Mboweni, the central bank governor and an ANC stalwart, said in 2001 that "the wheels have come off" in Zimbabwe.[15]

But Mbeki and his inner circle take a different line. To Western diplomats and journalists, they say that they find the events of the last few years in Zimbabwe very troubling, but they are working quietly behind the scenes for a diplomatic solution because it would be foolish to provoke unrest by criticizing Mugabe too explicitly.

Fair enough. But there seems to be more to it than this. South Africa's official observer missions at the elections Mugabe brazenly stole in 2000 and 2002 declared both to have been "free and fair." They did not have to do this. Nor were they forced to invite one of Mugabe's most thuggish lieutenants, Emmerson Mnangagwa, as a guest of honor to an ANC national conference in 2002. The crowd greeted him with tumultuous applause. Mbeki hugged him and described Zimbabwe's ruling party as "our ally and fellow liberation movement," which he said was doing everything it could "to address the challenge of ensuring a better life for all the people of this sister country, both black and white."[16]

Can he possibly believe this? I hope not. There are other plausible explanations for Mbeki's reluctance to criticize his neighbor. Mbeki's brother, Moeletsi, outlined a fairly cynical one during an interview. He argued that the South African government "doesn't want to take responsibility for the undoing of the present government in Zimbabwe, because if it undoes the present government, then it has a moral responsibility to reconstitute a new government." No one, he said, "wants to pay the price . . . of the clean up."[17]

Another possibility is that President Mbeki sees Zimbabwe's problems as primarily a clash between a black liberation leader and an old colonial power, Britain. He does not want to take the white man's side, according to this argument, partly out of racial and comradely solidarity, and partly because he fears black South African voters would disapprove.

Then again, perhaps Mbeki does not want to lean too hard on Mugabe because he does not want to see power won by an opposition party like Zimbabwe's, which has roots in the trade union movement. The most likely future threat to ANC dominance will come from South Africa's trade unions, which are currently part of the ruling alliance but are growing restless.

I suspect that all of these explanations are true. Mbeki could easily topple Mugabe, simply by turning off the electricity in Zimbabwe, much of which comes from South Africa. But he does not, because it would be too much trouble and might dent his African nationalist credentials. And he will not even talk to the Zimbabwean opposition (i.e., the rightful government of Zimbabwe) because that might give heart to the South African opposition.

Not that there is much hope of that. South Africa's opposition parties, though feisty, are midgets; Nelson Mandela calls them "Mickey Mouse parties." For now, important policy debates take place within the ANC. Disagreements are common: the ruling party is a broad church, including both communists and free-marketeers, both Africanists and liberals. All that its members really have in common is that they all opposed apartheid. With apartheid gone, so is the party's ideological glue. Mbeki hears constant grumbling from leftists within the ANC, particularly those who are also members of the unions or the South African Communist Party. The leftists want huge increases in taxes and spending, even tougher protections for workers, and an end to privatization. Some quite senior ANC leaders make no secret of their loathing of free enterprise. Kgalema Motlanthe, the party general secretary, told workers in May 2000 that "You must intensively hate capitalism and engage in a struggle against it."[18]

Such views are common within the ANC but are not party policy. Though himself a former member of the communist party, Mbeki realized several years ago that the hard left has no answers, and he has used his considerable political skills to neutralize it, co-opting the more able left-wingers with plum jobs. Mbhazima Shilowa, South Africa's most charismatic union boss, was made premier (governor) of Gauteng, the province that includes Johannesburg and Pretoria. In the Mbeki cabinet, several of the most Thatcherite tasks were given to members of the communist party. In 2001, communists were in charge of privatizing state-owned industries, lowering trade barriers, and refusing pay raises to public sector unions. Faced with the option of either ditching their beliefs or losing their jobs, they performed these tasks adequately, or at least better than you would have expected.

A greater risk than socialism is that the ANC's unchallenged hegemony could corrupt it. For as long as most South Africans remember apartheid, the liberators will keep on winning elections. If you are a South African who wants to get rich through politics, the ANC is obviously the party to join. If you are black, all the better. It is party policy to support black-owned firms, so you can hand out contracts to your relatives and claim to be promoting "transformation."

The top levels of the South African government seem quite clean. But in provincial and local governments, corruption is a huge problem. "Little did we suspect," sighed Nelson Mandela, "that our own people, when they got that chance, would be as corrupt as the apartheid regime. That is one of the things that has really hurt us."[19]

Comparison with the old days is tricky, because the new regime sets itself higher standards. If an apartheid-era bureaucrat did his job efficiently and honestly, this was not necessarily a good thing because his job might have been to bulldoze black people's houses. If, on the other hand, an ANC appointee snaffles funds intended for poverty relief, schoolchildren go without breakfast.

Chaos in local government helps crooked officials pilfer without fear of punishment. Some of this chaos dates back to the creation of black "homelands" by the apartheid government. The old regime, which was always trying to devise convoluted justifications for racial tyranny, came up with the idea that if it granted "independence" to a few blobs of South African territory, it could dump unemployed blacks there and disown responsibility for them. Pretoria spent vast sums building tinpot capital cities and propping up puppet black governments in these homelands, for the exercise was intended not merely to deceive outsiders but also to allow white South Africans to kid themselves that what they were doing was moral.

One of the results was to make South Africa more of a bureaucratic spaghetti-spill than it already was. In 1987, including all the homelands, South Africa had eleven presidents or prime ministers, eighteen health ministers and countless ambassadors sent from one part of the country to another.[20] Integrating the homelands into the new South Africa has been an administrative nightmare. For example, in the Eastern Cape, one of the poorest of South Africa's nine provinces, a white area (with a largely black population) had to be merged with two black homelands, each with their own bureaucracy, flag, anthem, army with more majors than privates, and so on. Homeland bureaucrats were notoriously slack and corrupt. White bureaucrats were notoriously slack and hostile to blacks. There were far too many of both groups, they were split between the provincial capital city and the two former homeland capitals, and they were almost impossible to sack.

To add to the confusion, there were nowhere near enough competent accountants in the province, and few of them wanted to work for the government. In 1998–99, ten out of fourteen provincial government departments in the Eastern Cape, which between them controlled 97 percent of the provincial budget, failed to submit proper accounts to the auditor-general.[21] Such laxity made it hard to catch light-fingered officials, of whom there were many. In 2000, South Africa's main anti-corruption watchdog had 27,000 cases outstanding in the Eastern Cape.[22]

Even when crooked bureaucrats are exposed, not much happens to them. After a tip-off from a bank, a senior official in the accounts division of an Eastern Cape department was arrested in 1996 for allegedly embezzling a million rand. But the police docket disappeared, the case was dropped, and the woman in question kept her job. Bureaucrats caught stealing are sometimes simply made to return the loot. "In many cases this amounts to being 'punished' by being given an interest-free loan," complained one academic.[23]

President Mbeki occasionally frets about "careerists" within the ANC but angrily disputes the idea that the party is too powerful. On the contrary, in 1998 an ANC discussion document, written by one of his closest advisers, gave the following insight into the party's ambitions. Transformation of the state, it said, "entails, first and foremost, extending the power of the NLM [National Liberation Movement, i.e., the party] over all the levers of power: the army, the police, the bureaucracy, intelligence structures, the judiciary, parastatals, and agencies such as regulatory bodies, the public broadcaster, the central bank and so on."[24]

This sort of comment fuels the worst fear about the ANC. One reason that so much attention has been paid to recent events in Zimbabwe is that some people see the place as an omen of what might happen to South Africa. Zimbabwe's ruling party was once, like the ANC, widely respected for supplanting a white racist regime and then preaching national reconciliation. But two decades of virtually unchallenged power turned ZANU into a giant patronage machine, with leaders convinced that their role in overthrowing white rule gave them the right to govern forever.

If, in twenty years time, the ANC looked like losing power, would it do a Mugabe? ANC leaders find the question insulting. We believe in democracy, they say, which is why we fought for it for so long. Maybe, but some ANC leaders have an odd view of what democracy is. After local elections in December 2000, S'bu Ndebele, the ANC chairman in KwaZulu-Natal province, threatened all the blacks, coloreds, and Indians who voted for the opposition that there would be "consequences for not voting for the ANC. When it comes to service delivery, we will start with the people who voted for us and you will be last." That threat was hardly in the spirit of the constitution, but it drew no rebuke from the party leadership.[25]

Black expectations, white fears

South Africa has changed dramatically since 1994, but blacks and whites see these changes rather differently. To oversimplify somewhat: blacks resent the fact that white South Africans are still richer and only grudgingly apologetic about the past. Whites resent the fact that they pay most of the nation's taxes and receive little in return.

Both grievances are real. Most white South Africans live in comfort, while jobless blacks live in squalor and die young. Many black South Africans argue that since whites' wealth was accumulated through the exploitation of voteless black workers, whites should be begging forgiveness and handing over more of their money.

Few white South Africans share this view. Many never voted for apartheid, and among those who did many feel that by handing over power without being forced to, they have settled their debt to their black compatriots. To the idea of paying reparations, many middle-class whites scoff that they already pay income tax at up to 42 percent each year, sales tax at 14 percent, dividends tax, capital gains tax, and a host of other levies. "And what do we get for it?" a white economist asked me. "The public schools are awful, so we educate our children privately. We pay for private health insurance because public hospitals are a nightmare. And we hire private security guards because the police are useless."

Of course, prosperous blacks pay taxes too, and the richest also pay for private schools, health insurance, and security guards. But they tend not to resent it as much as white South Africans do, because so many owe their prosperity to the government.

"Black economic empowerment" has, understandably, been one of the ANC's top priorities. Many thousands of blacks have been hired as civil servants or managers at state-owned firms. The government has also tried to create a black business class in record time.

It has tried to do this by fiat. Banks were leaned on to lend money to well-connected black businessmen, usually former ANC bigwigs, to buy chunks of white businesses. White-owned conglomerates, eager to please the government, sold mines, newspapers, and banks to black consortia. These businesses were expected to prosper under black control for three reasons. First, they would win more government contracts. Second, they would enjoy easier relations with black trades unions. Third, they would be better at selling to black consumers. The share prices of these so-called "black chip" firms were supposed to rise, and the owners were supposed to repay their bank loans out of dividends or capital gains.

The trouble with this theory was that it was nonsense. None of the new black tycoons had much experience of running large companies. Few made a success of it. When the Johannesburg stock exchange plunged after the Asian crisis of 1997, many new black businessmen found themselves unable to service the debts they had incurred to become tycoons in the first place. The banks could have foreclosed on them but decided that it would be politically unwise to do so.

As a result of all these "empowerment" deals, the black share of the value of firms listed on the Johannesburg stock exchange rose from nothing when the ANC came to power to 9.6 percent in 1998. It then fell again, to 5.3 percent in 2001, partly because investors noticed that many of these firms were badly managed.[26]

The drive for black empowerment has produced some perverse role models for young black entrepreneurs. The richest black businessmen have largely got that way by parlaying political influence into a share of someone else's business. Few new factories are built this way, and few new jobs are created. A few well-connected blacks have become honkingly rich overnight, but there is obviously a limit to how many people can be empowered this way.

What South Africa really needs is for members of the black majority to set up, starting from scratch, some firms of their own. There have been a few successes, such as Motswedi Technology Group (a computer firm) and Herdbuoys (an advertising agency). Encouragingly, the number of black franchise-holders doubled between 1995 and 2000.[27] But in general black townships, even the most densely populated, have remarkably little commercial buzz. I was always struck, when walking around Soweto, how few of its 3–4 million inhabitants ever tried to sell me anything. Compared to the mobbing one receives from street vendors in Brazil, India, or Thailand, Soweto seems pleasantly calm. But its calm may not augur success.

Frustrated at the slow pace of black empowerment, a commission led by Cyril Ramaphosa, a former ANC leader who is now South Africa's most prominent black tycoon, argued that the state should do more to speed it up. The commission recommended in 2001 that chunks of state pension funds be reserved for investment in black businesses and that white firms should be compelled to appoint more black directors and offer more contracts to black-owned firms.

Ramaphosa argues that that state-driven black empowerment will make the economy grow faster and so benefit everyone.[28] This is unlikely. Where contracts with black firms make commercial sense, white firms are likely to sign them without compulsion. The marginal effect of making such deals compulsory is to force firms to sign the contracts that they would not otherwise have signed, that is, the ones that do not make commercial sense.

Under pressure from the government, firms in some industries have drawn up "black empowerment charters," typically promising that, say, 25 percent of the industry will be in black hands by 2010. To achieve this, they will have to sell chunks of their businesses to blacks. The government insists that such deals will be made at "market" prices, but the market price of an oil firm or a mine is obviously affected by the fact that its owners are obliged to sell it. White firms submit because they fear that the alternative might be worse. They would rather surrender a quarter of their business now than have the whole thing nationalized in ten years' time.

But black business cannot rely on handouts forever. As a proportion of the total, South Africa's white population will shrink for the foreseeable future. The white birth rate is lower than the black one, and many whites are emigrating. Older whites, whose houses and savings are tied up in South Africa and who cannot afford the rent in London or Sydney, tend to stay. But the young and gifted, who do not see why they should be punished for their parents' crimes, head for countries where they can learn new skills, earn hard currency, and not be discriminated against. Some will spend a few years abroad, gain marketable experience, and return to South Africa's sunshine and cheap restaurants. But others will not.

Some South Africans rejoice at the "chicken run," arguing that emigrants are traitors – and probably racists, too – so the country is better off without them. But if South Africa is to prosper, the dwindling number of white taxpayers needs to be replaced by a black business class that is not dependent on the government for its profits. Someone has to pay for all those public works programs.

South Africa has a better shot at creating a genuinely entrepreneurial black business class than most other African countries. The roads in South Africa are better, the airlines run on time, and all the support services that businesses need are in place, more or less. What is missing is a wider understanding that wealth is something you have to create.

In late 2002, I found myself sitting at a table with South Africa's mining minister, Phumzile Mlambo-Ngcuka, and a group of up-and-coming black mining barons. She was trying to persuade me that a proposed forced march to black mine ownership would be good for business and good for the country. She sensed that I was not convinced.

"Why are you so cynical?" she asked.

I glanced to my left, at a suave representative of the new black entrepreneurial class who was sitting there. It was Bridgette Radebe, a cabinet minister's wife.

Conclusion: One Step at a Time

A Tanzanian child began to shake uncontrollably. The doctor guessed, correctly, that she was in the grip of malarial convulsions. But the child's mother diagnosed that her daughter had been seized by evil spirits and, knowing that if the doctor gave her an injection to calm her, those spirits would escape through the needle-hole and possess more victims, she clasped the girl to her chest and fled from the clinic.

The clinic staff were aghast. If the child was taken back to her village, she would surely be subjected to the traditional "cure" for convulsions, where the victim is put under a blanket and made to inhale the smoke from burning elephant dung until she passes out. This would probably not address the underlying cause of her sickness, namely the millions of malarial parasites cavorting in her bloodstream. So they chased after the mother and persuaded her to return to the clinic by promising that her daughter would not be given an injection. Instead, they gave her a tranquilizer, Valium, via a suppository. When the shaking stopped, they were then able to give her quinine to tackle the parasites, and she was cured.

I was told this story by Harun Kasale, a Tanzanian doctor, who was trying to explain some of the difficulties of delivering medicine to the poorest of the poor. Many rural Tanzanians believe that diseases have supernatural causes, which prompts them to seek supernatural remedies. Instead of trusting conventional medicine, they turn to traditional healers. Some traditional treatments may have healing properties, but many are useless and possibly dangerous. They remain popular, however, not least because they tend to be much cheaper and nearer than the nearest clinic.

Dr. Kasale was trying to make it easier for rural Tanzanians to get proper health care. He was working on a ponderously named scheme with a simple premise: the Tanzania Essential Health Interventions Project (TEHIP) set out to show that even a tiny health budget, if spent rationally, could make a big difference.

Backed by the Tanzanian health ministry and a Canadian charity called the International Development Research Centre (IDRC), Dr. Kasale and his colleagues carried out an experiment. They took two miserably poor rural districts, with a combined population of 700,000, and tried to find out how many lives could be saved by budgeting more logically. The results were so startling that I flew out to Tanzania to have a look.

The experiment was conducted in Morogoro and Rufiji, two sprawling slabs of bush the size of Belgium. I landed in Dar es Salaam, the commercial capital, and drove out westwards to Morogoro with Dr. Kasale. It was as beautiful as poor rural areas usually are. Coconut palms glistened in the morning mist, dazzling sunlight played on green-cloaked mountains, and every ten-dollar shack had a million-dollar view.

The people in Morogoro live much as they have since agriculture first reached Tanzania, growing starchy vegetables, eating what they need, and trading the surplus, if any.

Before the experiment began, annual health spending in Tanzania was about $8 a head. In Morogoro and Rufiji, IDRC added $2 a head to the pot, on condition that it was spent rationally. By this the donors meant that the amount of money spent on battling a particular disease should reflect the burden that disease imposed on the local population.

This may sound obvious, but it is an approach that few health ministries take, in Africa or in the West. In Morogoro and Rufiji, no one had a clue which diseases caused the most trouble, so TEHIP's first task was to find out. The traditional way of gathering health data in Tanzania was to collate records from clinics, but since most Tanzanians die in their homes this was not terribly accurate. So TEHIP sent researchers on bicycles to carry out a door-to-door survey, asking representative households whether anyone had died or sickened recently, and if so with what symptoms.

These raw numbers were then crunched to produce a "burden of disease" profile for the two districts. In other words, researchers sought to measure how many years of life were being lost to each disease, with a weighting to reflect the collateral damage to families when breadwinners die. They found that the amount the local health authorities spent on each disease bore no relation whatsoever to the harm that the disease inflicted on local people. Some diseases were horribly neglected. Malaria, for example, accounted for 30 percent of the years of life lost in Morogoro, but only 5 percent of the 1996 health budget. A cluster of childhood problems, including pneumonia, diarrhea, malnutrition, measles, and malaria, constituted 28 percent of the disease burden but received only 13 percent of the budget.

Other conditions, meanwhile, attracted more than their fair share of cash. Tuberculosis, for example, accounted for less than 4 percent of years of life lost but received 22 percent of the budget. No one wanted to cut spending on anything, but the research suggested that the extra $2 a head would be best spent on neglected diseases for which there were cost-effective treatments or preventive measures. As it turned out, the extra cash was ample: neither in Morogoro nor in Rufiji was the system able to absorb more than an additional 80 cents or so.

This tiny cash infusion smoothed the transition to a more effective approach to health care. Health workers, mostly nurses or paramedics rather than doctors, were given a simple procedure to show how to treat common symptoms. An illustration: if a child arrives coughing, and with a running nose and a hot brow, the nurse is instructed to work through a checklist of other symptoms to determine whether it is merely a cold or something worse. If the child is breathing more than fifty times a minute, for example, he is assumed to have pneumonia, given an antibiotic, and checked again after two days.

In most cases the cheapest treatments are offered first. Children with diarrhea are given oral rehydration salts, which cost a few cents. If the salts don't work, the child is referred to a clinic and put on a drip. For malnutrition, the first treatment offered is advice on breastfeeding. When this is not enough, the child is prescribed cheap vitamin-A pills. AIDS is tackled through education, condoms, and antibiotics to heal open sores caused by other venereal diseases, which present the virus with an open door into a new bloodstream.

Knowing which diseases people are actually suffering from enables clinics to order the right drugs. Previously, the government sent out the same package of pills to all dispensaries, which meant that popular drugs ran out while others gathered dust. Non-malarial mountain villages used to receive as many malaria drugs as mosquito-infested lowland ones, and villages where no one had ever suffered from asthma received asthma medication. "We did things blindly," a doctor in Morogoro recalled.

Perhaps most important, health centers in Morogoro now encourage people to use bednets impregnated with insecticide, which fight mosquitoes in several ways. If the bug hits the mesh, it dies. If it merely flies close to the bednet, it feels dizzy and either falls to earth, where it is eaten by ants, or buzzes off to rest and recuperate, which means that it will bite no one that night. A bednet's mosquito-repelling effect stretches for 500 meters in all directions, so netless villagers gain some protection from their better-equipped neighbors.

Conservative types at first shunned bednets in favor of the *mtuti*, a hot, itchy traditional sleeping bag woven of palm leaves. But with a bit of urging from nurses they discovered that cotton bednets are softer on the skin and better at beating back bugs.

Despite the cost – about $3 for a locally made net, with the insecticide somewhat subsidized – the nets are popular. Village shops sell them. Peasants hang them in huts on stilts in their rice-fields, where they sleep during harvest season, so as to be at hand to scare off crop-munching hippos. In Morogoro, even the Masai, a fiercely conservative tribe of nomadic cattle-herders, have started draping themselves in insecticide-soaked bednets when sleeping under trees.

The results of all this were stunning. In Rufiji, infant mortality fell by 28 percent between 1999 and 2000, from 100 deaths per 1,000 live births to seventy-two. The proportion of children dying before their fifth birthdays dropped by 14 percent, from 140 per 1,000 to 120. The figures for Morogoro are thought to be equally good, although they had not been properly checked when I was there. In nearby districts, and in Tanzania as a whole, there is no evidence of a similar improvement over the same period.

The stories I heard in Morogoro suggested that better health care had made people less poor. Everyone agreed that the fall in malaria had had especially happy effects.

Like most of Tanzania, Morogoro is a holiday camp for mosquitoes. While Dr. Kasale and I were there, we were caught more than once in booming rainstorms. When each downpour stopped, it left stagnant puddles everywhere, which swiftly became hatcheries for mosquitoes. The locals stay dry-ish by using big palm leaves as umbrellas but until recently had little protection against the swarms that follow storms.

I asked people if their lives had changed since the TEHIP experiment began. They all said they had. A young peasant called Mustapha Dangeni told me that his two children used to be smitten with fever almost every month before he got a bednet. Now, he said, they had been healthy for a whole year. He and his wife had found that, because they did not have to spend time nursing sick children, they could work longer in their fields, so they had produced more spare corn and millet. They earned more money than usual and did not have to spend any of it on anti-malarial drugs. Dangeni invited me into his hut to show me all the things he had bought with the extra cash: a radio, a bicycle, some rough furniture, better tools, and so on. "Things are continually improving." He beamed, leaning shirtless against a sack of charcoal.

Health and efficiency

The lesson from Morogoro and Rufiji is that simple ideas, rigorously applied, can yield dramatic results. Africa's problems are huge but, if tackled rationally, not insoluble. The Tanzanian government is keen to roll out TEHIP-like programs across the whole country. That would be a good start. Other countries should follow suit. And they should also apply the same rational approach to more or less everything they spend money on.

Too often, they won't. Governments everywhere waste money, but in Africa the problem is especially grave because there is less cash to waste and because it is wasted so flagrantly.

Given finite funds and potentially infinite demands for them, a government has to decide what is really important and what is not. Needs vary from country to country, but most African countries still need the basics: primary education, primary health care, passable roads, piped water, and a functional legal system. Such bare necessities should be given priority but often aren't.

Even in the most indebted countries, there is always money for ministerial limousines and mansions or for first-class flights to pointless conferences. After an unexpected upgrade on a plane bound for Lusaka, I once found myself sitting next to one of the top men at the Zambian finance ministry. When he found out who I was, he spent the next half an hour hectoring me about Zambia's need for deeper debt relief, before the complimentary champagne put him to sleep. Around that time, his country's annual budget for dealing with its AIDS crisis was half the sum earmarked for building villas for heads of state attending a talking-shop Zambia was hosting.

In 2001, some 18,000 delegates gathered to trumpet their grievances and demand "remedial measures" at a "UN World Conference Against Racism" in Durban. Some Africans and black Americans demanded that compensation for slavery should be paid by the American government. Others demanded that reparations for the Rwandan genocide should be paid, also by the American government. Several African presidents dwelt at great length on the iniquities of colonialism while omitting to mention their own countries' current ethnic violence.

In itself, the conference was not important. But it did highlight two big problems. First, the tendency of African elites to spend other people's money on themselves – a suite at one of the hotels on the Durban waterfront does not come cheap. Second, their tendency to believe that Africa's problems are someone else's fault.

I hear this argument often, at least from the educated middle class: civil servants, politicians, academics, journalists, and so forth. African newspapers are full of it, as is my email inbox. A good way of keeping up with the trends in this school of thought, I have found, is to subscribe to the *New African*, a glossy magazine published in London. It makes fascinating reading.

The latest issue to land on my desk contains the following. An editorial denouncing the "secret groups" from "the nations of European stock" who "meet each year and fix the rules and order of the world." An article praising Robert Mugabe's land reform program. Another installment in a long series on German massacres in Namibia around the beginning of the twentieth century. An article on the American presidential election of 2000 entitled "So who stole the black vote in Florida?" A piece on water privatization in Ghana, subtitled "Why does the West want to take away from the people the most precious and indispensable commodity of all – water?" A book review arguing that "the current geopolitical order . . . has ensured that Africa [is] at the eternal mercy of the big powers and their multinational corporations." And a report that a Cameroonian doctor has discovered a cure for AIDS.[1]

The magazine's editor, Baffour Ankomah, a Ghanaian with a colorful turn of phrase, acknowledges that many African governments are corrupt and undemocratic but seems to resent it when foreigners point this out. If an African leader is particularly vilified in the West, Ankomah tends to applaud him for standing up to the neo-imperialists. When interviewing such leaders, Ankomah's journalistic scepticism tends to fail him.

In the issue of July/August 2002, for example, he devotes the magazine's cover and sixteen inside pages to a "ground-breaking world exclusive interview" with Charles Taylor, who at the time was the president of Liberia. Readers are assured that the piece is "a collector's item" and treated to a dozen shiny pictures of Taylor, snappily suited, comfortably enthroned, and parrying tough questions such as, "How has life been at the top, as the democratically elected president?"

While it is quite true that Taylor was elected, one feels there is a bit of background missing here. In 1989, Taylor led a rebellion against the corrupt and murderous regime of Samuel Doe. After an eight-year civil war, during which soldiers in Mickey Mouse masks played "guess the sex" of unborn babies before cutting their mothers open to see, Taylor emerged as the most powerful warlord in Liberia. An election was held in 1997, which Taylor won by making it clear that if he lost he would start fighting again. "He killed my ma, he killed my pa, I'll vote for him," ran one of his campaign slogans.

Two years later, a new civil war broke out, pitting Taylor's government against rebels backed by neighboring Guinea. Taylor's ability to fight back was hampered by UN sanctions imposed on his regime for supporting the hand-chopping rebels in another neighboring country, Sierra Leone, and for his alleged involvement in the illicit trade in "conflict diamonds."

Taylor tells the *New African* that he thinks these sanctions unfair, particularly since Sierra Leone's civil war has ended. Ankomah agrees and lets Taylor ramble on about his theory that "there has been a conspiracy out there to destroy this country and our people," and, furthermore, that the imbalance in power between America and the rest of the world is "the root of all crises throughout the world."

The *New African* quotes, without comment, Taylor's assertion that "there are no political prisoners in any jails in this country. We have freedom of speech, we have freedom of the press." Gugu Radebe, a colleague of mine from Johannesburg, tells a different story. In 2000, while filming a documentary in Liberia, he was arrested, along with three other journalists, Tim Lambon, Sorious Samura, and David Barrie, for allegedly plotting to defame the regime.

Prison was not comfortable. The cells were tiny, the windows had been blocked up, and only an airhole the size of a brick allowed them to breathe the hot, wet Liberian air. Gugu recalls: "We were locked up in the cells and people kept coming to look and peek. These guys were coming around and holding their dicks and looking at the white guys thinking: 'Hmmm, supper.' Things like that. We then looked for the main man there, and we found him quite quickly. . . . I called him across and said, 'Look, I've been in prison before, I know what goes on in here, can we buy our protection?'"[2]

For $150, the four bought themselves some watchful muscles. Fortunately, Nelson Mandela and Jesse Jackson appealed for their release, and after a week behind bars they were freed. Gugu vowed never to go back to Liberia.

Ankomah does, to be fair, raise a couple of sensitive topics, such as the almost complete lack of development in Liberia in the 155 years since independence. Taylor's explanation for this is that America has done "nothing" for its former colony in the last century and a half. This is not entirely accurate, Ankomah interjects, prompting Taylor to backtrack a bit. He concedes that the Americans built Liberia's main airport but stresses that this was only so they could use it as a military base. He admits that they built a seaport, too, but this does not count because it was "built to export rubber."

I hear this argument quite often: that because the colonists built infrastructure to suit their own needs, it was therefore of no benefit to the locals. This does not follow. Doubtless many ancient Britons objected when Roman invaders built roads all over their country. The Romans did not build them to please the natives; rather, they wanted to make it easier to govern their new colony and easier to trade with other parts of the empire. Nonetheless, after the Romans left, their roads remained the best in Britain for 1,000 years.

Anyway, back to Taylor. "We have not had any major long-term assistance," he moans. "Liberia has natural resources. People now have to come in to invest in the country long term. Don't come and dig the iron ore and take it out. You dig the iron ore, you must smelt it here and you must produce steel rods here. That's long-term economic development for our country."

One reason why investors might not be keen to do this, which you would never guess from reading the *New African*, is that Taylor passed a law giving himself the right to dispose of all "strategic commodities" in Liberia. These include all minerals, all forest products, all agricultural and fishery products, and anything else the president chooses to call "strategic." Until his overthrow in August 2003, Liberia was, as one of my colleagues at the *Economist* put it, "Charles Taylor, Inc."

Why ideas matter

Few people succeed unless they believe that they can, and no nation ever has. Top athletes exude a self-confidence that often

248

elides into arrogance. So do countries that are doing well: think of Britain in the nineteenth century, Japan in the 1980s, or America today.

Much of Africa, by contrast, is seized by the uniquely disempowering notion that foreigners are to blame for most past and present ills. Of course, foreigners sometimes really are to blame. Africans have suffered, and it is only natural that many should bear grudges for the wrongs of the colonial period. Many people in other parts of the world also nurse old grievances, and it has not necessarily held them back. Britons who were born long after 1945 still harp on about the Second World War, and some Koreans have still not forgiven Japan for invading Korea in 1592. But there are few places besides Africa where intellectuals are so consumed by the past. Nor are there many non-Africans who have devoted as much time, effort, and diplomatic capital to the pursuit of various forms of reparation for historical crimes.

Railing against outsiders may be cathartic, but it does not achieve much. The politician who makes the most ferocious speeches denouncing Whitey is not necessarily going to be the best at balancing the budget or fixing the drains. More often, the opposite is true: bad rulers often cloak themselves in nationalism to distract attention from their failures.

The quest for reparations is likely to be counter-productive. Rich countries give aid mostly for reasons of charity, not contrition, and will not open their purses wider just because African campaigners demand that they take responsibility for their ancestors' misdeeds.

Campaigners may retort that other victimized groups have succeeded in winning reparations from Western governments. The aborigines of Australia, for example, and the indigenous peoples of America and Canada have wrung a continuous flow of handouts from their fellow citizens. True, but it is not clear that the money has done them much good. Some people argue that, on the contrary, it has fostered dependency and alcoholism.[3]

A few small groups of Africans have won compensation for

historical wrongs, but sudden payouts can be as disruptive as winning a lottery. In 2002, the British government agreed to pay $7 million to 228 members of the cattle-herding Samburu tribe in Kenya, to compensate them for deaths and injuries caused by mines in an area used as a training ground by the British army. Hundreds of them walked miles to Nanyuki, the nearest town with a bank, to collect payouts ranging from $13,000 to $430,000. The average annual income in Kenya is $360.

With the first payout, the Samburu held the biggest party Nanyuki had ever seen. They scattered banknotes around bars, ate every cow in town, slept with the horde of prostitutes who had come from afar to join the frolics, and bought old clunkers for huge sums with the vague idea that they might start taxi businesses, although few had driving licenses. After the mother of all binges, they left, singing, in their worn-out taxis.[4]

Wiser Africans do not wish to be seen as victims. At the Durban racism conference, Abdoulaye Wade, Senegal's president and a descendant of slave-owning African kings, pooh-poohed the idea that modern Africans should be paid compensation for nineteenth-century slavery. "If one can claim reparations for slavery," he said, "the slaves of my ancestors, or their descendants, can also claim money from me. Slavery has been practised by all people in the world."[5] George Ayittey goes further, arguing that "Almost every black problem is placed or explained in terms of a racialist paradigm, giving the false impression that black problems cannot be solved until racism is totally eradicated. This is painfully unrealistic. Regrettably, there will always be racism in the West and elsewhere. Must we blacks wait for its end before we take the initiative ourselves to solve our own problems?"[6]

Even some of the loudest grievance-shouters, such as Thabo Mbeki, recognize that Africa cannot grow rich from reparations. As I argued earlier, if Africa is to prosper, it must do so the way all prosperous countries, barring a few oil sheikhdoms, have done: by making things and providing services that other people want to buy.

This idea does not get much play in the African media, but it gets some, and as the press grows freer it may get a bit more. One of the most cheering stories of the last decade has been the steady liberation of the African press.

In the 1980s, governments completely dominated Africa's airwaves and printing presses. Broadcasters were state-owned and pumped out dreary propaganda. Independent newspapers were either banned or subject to frequent run-ins with the secret police. But since the end of the Cold War and the demise of the one-party state, dozens of lively, irreverent, and sometimes scurrilous papers have popped up. Private radio stations are also booming, which is important because most Africans cannot afford a daily paper but every village has a radio. In 1985, there were only ten community broadcasters in the whole of Africa; in 2000 there were more than 300. In Uganda alone there are more than thirty private stations pumping out hip music and frank chit-chat, and 100 more have won licenses.

A hack's life is freer and safer than ever before. In 2001, no African journalists were killed because of their work, although four were murdered for motives unknown. Less encouragingly, over 180 were jailed, but most were released within forty-eight hours without charge. Several countries still have censorious laws. In Congo, those who "insult the army" face the death penalty. In Angola, it is an offence to "slander . . . the memory of the dead," and for those charged with defaming the Mozambican president, "truth is not a defence." But only in Zimbabwe and Eritrea has press freedom been seriously curtailed in recent years.

Our brave correspondent in Harare, Andrew Meldrum, was arrested in 2002 for allegedly "publishing a falsehood." He spent a night in a cold, lice-ridden police cell, where he says he found the company extremely pleasant. His cellmates were two Zimbabwean journalists, equally innocent of any wrongdoing.

They found a copy of the state-owned newspaper, the *Herald*, on the cell floor and started chatting about its contents. A guard ordered them to stop, adding that prisoners were allowed to use newspapers only for toilet paper.

Andy was eventually acquitted, but within minutes of his acquittal he was served with a deportation order. In May 2003, while he was still appealing against the order, he was abducted by the police, bundled on to a plane, and expelled from the country. He is the first to admit, however, that had he not been an American citizen he would probably have suffered far worse.

In less tyrannical countries than Zimbabwe, the main problem for African journalists is not censorship but money. I spoke with Diallo Souleymane, the editor of two newspapers in Guinea, *Le Lynx* and *La Lance*. He told me that not many Guineans could afford to pay the fifty cents or so that he charged for his papers but that news vendors hired copies out for a fraction of the cover price. "A guy takes the paper to his office, reads it for half an hour, and returns it when he's finished," he said. Each copy, he reckoned, was read by thirty people.

But still, his papers are not exactly drowning in cash, and this affects their capacity to gather news. Souleymane told me that he had fifteen reporters in the capital, Conakry, but that he could rarely afford to send them to other parts of the country to find out what was going on. He tried recruiting freelancers in provincial towns, but the local political leaders were usually able to co-opt them by paying far more than *La Lance* could afford in return for sycophantic coverage.

Private newspapers and radio stations, being businesses themselves, are quite likely to promote business-friendly values. Many don't, of course, but there is a much broader range of ideas circulating now than in the days when the state had the only megaphone in town. Independent journalists are also much better at exposing corrupt officials, criticizing government policies, and generally holding their rulers to account. One of the surest signs that they are doing a good job is that African politicians, by and large, detest them.

The feeling is particularly strong among the more recently victorious liberation movements, who remember being lionized when they were rebels and resent being lambasted now they are in government.

I encountered this regularly in South Africa. The ANC received little but adulation from the foreign media while it was a rebel movement, simply because it was opposed to apartheid. But when it formed a government, the press started to assess it on the basis of how well it governed. For some ANC leaders, the ensuing criticism was hard to stomach.

I once managed to secure an interview with President Mbeki by politely and persistently nagging his deputy press secretary. The day before the interview was to take place, I was summoned to Pretoria for a briefing with his chief spokesman, Parks Mankahlana. Ushered into his office, I extended a hand and introduced myself. Perhaps because he had been gravely ill, Mankahlana appeared to have had no idea that he had an appointment with me. He turned to his deputy in fury and asked her, "Why on earth did you let *him* in here?"

He then gave me a lecture on how much he hated the *Economist* for its arrogance and Afro-pessimism, before moving on to the subject of how much he hated the entire Western press corps for the same reason. A recent incident particularly rankled: he told me that he had invited all the foreign hacks in South Africa to a press conference about a new presidential advisory panel, but no one showed up. Perhaps unkindly, I pointed out that the conference had been held on the same day as a violent election in Zimbabwe that had captured global headlines and that if any of us had stayed in South Africa, we would probably have been sacked. Then he really lost his temper.

Sadly, Mankahlana died a few months later of AIDS. Possibly, when I spoke to him, illness had already affected his judgment. But I suspect that the sentiments he expressed were sincere, even if he might not have chosen, had he been healthy, to express them so bluntly.

Being a journalist in Africa is no way to make friends. Many politicians have berated me for the *Economist*'s Africa coverage, which they say dwells too much on wars, famines, and Zimbabwe and so scares off investors. When on holiday in Africa, as soon as I reveal what I do for a living I am usually harangued by the tour operator for the excessive attention Western hacks pay to stories of bloodshed and particularly to stories of Western tourists getting murdered.

I can see their point, and I sympathize with it. Some journalists are irresponsible, some are lazy, some report in a highly misleading way. But most, in my experience, try quite hard to find out what is happening and to convey that information as accurately as possible. They may oversimplify, they may sacrifice nuance to make the story more gripping, but they don't usually lie. The reason they report that Africa is plagued by war, famine, and pestilence is that Africa is plagued by war, famine, and pestilence. They will stop reporting this when it stops being true.

Of course there is much that is good going on in Africa, and some news organizations go out of their way to report it. CNN regales viewers of *Inside Africa* with plenty of upbeat stories, and BBC World devotes a regular slot to African business. But these are not the stories that people remember. Thumbing through my own cuttings, I am reminded that I have written about African novels, theater, radio, advertising, drinking games, banking, corporate governance, rugby, soccer, sex, golf, cricket, cartoons, car manufacturing, platinum mining, migration, music, information technology, tourism, education, and countless other everyday topics. I don't need a cuttings file, however, to remind me of the charred bodies on Kinshasa's pavements or the sunken, subdued faces of AIDS patients in Ndola. I could be wrong, but I suspect that you, too, recall the ghastly images of Ethiopia's famine of 1984 more sharply than you can the last article you read on microcredit.

Some Africans have suggested to me that journalists, local and foreign, should go easy on Africa's rulers because it is not reasonable to expect the governments of poor countries to be as efficient or clean as those of rich countries. I take the opposite view. In poor countries, bad government is a matter of life and death. If someone defrauds the French government of a few million euros, this is a crime, and he should be jailed, but life for the average Frenchman will continue to be comfortable. If, on the other hand, a Malawian politician is looting the emergency grain reserve, people will starve as a consequence of his actions. An aggressive press is a crucial check on corruption.

Out of Africa, hope for something new

I will always be an outsider in Africa. I have never been poor or oppressed, and I grew up in a country where African-style poverty has been unknown for generations. When I wander around Africa, I do so wrapped in the armor that money provides. Where there is violence, I can afford to stay in a hotel with security guards. Where there is sickness, I can buy medicine. Where there is hunger, I can always find something to eat.

Africa constantly reminds me how lucky I am to have grown up in a rich, peaceful country. If I'd been born in Africa, there's a good chance that I'd be dead by now and almost no chance that I'd be racking up so many frequent-flyer miles. I'm a foreigner, so this is an outsider's perspective, for what it is worth.

I believe that Africa can grow rich. Most African countries are not yet on the right path, but several are at least hacking through the undergrowth looking for that path. Where exactly it will lead is up to Africans; only they can choose what kind of society they want to live in. But whatever the details it is clear that the society most Africans want to build is an industrialized one. I do not think I have met any Africans, whether peasants, bishops, or bankers, who do not want their countries to enjoy a standard of living like the West's. And this will take time. Nations do not suddenly wake up industrialized. To join the modern world, Africans will have to study, toil, save, and invest.

In Europe, the process was excruciatingly slow. After the sack of Rome in 410, Europeans almost entirely forgot how to read, write, or lay bricks. For 1,000 years, they huddled in freezing huts of sticks and straw, terrified of the wolves and evil spirits that lurked in the forests around them. Their lives were so static and insular that they often could not understand the dialects spoken by the peasants in the next village. The local warlords who ruled them did so with unreflecting cruelty. It would never have occurred to an English king of the fourteenth century that public money was not his to spend as he pleased, though he might have had difficulty counting it, math skills being rare in those days.[7]

During the fifteenth and sixteenth centuries, Europeans rediscovered the great works of classical literature and philosophy and hauled themselves back up to the level of civilization their ancestors had enjoyed in Roman times. A trickle of technological advances over the next two centuries turned into a stream in the 1800s and a torrent in the 1900s. In mid-century, communism and fascism slew millions and threatened to halt the continent's progress, but both ideologies were eventually vanquished.

At the beginning of the twenty-first century, life in Europe and most of its offshoots, particularly America, is peaceful and prosperous. East Asia, which started industrializing later but had the advantage of being able to learn from the West's example, is catching up fast.

In all these places, change has been traumatic. Mass affluence has shaken up the old social order. British plumbers can earn more than professors or archdeacons. Mass mobility has loosened family ties. Religious faith has waned in much of the rich world, with the striking exception of America.

In Africa, too, as progress comes, it will involve pain. New technologies will kill old industries; cost-cutting governments will lay off legions of un-needed employees. As Africa grows less poor, its people will probably become more individualistic, for money allows individuals to make more choices for themselves. A peasant typically spends his whole life farming the strip his chief allocates to him. But if he hops on a bus, moves to a city, and learns a skill, he has a much wider range of options as to what kind of work he will do, where he will live, who he will marry, and so on.

Some Africans already fret that modernization will mean the Westernization of their culture: that television will kill traditional songs and festivals or that the empty materialism of American soap operas will infect their children. It is a worry. African folk tales, if not written down, may be lost. Some of Africa's many languages will disappear, too. People find it easier to communicate if they speak tongues that many others speak, which is why billions learn English, whereas Khoi will probably go the same way as Cornish.

But a glance at the rich world suggests that the new does not necessarily drive out the old. Japanese teenagers watch American movies, but they watch more Japanese ones. Television has not killed *kabuki* theater; it has projected it to a wider audience. People tend to preserve the traditions they value and quietly ditch the ones they do not care about. People are not usually forced to join the modern world, although the modern world's bulldozers do sometimes destroy the forests where traditional hunter-gatherers live. For the most part, the drift from traditional to modern ways of living is voluntary. People migrate to towns because they prefer the greater material well-being, the greater freedom, and the greater variety of opportunities that an industrialized society offers.

Which is why the vast majority of Africans are striving, step by step, to get richer. For some reason, the African go-getter who sticks most in my mind is a young man I met on a hill in rural KwaZulu-Natal. This South African province used to be riven by political violence: as apartheid crumbled, followers of the African National Congress fought a sporadic guerrilla war against Inkatha, a Zulu tribal party. The apartheid security forces sent arms and agents provocateurs to stir things up: between 1985 and 1994, some 12,000 people were killed.

Many young men dropped out of school and spent their adolescence burning down neighboring villages. Tens of thousands endured such a bloody upbringing that they are now emotionally damaged and practically unemployable. But despite this tough start many are straining diligently to lift themselves out of poverty.

The one I spent the longest talking to was a veteran of the local war, a nineteen-year-old who had seen more deaths than he had worn neckties. When the conflict ended, he started raising chickens, which he slaughtered, cooked, and sold. He had big plans: he had been studying basic accounting and wanted to expand his business, save, and put his children through university. He told me that if South Africans worked hard, the country could grow rich, like Japan.

I cautioned, pedantically, that the Japanese had labored for a century before they caught up with the West. He shrugged. "We can do it, too," he said. "And besides, raising chickens is better than fighting."

NOTES

Introduction: Why is Africa so poor?

1. World Bank, *Can Africa Claim the 21ˢᵗ Century?* Washington, 2000, pp.6–17.
2. Jeffrey Sachs, "Helping the World's Poorest," *Economist*, 14 August 1999.
3. C. Meillassoux, (ed.), *The Development of Indigenous Trade and Markets in West Africa*, London, 1971, cited in John Reader, *Africa: A Biography of the Continent*, Alfred A. Knopf, New York, 1998, p.291.
4. World Bank, 2000, p.14.
5. For an account of the more gruesome aspects of Japanese colonial rule, see George L. Hicks's *The Comfort Women: Japan's Brutal Regime of Enforced Prostitution in the Second World War*, W.W. Norton, New York, 1995.
6. Address to UN university, Tokyo, 1998, reprinted in Thabo Mbeki, *Africa: The Time Has Come*, Tafelberg/Mafube, Cape Town, and Johannesburg, 1998, p.248.
7. Chinua Achebe, *The Trouble with Nigeria*, Heinemann, Oxford, 1984, p.1.
8. George Ayittey, *Africa Betrayed*, St. Martin's Press, New York, 1992, pp.168–9.
9. Hernando de Soto, *The Mystery of Capital: Why Capitalism Triumphs in the West and Fails Everywhere Else*, Basic Books, New York, 2000, pp.35–7.
10. UNAIDS, *AIDS Epidemic Update*, December 2002, *www.unaids.org*.
11. "Stop denying the killer bug," *Economist*, 21 February 2002.
12. Everyone agrees that Uganda has done well in curbing AIDS, but Justin Parkhurst of the London School of Hygiene and Tropical Medicine argued, in an article in the *Lancet* in July 2002, that the miracle was exaggerated. HIV prevalence was never quite as high as 30 percent, he said; the data were taken chiefly from testing women in urban antenatal clinics, which was not a fair sample of a population that is half male and 87 percent rural.

13. Achebe, 1984, p.19.
14. John Murphy, "Making a Splash in South Africa," *Baltimore Sun*, 13 November 2000.
15. In 1993, when I was living in Seoul, a gallery there displayed a piece of installation art called *Have you ever seen the president?* It consisted of dozens of little black loudspeakers, arranged against a blank white wall in the shape of the South Korean president's silhouette. Through the speakers were played grunts, moans, and expletives; the sound-track of a porn film. If the artist, Hong Sung Min, was expecting to get a rise out of the president, Kim Young Sam, he was disappointed. The president ignored him. Artists are a little less bold in North Korea. In 1995, I visited a gallery in Pyongyang. In the entrance hall was a masterpiece of socialist realism, *Kangson Twilight*, a painting of a steel-works against a fiery sunset. Someone had clearly decided that, although this was ideologically correct, there was something missing. So they ordered the artist to add a large image of Kim Jong Il, North Korea's "Dear Leader," in the foreground.
16. Santi Chakrabati, Botswana finance ministry, author interview, March 1999.

Chapter 1. The vampire state

1. Some Africans disagree. George Ayittey (who coined the phrase "vam-pire state" to describe the typical post-colonial African government) points out that Africans have traded enthusiastically with each other for centuries and that the continent's marketplaces prospered better before modern African governments tried to regulate them. See George Ayittey, *Africa Betrayed*, St. Martin's Press, New York, 1992.
2. Some bakers tried to dodge this rule by, for example, putting raisins in their dough and calling the result "raisin bread," which was not price-controlled. So the government kept lengthening the list of price-controlled goods.
3. The government denied that it had fixed the prices either of gasoline or of the Zimbabwe dollar. (Interview with Simba Makoni, the Zimbabwean finance minister, 6 March 2001.) The official line was that banks voluntarily agreed to deal in currency only at or around the rate recommended by the central bank. But the banks knew full well that if they failed to toe the line "voluntarily," the government would formal-

ly oblige them to. So they all but stopped dealing in foreign currency. If important customers came to them asking for American dollars, they would put them in touch with other customers who were exporting and leave the two parties to work out a deal in private. Fuel prices, meanwhile, almost made sense if you believed that the official exchange rate reflected reality, which it didn't. Supplies were further constrained by the fact that NOCZIM, a state-owned firm, had a monopoly over the import of gasoline into Zimbabwe. Being state-owned, it set prices as the government dictated, even if that meant that it could not pay for further imports.

4. IMF estimate, 2001.

5. Mugabe's government had not, at the time of writing, got round to seizing mines and factories. But the regime did pull off some more stealthy heists. Pension funds, for example, were forced to invest a large part of their portfolios in ten-year government bonds that paid only 15 percent annually. At a time when inflation was over 200 percent, this was simple theft. Forcing pension funds to buy worthless paper is not quite the same as hitting grandma over the head and stealing her handbag – it leaves fewer bruises – but it had the effect of robbing many more present and future pensioners than any gang of muggers could, no matter how well organized. And each pensioner was robbed of much more than she usually carries in her purse.

6. In 1999, an independent MP, Margaret Dongo, managed to obtain a list of those who had received land under the land reform program. In the late 1990s, most land was given to rich, well-connected people, including cabinet ministers. See *Land, Housing and Property Rights in Zimbabwe*, Centre on Housing Rights and Evictions, Geneva, 2001, p.16, www.cohre.org. An idea of what happened after the stolen election in 2002 can be gleaned from a secret audit, commissioned by the government itself and leaked in 2003, which described a thuggish free-for-all as Mugabe's closest allies assembled vast country estates for themselves on land seized from white farmers. Black peasants who took the government's promises of free land at face value were sometimes violently evicted to make way for generals and ministers. See *Africa Confidential*, 21 February 2003.

7. A figure often incorrectly given as 70 percent, or misleadingly given as "70 percent of the most productive farmland." Commercially farmed land in Zimbabwe is productive largely because it is commercially farmed.

NOTES

8. In 2000, there were about 70,000 whites in Zimbabwe and 75,000 elephants.
9. "The mess one man makes," *Economist*, 22 April 2000.
10. Ayittey, 1992, p.65.
11. George Ayittey, *Africa in Chaos*, St. Martin's Griffin, New York, 1999, p.52.
12. The best-written, though tongue-in-cheek, account of why Tanzania is so poor can be found in *Eat the Rich*, P. J. O'Rourke, Atlantic Monthly Press, 1998.
13. World Bank, *Can Africa Claim the 21ˢᵗ Century?* 2000, p.53.
14. Ayittey, 1999, p.114.
15. Ayittey, 1999, p.246.
16. Cited in International Crisis Group, *Zimbabwe: The Politics of National Liberation and International Division*, Harare/Brussels, 17 October 2002, p.4, *www.crisisweb.org*.
17. Ibid., p.4.

Chapter 2. Digging diamonds, digging graves

1. This chapter draws on the work of a former World Bank economist, Paul Collier, who was the lead author of, among other studies, *Breaking the Conflict Trap; Civil War and Development Policy*, World Bank, Washington, 2003. A conversation I had with Collier in May 2003 was also very helpful.
2. World Bank, *Can Africa Claim the 21ˢᵗ Century?* Washington, 2000, p.55.
3. World Bank, 2003, pp.53–91.
4. World Bank, 2000, p.57.
5. One study found that a country whose exports of primary products (i.e., unprocessed ones, such as minerals, oil, and coffee) accounted for as much as 28 percent of GDP was more than four times as likely to be at war than a country with no primary exports. Paul Collier, *Justice-Seeking and Loot-Seeking in Civil War*, World Bank, Washington, 1999. Unpublished manuscript, cited in Jakkie Cilliers and Christian Dietrich (eds.), *Angola's War Economy: The Role of Oil and Diamonds*, Institute for Security Studies, Johannesburg, 2000, p.41n.
6. This marvelous phrase was coined by Declan Walsh, an intrepid Irish scribbler. Declan Walsh, "Expensive but Never Boring Hotel Is Centre

Stage for Kinshasa's Unfolding Story," *Sunday Independent* (South Africa), 11 February 2001.

7. Zapiro (Jonathan Shapiro), editorial cartoon, 4 May 2000. Reprinted in David Philip, *The Devil Made Me Do It*, Johannesburg, 2000, p.91.

8. *The Report of the Panel of Experts on the Illegal Exploitation of Natural Resources*, UN Security Council, April 2001. Cited in *Financial Times*, 18 April 2001.

9. *Final Report of the Panel of Experts on the Illegal Exploitation of Natural Resources and Other Forms of Wealth of the Democratic Republic of the Congo*, UN Security Council, 16 October 2002.

10. Human Rights Watch, *War Crimes in Kisangani*, Washington, August 2002, p.4, *www.hrw.org*. Some observers put the figure even higher. In April 2003, the International Rescue Committee (*www.threirc.org*.) estimated that the death toll was between 3 and 4.7 million. Even the lower of these numbers would make Congo's war the most lethal since the Second World War. The true scale of the calamity will probably never be known. As one UN worker put it: "Congo is so green, you don't even see the graves," "Africa's Great War," *Economist*, 4 July 2002.

11. In January 2003, at least twenty-six alleged conspirators, including Colonel Eddy Kapend, a former aide to Kabila, were convicted of plotting the assassination and sentenced to death. The trial was grotesquely unfair, however, so the mystery is far from solved.

12. Fred Bridgland, *Jonas Savimbi: A Key to Africa*, Mainstream Publishing, London, 1986, p.30.

13. Angola Country Report, Economist Intelligence Unit, third quarter, 1998, p.16f.

14. Ibid., p.14.

15. George Ayittey, *Africa in Chaos*, St. Martin's Griffin, New York, 1998, pp.313–14.

Chapter 3. No title

1. For a longer account of this process, see Jared Diamond's *Guns, Germs, and Steel*, W.W. Norton & Co., New York, 1997.

2. Hernando de Soto, *The Mystery of Capital: Why Capitalism Triumphs in the West and Fails Everywhere Else*, Basic Books, New York, 2000, pp.35–7.

NOTES

3. Government of Malawi, *Report of the Presidential Commission of Inquiry on Land Policy Reform*, March 1999, pp.54 and 116.
4. de Soto, 2000, pp.18–20.
5. Personal communication, March 2003.

Chapter 4. Sex and death

1. The AIDS statistics in this chapter are largely taken from *Epidemic Update* reports issued by UNAIDS, *www.unaids.org*.
2. The best account of this under-reported horror is Jasper Becker's book *Hungry Ghosts: China's Secret Famine*, John Murray, London, 1996.
3. Steven Swindells, "Mogae warns Botswana faces extinction from AIDS," Reuters, 14 March 2001.
4. Some of these quotes appeared in "Stories of the People," an article by Emma Guest in *African Decisions*, July–September 2000. My wife and I visited Beitbridge together.
5. UNICEF, *Orphans and HIV/AIDS in Zambia*, Lusaka, 1998, p.2.
6. Ibid., p.17.
7. AIDS has also led to a dramatic increase in the number of homeless children: perhaps 90,000 live on Zambia's streets or in the bush, scratching a living by recycling broken bottles or through petty theft (UNICEF, 1998, p.2). Too poor to afford glue to dull the evening chill, they sniff "jenkem" – fermented sewage. A British aid worker in Lusaka, the Zambian capital, predicts appalling social consequences: "We will have a generation of illiterate kids whose only formative experience has been one of sickness, death and marginalisation. We're not talking about individual children. We're talking about a group mentality, and their own nurturing ability in the future as parents, if they're not seeing positive role models and being parented." (Quoted in Emma Guest, *Children of AIDS: Africa's Orphan Crisis*, Pluto Press, London, 2001, p.158.)
8. Console Tleane, "Racist Ideology Lurks Behind AIDS Research," *City Press* (South Africa), 28 July 2002.
9. Human Rights Watch, *Scared at School: Sexual Violence Against Girls in South African Schools*, New York, 2001, *www.hrw.org*.
10. UNAIDS, *Report on the Global HIV/AIDS Epidemic 2002*, pp.25–6.
11. Robert Thomson, "A Rebel with a Capitalist Cause," *Times* (London), 2 January 2003.

12. World Bank, *African Development Indicators 2001*, Washington, 2001, p.320.
13. As mentioned above in a note to the introduction, although everyone agrees that Uganda has done well in curbing AIDS, some think the miracle was exaggerated. Justin Parkhurst of the London School of Hygiene and Tropical Medicine argued, in an article in the *Lancet* in July 2002, that HIV prevalence was never quite as high as 30 percent. The data were taken chiefly from urban antenatal clinics, which were not representative of a population that is 87 percent rural.
14. This figure is from the Human Sciences Research Council's *Study on HIV/AIDS*, December 2002, *www.hsrc.ac.za*, which puts adult HIV prevalence in South Africa at 16 percent and total prevalence at 11 percent. Previous estimates based, like other African AIDS data, on tests in antenatal clinics were much more alarming.
15. Chenjerai Hove, *Shebeen Tales*, Baobab Books, Harare, 1994, p.52.

Chapter 5. The son of a snake is a snake

1. Basil Davidson, *The Black Man's Burden; Africa and the Curse of the Nation-State*, Three Rivers Press, New York, 1992, p.12.
2. Philip Gourevitch, *We Wish to Inform You That Tomorrow We Will Be Killed With Our Families*, Farrar, Straus & Giroux, 1998, pp.147–9.
3. It is hard to say exactly which individuals gave which orders. Some of the alleged ringleaders are still on trial, others are on the run, and most claim they are innocent. At the time of writing, an international tribunal for the most important *génocidaires* had secured only sixteen convictions, including that of Jean Kambanda, a former prime minister. The alleged mastermind of the genocide, Colonel Theoneste Bagosora, was facing twelve charges, all of which he denied. The director of Radio Mille Collines, Ferdinand Nahimana, was on trial, while the alleged moneyman behind the massacres, Felicien Kabuga, had been sentenced to life in prison. The international tribunal, which is in Arusha, Tanzania, hands down maximum sentences of life imprisonment; middle-ranking *génocidaires*, tried in Rwanda, face execution.
4. Gérard Prunier, *The Rwanda Crisis: History of a Genocide*, Hurst & Co., 1997, pp.1–35.
5. John Reader, *Africa: A Biography of the Continent*, Alfred Knopf, 1998, p.621.

6. Prunier, 1997, pp.80–81.

7. Ibid., pp.75–7.

8. If this seems implausible, see ibid., pp.102–7.

9. Ibid., p.223.

10. Ibid., p.224.

11. Ibid., p.250.

12. "Prosecutor Accused," *Economist*, 21 August 2003.

13. Eghosa Osaghae, *Crippled Giant: Nigeria Since Independence*, Hurst & Co., London, 1998, p.21.

14. Ibid., p.5.

15. Thomas Sowell, *Preferential Policies: An International Perspective*, William Morrow & Co., New York, 1990, p.71.

16. UNDP, *Human Development Report 2002*, pp.151 and 158–9.

17. Wole Soyinka, *The Open Sore of a Continent*, Oxford University Press, Oxford, 1996, p.124.

18. Ken Saro-Wiwa, quoted in Abdul Rasheed Na'Allah (ed.), *Ogoni's Agonies: Ken Saro-Wiwa and the Crisis in Nigeria*, Africa World Press, Trenton, NJ, 1998, p.339.

19. The two men have even written a book together: *The Pastor and the Imam: Responding to Conflict*, Muhammad Ashafa and James Wuye, Ibrash Press, Lagos, 1999.

20. Ben Maclennan, *Apartheid: The Lighter Side*, Carrefour, Cape Town, 1990, p.153.

21. The best short account of the transition to majority rule is Patti Waldmeir's *Anatomy of a Miracle: The End of Apartheid and the Birth of the New South Africa*, Penguin, London, 1997.

22. See, for example, Lawrence Schlemmer's survey for the South African Institute of Race Relations in 2001, *www.sairr.org.za*.

23. Speech to the national assembly, May 1998. Quoted in Thabo Mbeki, *Africa: The Time Has Come*, Tafelberg/Mafube, Cape Town, and Johannesburg, 1998, p.71.

24. Thabo Mbeki, address to the fifty-first national conference of the ANC, 16 December 2002, *www.anc.org*.

25. House of assembly debate, 1953, quoted in Allister Sparks, *The Mind of South Africa*, Arrow Books, London, 1997, p.196. Verwoerd's vision had started to fade long before 1994, however. From the 1970s, white governments spent much more on black education, although the racial gap was never eliminated. See John Kane-Berman, *South Africa's Silent Revolution*, SAIRR, 2nd edition, 1991.

26. See "Race, Law and Poverty in the New South Africa," *Economist*, 30 September 1999, and Tom Lodge, "ANC Factionalism: Curse or Blessing?" *Focus*, March 2003, *www.hsf.org.za*.

27. South African Institute of Race Relations (SAIRR), *South Africa Survey 2001/2002*, p.240, *www.sairr.org.za*.

28. SAIRR, 2001/02, pp.268 and 275.

29. Quoted in *Focus*, the magazine of the Helen Suzman Foundation, September 2000, pp.20–21, *www.hsf.org.za*.

30. *Sunday Times* (Johannesburg), "The Yummy and the Crummy," 13 May 2001.

31. Themba Sono, *From Poverty to Property*, FMF Books, Johannesburg, 1999, p.9.

32. SAIRR, 2001/02, pp.213–15.

33. Although it spent much more after the Soweto revolt in 1976, hoping to defuse black insurrectionary fervor.

34. Another 25 percent was listed in March 2003, with a discount for non-white South African buyers.

35. Patrick Chabal and Jean-Pascal Daloz, *Africa Works: Disorder as a Political Instrument*, International African Institute and James Currey, Oxford, 1999, pp.38–9.

36. Paul Collier and H.P. Binswanger, "State Reconstruction, Civil Wars and Ethnic Conflicts," paper presented at a World Bank conference in Abidjan, July 1999, cited in World Bank, *Can Africa Claim the 21st Century?* Washington, 2000, p.25.

37. Quoted in Sparks, 1997, p.70.

Chapter 6. Fair Aid, Free Trade

1. Andrew Roberts, *A History of Zambia*, Heinemann, London, 1976, pp.185–94.

2. Tim Wadeson, CEO, Konkola Copper Mines, interview with the author, March 2001.

3. Faysal Yachir, *Mining in Africa Today: Strategies and Prospects*, London, 1988.

4. Lise Rakner, Nicolas van de Walle, and Dominic Mulaisho, "Zambia," in *Aid and Reform in Africa*, World Bank, Washington, 2001, p.555. See also *African Development Indicators 2002*, World Bank, Washington, 2002.

5. Rakner *et al.*, 2001, table 9.7 in appendix 9.5. *www.worldbank.org*.

6. George Ayittey, "Why Africa Is Poor," *Daily Telegraph* (London), 27 August 2002. Between 1960 and 1997, Africa received aid totaling roughly $400 billion (adjusted for inflation).

7. World Bank, *Assessing Aid: What Works, What Doesn't, and Why*, Oxford University Press, New York, 1998, p.14.

8. Several African officials have complained to me about this, but most seemed to think that there was little they could do about it.

9. Graham Hancock, *Lords of Poverty: The Power, Prestige, and Corruption of the International Aid Business*, Atlantic Monthly Press, 1992.

10. Hendrik van der Heijden, *The Ineffectiveness of Economic Policy Reform, Foreign Aid and External Debt Relief in Zambia*, report for the Swedish embassy in Lusaka, June 2000, p.8.

11. Ibid., 2000, p.9.

12. Interview with Theo Bull of *Profit* magazine (Lusaka), April 2000. Bull added together the aid foregone because of the delay, the mines' operating losses, and the $45 million difference between the price received and an earlier (rejected) offer of $135 million.

13. I visited Zambia several times while Chiluba was in power and was struck by how few of the people I interviewed were prepared to be quoted by name – mindful, perhaps, that a number of prominent Zambian dissidents had died in mysterious circumstances. Among the courageous few who shunned anonymity, Fred M'membe, editor of the *Post* newspaper, and Dipak Patel, the former minister of commerce, were the most helpful. The November 2000 *Report of the* [Parliamentary] *Committee on Economic Affairs and Labour on the Review of the Privatisation of Zambia Consolidated Copper Mines Ltd*, which the government suppressed, also makes interesting reading, if you can get hold of a copy.

14. William Easterly, *The Ghost of Financing Gap*, Policy Research Working Paper 1807, World Bank, Development Research Group, Washington. Cited in World Bank, 1998, p.10.

15. W.A. Edge and M.H. Lekorwe (eds.), *Botswana: Politics and Society*, J.L. van Schaik Publishers, Pretoria, 1998, p.444.

16. Several interviews with economists and officials in Botswana helped flesh out this section. Among the most helpful were Kenneth Matambo of the Botswana Development Corporation, Charles Harvey and Keith Jefferis of the Botswana Institute for Development Policy Analysis, and Santi Chakrabati of the finance ministry.

17. World Bank, 1998.

NOTES

18. Ibid., p.3.
19. Alberto Alesina and David Dollar, *Who Gives Aid to Whom and Why?*, NBER Working Paper 6612, National Bureau of Economic Research, Cambridge, Mass. Cited in World Bank, 1998, p. 16.
20. World Bank, 2000, p.5.
21. Rakner *et al.*, 2001, pp.551–5.
22. Ibid., p.537.
23. World Bank, *Annual Review of Development Effectiveness, 1997.*
24. "Reform school," *Economist,* 5 April 2001.
25. David Dollar and Jakob Svensson, *What Explains the Success or Failure of Structural Adjustment Programs?*, World Bank, Development Research Group, Policy Research Working Paper 1938, Washington, 1998, cited in World Bank, 1998, p.52.
26. Howard and Janet Pack, "Is Foreign Aid Fungible? The Case of Indonesia," *Economic Journal* 100, March 1990.
27. Various sources, cited in World Bank, 1998, p.68.
28. World Bank, *African Development Indicators 2002*, p.289.
29. A few hours later, during an interview with the author in the back of a darkened minibus, May 2002.
30. The only other time was when I was a young freelancer, and I was asked to interview a South Korean rock band called the Seoh Taeji Boys for an entertainment magazine. I'd never heard of them, but they seemed nice. I've no idea if the piece was ever published.
31. Brian Reidl, *The Case Against the Farm Bill,* Heritage Foundation web memo, 5 February 2002, *www.heritage.org.*
32. Consumers' Association, 2003, *www.which.net/campaigns/food/production/page2.html*
33. P.J. O'Rourke, *Eat the Rich,* Picador, 1998, pp.116–18.
34. For more details, see *Economic Freedom of the World: 2001 Annual Report*, Cato Institute, Washington, 2001, pp.74–9, *www.cato.org.*
35. Jeffrey Sachs and Andrew Warner, *Economic Reform and the Process of Global Integration,* Brookings Papers on Economic Activity, No. 1, 1995. Cited in Aaron Lukas, *WTO Report Card III: Globalization and Developing Countries,* Center for Trade Policy Studies, Cato Institute, Washington, June 2000.

NOTES

Chapter 7. Of potholes and grasping gendarmes

1. Naomi Klein, *No Logo*, Picador, 2000, p.334.
2. Edward M. Graham, "Trade and Investment at the WTO: Just Do It!," in *Launching New Global Trade Talks: An Action Agenda*, Special Report No. 12, Institute for International Economics, Washington, September 1998, p.158. Cited in Aaron Lukas, WTO Report Card III: *Globalization and Developing Countries*, Center for Trade Policy Studies. Cato Institute, Washington, 2000, p.7.
3. Philippe Legrain, *Open World: The Truth about Globalization*, Abacus, 2002, p.21.
4. UN Conference on Trade and Development, *World Investment Report 2002*.
5. Interview with Bunmi Oni, October 1999.
6. UNCTAD, *World Investment Report 1999*.
7. Interview with Mark Hill, CE, Microsoft South Africa, February 2000.
8. A fine account of Shell's troubles in Nigeria can be found in Daniel Litvin's book *Empires of Profit: Commerce, Conquest and Corporate Responsibility*, Texere, New York, 2003.
9. For a longer account, see Karl Maier, *This House Has Fallen: Nigeria in Crisis*, Allen Lane, London, 2000, pp.75–110.
10. Interview with Bobby Danchin, February 2000.
11. De Beers might be an exception. If an NGO campaign made diamonds unfashionable, thus reducing the value of De Beers' stockpile (valued in 2000 at about $4 billion), the damage would be quantifiable and therefore, in theory at least, insurable.
12. "Ethically Unemployed," *Economist*, 30 November 2002.
13. George Ayittey, *Africa Betrayed*, St. Martin's Press, New York, 1992, pp.122–3.
14. Patrick Chabal and Jean-Pascal Daloz, *Africa Works: Disorder As a Political Instrument*, International African Institute, 1999, pp.102–3.
15. *The Economist*, Survey of Nigeria, 15 January 2000, p.10.

Chapter 8. Wiring the wilderness

1. Shereen El-Feki, "Biting the Silver Bullet," *Economist*, Survey of Agriculture and Technology, 23 May 2000.

2. Most of the modern statistics in this chapter are taken from the UNDP's *Human Development Report 2001: Making New Technologies Work for Human Development*.

3. All the truly ancient statistics in this chapter are culled from Angus Maddison's magisterial *The World Economy: A Millennial Perspective*, OECD, 2001.

4. I lifted the facts in this paragraph from Stephen Moore and Julian Simon's excellent book *It's Getting Better All the Time: 100 Greatest Trends of the Last 100 Years*, Cato Institute, Washington, 2000.

5. Interview with John Kabayo, August 2002.

6. Economist Intelligence Unit, country reprints, 2003.

7. "Wireless warriors," *Economist*, 14 February 2002.

8. See David Bevan, Paul Collier, and Jan Willem Gunning, *Nigeria and Indonesia: The Political Economy of Poverty, Equity, and Growth*, Oxford University Press, 1999.

9. *Sunday Times* (Johannesburg), 28 May 2000.

10. "Leave Them Be," *Economist*, 4 April 2002.

11. Interview with *Focus*, the magazine of the Helen Suzman Foundation, Issue 23, September 2001.

12. P. J. O'Rourke, *Eat the Rich*, Atlantic Monthly Press, New York, 1998, p.187.

13. World Bank, *Can Africa Claim the 21ˢᵗ Century?* Washington, 2000, pp.20–1.

14. *The Oxfam Education Report*, p.214, *www.oxfam.org*.

15. World Bank, 2000, p.44.

16. UNDP, *Human Development Report 2002*, p.169.

17. Liz McGregor, "Risky Business," *Guardian* (London), 30 November 2002.

Chapter 9. Beyond the rainbow nation

1. Ben Maclennan, *Apartheid: The Lighter Side*, Carrefour Press, Cape Town, 1990.

2. Tom Sharpe, *Indecent Exposure*, Martin Secker & Warburg, 1973.

3. Paul Kirk, "Mutilation by the Military," *Mail and Guardian*, Johannesburg, 28 July 2001.

4. South African Institute of Race Relations (SAIRR), *South Africa Survey 2000/2001*, p.166.

5. National Electricity Regulator. Cited in ibid., p.338.

6. Budget estimate, cited in ibid., p.172.

7. Ibid., pp.213–15.

8. Thabo Mbeki, interview with the author, July 2000.

9. *Scared at School: Sexual Violence Against Girls in South African Schools*, Human Rights Watch, New York, 2001, pp.21–8.

10. "Beating Crime, Not Suspects," *Economist*, 22 January 2000.

11. South Africa's *Bill of Rights*, 32, 1a.

12. *Final Report of the Truth and Reconciliation Commission*, October 1998, *www.truth.org.za*.

13. *Saturday Star* (Johannesburg). Peter Fabricius, "Mbeki Hails Cuba's Humanism," 31 March 2001.

14. BBC News Online, *Mandela Adds to Mugabe Pressure*, 7 May 2000, *news.bbc.co.uk*.

15. "Mboweni Slams Zimbabwe," Reuters, 23 August 2001.

16. Speech to the Fifty-first National Conference of the ANC, 16 December 2002, *www.anc.org.za/ancdocs/speeches/2002*.

17. *Mugabe's Secret Famine*, documentary written by Peter Oborne, produced by Juniper, broadcast on Channel 4 (UK), 12 January 2003.

18. Victor Mallet, "Rainbow Nation in Search of Self-assurance," *Financial Times* (London), 6 October 2000.

19. Howard Barrell and Sipho Seepe, "A Sense of Hope," *Mail and Guardian* (Johannesburg), 2 March 2001.

20. Maclennan, 1990, p.65.

21. Public Service Accountability Monitor, Rhodes University, *www.psam.ru.ac.za*.

22. Interview with Judge Willem Heath, head of the Special Investigating Unit, December 1999, and telephone interview with his spokesman, March 2000.

23. Colm Allan, head of the Public Service Accountability Monitor at Rhodes University, quoted in *Focus*, the magazine of the Helen Suzman Foundation, Issue 17, March 2000, *www.hsf.org.za*.

24. *The State, Property Relations and Social Transformation*, ANC discussion document, 1998, *www.anc.org.za* (archive).

25. Victor Mallet, "South Africa Opposition Attacks ANC Voter Threats," *Financial Times* (London), 8 December 2000.

26. McGregor's *Who Owns Whom*, cited in SAIRR, 2001/2002, p.188.

27. David Christianson, "Liberals Can Espouse Black Empowerment," *Focus*, March 2003.

NOTES

28. Patrick Wadula, "Empowerment Needed at Company Level," *Business Day* (Johannesburg), 6 June 2001.

Conclusion: One step at a time

1. *New African* (London), January 2003.
2. Interview in *Carte Blanche*, a South African television news program, 3 September 2000.
3. See, for example, Doug Bandow, *Native American Success Stories*, 11 May 1998, *www.cato.org*.
4. Adrian Blomfield, "Tribesmen Paint the Town Red After MoD £4.5m Windfall," *Daily Telegraph* (London), 28 November 2002.
5. Anton La Guardia, "African Rift Over Calls for Slavery Reparations," *Daily Telegraph* (London), 31 August 2001.
6. George Ayittey, *Africa Betrayed*, St. Martin's Press, New York, 1992, p.6.
7. For a lively account of life in Europe between the collapse of Rome and the Renaissance, see William Manchester's *A World Lit Only By Fire*, Little Brown, Boston, 1992.

Index

INDEX

INDEX

INDEX

INDEX

INDEX